A PASSION FOR POISON

In the summer of 1962, fourteen-year-old Graham Young stood in the Old Bailey dock charged with poisoning family members and a schoolfriend by methodically lacing their food and drink with such substances as thallium and antimony. Diagnosed with 'a psychopathic disorder', he was detained under the Mental Health Act and committed to Broadmoor, the youngest patient there since 1885.

Nine years later, Graham was released, believed to be no longer a danger to others. He found employment at Hadlands, a photographic supplies firm. In his role as an assistant storekeeper, Graham's duties included collecting and serving his colleagues' morning and afternoon tea. Very soon, members of staff began falling ill, experiencing debilitating pain — and dying ...

CAROL ANN LEE

A PASSION FOR POISON

Complete and Unabridged

CHARNWOOD
Leicester

First published in Great Britain in 2021 by
John Blake Publishing
an imprint of Bonnier Books UK
London

First Charnwood Edition
published 2022
by arrangement with
Bonnier Books UK
London

A catalogue record for this book is available
from the British Library.

ISBN 978–1–4448–4836–6

Published by
Ulverscroft Limited
Anstey, Leicestershire

Printed and bound in Great Britain by
TJ Books Ltd., Padstow, Cornwall

This book is printed on acid-free paper

'The whole story is too terrible.
You'll be disgusted and amazed.'

GRAHAM YOUNG
POLICE INTERVIEW NOTES, 1972

Contents

Contents

Introduction

A SHORT HISTORY
OF POISON

It's November 1971, the turning to ash of an already grey year. Hostilities in Northern Ireland are still on the rise; decimalisation means older people are asking 'What's that in real money?' every time a transaction is made; President Nixon watches as half a million people march on Washington DC to protest against the war in Vietnam; ultra-violent films *Straw Dogs* and *A Clockwork Orange* pack the cinemas; kids are glued to *Magpie*, *Mr Benn*, *The Clangers* and *Crackerjack*, while their parents favour *Z-Cars*, *Opportunity Knocks*, *Look: Mike Yardwood!* and *The Onedin Line*; and glam rock makes its shimmering, androgynous debut on *Top of the Pops*, in the form of Marc Bolan, all bombast, boots and feather boas.

Even in a dull year, the arrest of a Hertfordshire storeman called Graham Young seems unlikely to make much of an impact on British history. But here we are, on a dismal afternoon in Hemel Hempstead, where that same young man — reasonably tall, dark-haired, slim of limb and sharp of feature — sits in the police station on central Combe Street. Cigarette hooked between his nicotine-stained thumb and forefinger, he asks the detective sitting opposite, 'Do you know 'The Ballad of Reading Gaol', Superintendent?' He then recites Oscar Wilde's famous verse: 'Yet each man kills the thing he loves/By each let this be heard/

1

Some do it with a bitter look/Some with a flattering word/The coward does it with a kiss/The brave man with a sword.'

He pauses, then admits, 'I suppose I could be said to kiss.'

We will find out in due course why the crimes of this unprepossessing young man effected change in several crucial aspects of our laws, forensic science and institutions, but Graham Young's choice of words echo those of dramatist John Fletcher, whose comedic 1617 play *The Chances* is subtitled 'The Coward's Weapon, Poison'. Murder by poisoning is the method most favoured by fiction writers for the killing of one character — or more — by another. Stealthy, arcane and chillingly abstract in allowing the killer to be miles from the victim when the death blow is delivered, poison is the ink that flows through many a crime writer's pen, a symbol of sin and treachery. And very often, those stories are inspired by real-life murders, for poisoners are strangely unique among their homicidal peers, possessed of a macabre decadence that imbues their crimes with an eerie, inappropriate nostalgia.

The history of poison is as old as time itself. In the prehistoric world, hunters dipped their arrows in snake venom while the ancient indigenous people of South America fashioned poison darts from plant sap and the venom of frogs (there are over 200,000 poisonous animals, including fish, spiders, bees, snails and birds, whose feathers are toxic to the touch). The Greek word *toxicon* refers to poison arrows and has given us the words 'intoxicated' (sickened by poison arrows) and 'toxin'. These poison arrows appear in the works of Greek philosopher Aristotle, who refers to the nomadic Scythians and their weapons, infused

2

with a blend of decomposing blood liquid waste and fluid from rotting snakes, which could result in septicaemia. Aristotle also mentions his fellow Greek philosopher Socrates, sentenced to death in 399BCE for allegedly corrupting Athens' young people. Socrates chose poison as a form of execution and died among friends after imbibing hemlock, a plant said to have turned deadly after Jesus' blood was spilled upon it where it grew on the hillside of his crucifixion.

Earlier still, we find 'recipes' for poison written in hieroglyphics on one of the world's oldest medical documents, the Ebers Papyrus. The first known Egyptian pharaoh, Menes, took a keen interest in poison and one of the most famous self-inflicted deaths in history is Cleopatra's alleged suicide using asp venom. The father of Chinese herbal medicine, Shen Nung, experimented with 365 herbs before one killed him, while the first Chinese emperor, Qin Shi Huang, poisoned himself in his search for the elixir of life. Poison was the weapon of choice for assassins of the ancient civilisations of Greece, Persia and India, where Mughal emperors would present their enemies with poison-infused robes and criminals were sentenced to death using toxins.

Ancient Roman law contains the first legislation against poisoning. The dictator Sulla issued the Lex Cornelia de Maiestate in response to the rash of assassinations; no less than six emperors were poisoned to death. Claudius' wife Agrippina poisoned him to advance the career of her son, Nero, who then employed a woman named Locusta to act as his personal advisor on the matter; with her expertise, he was able to dispose of his mother, brother and several wives. To gain the throne, Nero also poisoned his stepbrother. In all, 170 women were found guilty of maliciously administering poison during Roman rule, and one theory holds that the empire's decline and fall was due to lead poisoning from the water pipes; there may be some truth in that, since symptoms include depletion of mental skills and loss of libido, with some emperors displaying signs of madness and the population as a whole suffering decreased fertility.

Renaissance Rome saw the emergence of an infamous poisoning dynasty: the Borgias. Led by Rodrigo Borgia (Pope Alexander VI), the family were ruthless in their determination to retain power within the Catholic clergy, dispatching their enemies — cardinals, bishops and noblemen — with such astonishing regularity that English essayist Max Beerbohm observed: 'The Borgias selected and laid down rare poisons in their cellars with as much thought as they gave to their wines.' Recent research suggests that Lucrezia Borgia probably did not deserve her fearsome reputation, but her brother, Duke Cesare, was a serial poisoner who killed dozens of people. The Borgias liked to test toxins on the poor, experimenting with aconite, strychnine and other poisons. They eventually devised a concoction known as 'cantarella', thought to contain blister beetles and arsenic, which was served to victims in the wine that accompanied dinner.

Italy in the 16th century was the location of an extraordinary guild: the Council of Ten. Comprised of alchemists, the clique offered to commit murder by poison for a fee, keeping accounts in a thin ledger marked '*Secreto Secretissima*' (top, top secret). Another Italian noblewoman, Catherine de Medici, was widely believed to have carried furtive knowledge about poisons with her to France, where she was known as the

'Black Queen' after marrying King Henry II. Her potions were kept in small vials hidden in cabinets within the royal residence, brought out for experiments on prisoners and animals. The King lived in fear of his wife, who was suspected of murdering his brother and her daughter's prospective mother-in-law, the latter with poisoned gloves. By the end of the 16th century, France had become a veritable hotbed of poisoners; noble men and women, and the wealthy, were frequently the victims of arsenic plots. The substance became known as the *poudre de succession* or 'inheritance powder', and if given to a wet nurse in discreet quantities would kill a suckling infant rival.

In England, failed assassination attempts beset Queen Elizabeth I, including a Spanish plot to hire a go-between who would smear the pommel of her riding saddle with an opium-infused poison. On the other side of the world, Chinese emperors were so fearful of being murdered by such means that they pushed small squares of silver into their meals, which they would then scrutinise, believing that the presence of poison would cause the silver to tarnish immediately. But it was in France where poison continued to be a prolific threat to royals and nobility. The priests of Notre-Dame heard countless confessions involving poisons, leading to the establishment of a *chambre ardente* ('burning chamber'), essentially a poisoners' inquisition. Over 400 people were charged with murder as a result. At the heart of the matter was fortune-teller Catherine Deshayes. Known as 'La Voisin', Deshayes sold her unique brew of arsenic, opium, belladonna and aconite to wealthy women wanting rid of a husband or child. Found guilty of attempting to kill King Louis XIV, Deshayes was tortured and burnt at the stake.

5

It was women too, who were the focus of the secret poison societies that emerged in Italy around this time and provided them with toxins and advice on how best to dispense them. Another fortune-teller, Hieronyma Spara, ran a secret society in Rome that offered means and method to disgruntled wives. The most notorious peddler of poisons was Madame Giulia Tofana, who created her own deadly potion, which she named 'Aqua Tofana'. She was a popular figure until a rumour spread that she had poisoned the water supply in Rome; under torture she confessed to murdering 600 people, including two popes. She and her daughter were executed in 1659, along with three helpers; other accomplices were bricked up alive inside the dungeons of Palazzo Pucci.

Madame Tofana's potion was thought to contain arsenic, used both medicinally and murderously for centuries. Colourless, tasteless and odourless, it was administered as part of Chinese medicine hundreds of years ago and used by Greek physician Hippocrates in the fifth century BCE to treat stomach ulcers. Medieval alchemists, however, believed it could be used in an elixir to achieve immortality. By the 18th century it was once more employed in medicine when it appeared as an ingredient in Fowler's solution, a remedy used to treat a wide variety of ailments, including asthma and syphilis. In 1890, arsenic was declared to be the best treatment for leukaemia and remains part of chemotherapy for acute forms of the cancer. The substance was also a popular element in women's beauty, whether as an ingredient in face cream or something more unusual, such as the use to which it was put by Diane de Poitiers, the mistress of King Henry II of France (who was married to poison expert

Catherine de Medici). The King's senior by 19 years, de Poitiers drank a potion of liquid gold every day in order to maintain her looks, believing it to have magical properties if used circumspectly. In 2009, her remains were disinterred by French experts who were astonished to find gold in her hair and on the ground where it had seeped out of her cadaver.

Arsenic was often a feature in sensational trials during the Victorian era. Indeed, it was a part of many people's daily lives, whether for good or bad, or simply (and literally) as part of the wallpaper. The introduction of life insurance schemes, coupled with the easy availability of arsenic, led to multiple murders and attempted murders involving the toxin. Poisoners seemed to abound in greater number than ever before: Florence Bravo, Madeleine Smith, Mary Ann Cotton, Florence Maybrick, Dr Crippen and William Palmer are just a handful of the infamous names at the forefront of this particular branch of murder. And yet again, it was women who seemed to present the deadlier threat, perhaps because divorce was harder and more expensive to obtain than arsenic. The government attempted to address the problem by introducing the Arsenic Regulation Act of 1851, wherein a clause suggested that only men should be permitted to purchase the substance. Nonetheless, poisoning was declared to have 'become epidemic; the witchcraft, as it were, of modern times'.

In the end, science brought about the downfall of the 'white widow-maker'. For centuries, physicians had been at a loss to know how to detect or treat arsenic poisoning; one technique involved throwing the contents of a suspected victim's stomach into a fire to ascertain whether they smelled of garlic. But in 1836, English chemist James Marsh discovered a much more reliable method to detect traces of arsenic in human tissue. A French woman suspected of killing her husband with arsenic-laced cakes was the first poisoner to be proven guilty using the Marsh test, which developed as the years rolled by, resulting in a significant drop in deaths caused by deliberate arsenic poisoning.

Ironically, as science advanced to save lives that might otherwise have been lost to poisoning, on an industrial scale it led to millions of deaths. The use of toxins in warfare is centuries old; the ancient Greeks, Romans and Chinese were among those who employed burning sulphur to smoke out an enemy, while seventh-century Byzantines invented 'Greek fire', chemicals that could float and burn, destroying wooden ships and their crews with a substance described as 'ancient napalm'. Two centuries later, poison was added to a new weapon invented by the Chinese: gunpowder.

But it was the early years of the 20th century that saw governments turning to poison on a mass scale. On 22 April 1915, just as the sun was setting over the Belgian fields of Ypres, the German army released their new weapon: 168 tons of chlorine gas. A Canadian officer recalled that it appeared as 'a deadly wall' that 'rolled slowly over the ground, turning the budding leaves of the trees, the spring flowers and the grass a sickly white'. The wind carried the vapour to the Allied trenches, where it poured into the eyes and throats of the unsuspecting troops. The poison gas inflicted unimaginable pain, blindness and a feeling of being strangled or burned alive. Over 5,000 soldiers were asphyxiated.

Chemist Fritz Haber had worked throughout the war at developing what he called 'a higher form of killing'. He took a personal interest in the deployment of chlorine gas at Ypres and went on to lead the evolution of even more noxious chemicals, including mustard gas and phosgene, which caused the sufferer to choke while his body burned and could also produce psychological terror. German-Jewish Haber was regarded as a hero in Berlin following the attack at Ypres; a party was held in his honour one month later to celebrate. But among those who were repelled by the uses to which Haber had put his brilliance was his wife, Clare, a renowned chemist in her own right. She called the poison gas 'a sign of barbarity, corrupting the very discipline which ought to bring new insights into life'. As the party got under way, Clare shot herself through the heart, dying instantly.

Haber was awarded the Nobel Prize in Chemistry in 1918. Fifteen years later, he was forced to flee his homeland when the Nazi Party came to power. He died of a heart attack while in exile; his laboratory and research papers were seized by the Nazis and used in the development of Zyklon B, a form of hydrogen cyanide that was shipped out to concentration camps across Europe, where it killed millions of Jews — including members of Haber's own family — in the gas chambers. At Auschwitz-Birkenau, around 8,000 people a day were murdered by the gas, which took just 20 minutes to kill all the occupants of a single chamber.

Towards the end of the war, as Germany's defeat loomed, Nazi leaders took to poisoning themselves with the use of cyanide pills. As a chemical compound, cyanide has been used for nefarious means since time immemorial, largely because of its efficiency, potency and speed of effect, but it is immediately detectable after death, giving off a distinctive smell during autopsy. There was one instance where its strength failed: Russian faith-healer Rasputin survived attempts to kill him in 1916 with the use of cyanide-topped cakes and poisoned wine; he was subsequently shot and thrown into the Malaya Nevka river. But in 1945 cyanide proved effective as a suicide pill, ending the lives of Hitler, his wife and his dog in their Berlin bunker, with countless military leaders, government officials and Nazi sympathisers following suit. The 'architect' of the Holocaust, Heinrich Himmler, killed himself with a cyanide pill during Allied capture, as did German military leader Hermann Goering on the eve of his execution at the Nuremberg Trials. Reich Minister of Propaganda Joseph Goebbels and his wife Magda murdered their six children in Hitler's bunker on 1 May 1945 before jointly committing suicide with cyanide pills.

Twenty years later, a single case of murder involving cyanide terrified generations of Americans. On Halloween 1974, eight-year-old Timothy O'Bryan was given a Pixy Stix by his father, Ronald Clark O'Bryan; it contained potassium cyanide. The little boy died in hospital that night, killed by his debt-ridden father who had hoped to collect his son's life insurance. 'Candyman' Ronald Clark O'Bryan was executed by lethal injection in 1984, but the killing haunted America, giving substance to already existing urban legends about poison-laced sweets, and led to some hospitals and sheriff's departments offering free analysis of treats on Halloween. Four years after the murder, potassium cyanide featured in a horror story on a much larger scale when American preacher Jim Jones directed the murder-suicide of more than 900 'disciples' of his People's Temple in Guyana. Parents fed the poison-infused fruit punch to their children before drinking it themselves. Jones died with his followers but chose a gunshot to the head instead. The mass poisonings were instigated by the visit of US Congressman Leo Ryan and a delegation of journalists determined to investigate stories of human rights abuses at the temple. Four of those who had flown to Guyana, along with Ryan, were murdered on the airstrip as they attempted to leave.

By then, poison and politics were often inextricably intertwined. In the 1950s, the CIA and KGB equipped spies with L-pills to kill themselves if captured. With the 'L' standing for 'lethal', these poisons were concealed in objects such as spectacles and fountain pens, which wouldn't normally attract attention but, if bitten, released a deadly toxin. Cyanide gas was contained in a spray gun fired by a former KGB agent at two Ukrainian nationalist leaders in the late 1950s and in the decade that followed, the CIA spent endless hours devising poison-laden means of assassinating Cuban revolutionary Fidel Castro, including lacing his cigars with botulinum, sprinkling his shoes with thallium salts and contaminating his scuba-diving apparatus with tubercle bacilli. In the event, Castro survived until 2016, dying at the age of 90.

The world of espionage utilised poison on innumerable occasions throughout Castro's lifetime, with some notorious instances, such as in the case of Bulgarian dissident Georgi Markov, killed in 1978 when a passing stranger poked him with an umbrella that fired a deadly pellet of ricin. Political assassins and

11

terrorists found new ways to deploy poison, plotting destruction with the use of nerve agents such as sarin and anthrax. Polonium-laced tea brought about the slow and agonising death of Alexander Litvinenko, the former officer of the Russian Federal Security Service, who was photographed emaciated and bald in his hospital bed shortly before he passed away in November 2006. In 2018, Russian dissident Sergei Skripal and his daughter Yulia were found unconscious on a bench in Salisbury, England, having been poisoned by a Novichok nerve agent. They recovered eventually but further deposits of Novichok were discovered throughout the city, and a 44-year-old woman, Dawn Sturgess, died following contact with a poisoned perfume bottle.

In recent years poison has seen a resurgence in its cosmetic usage. One of the most toxic substances known to humanity, the bacterium *Clostridium botulinum* could kill 20 million people with a single gram if it were swallowed. Today, however, we know it better in diluted form as the source of Botox, used to treat serious health issues such as cerebral palsy and multiple sclerosis but also to immoblise facial muscles in order to reduce wrinkles. The employment of poison in pursuit of beauty has extensive roots, taking us back to a time when it was regarded as belonging to the realm of magic rather than science and the Sumerian goddess of healing, Gula, who was also the mistress of charms and spells and often called upon to deal with those who used poison for nefarious means. Hence its widespread use as a plot device in literature, from the scheming witches of Macbeth and their incantation, 'Double, double toil and trouble/Fire burn and cauldron bubble' to Madam Bovary's suicide by arsenic and the poisoned red apple, familiar to all children from the fairy-tale of Snow White. Even a character as seemingly harmless as the 'mad Hatter' in Lewis Carroll's *Alice in Wonderland* has his origins in real-life tragedy: in centuries past, hatmakers treated felt using mercurous nitrate — a form of mercury, the metal that can turn to vapour as if by magic at room temperature. Those vapours inadvertently inhaled by the hatmakers often induced symptoms of mercury poisoning, affecting the brain and nervous system, hence the saying 'mad as a hatter'.

But of all those authors turning to poison as inspiration for their writing, none is more famous than Agatha Christie. Her knowledge of poisons arose from the offer of a job at a dispensary while she was working as a nurse in her local hospital during the First World War; thus she became an apothecary's assistant, which provided her with ample opportunity to learn about toxins. During the Second World War, she volunteered again to work in the dispensary at the University College hospital in London, where she renewed her training. A prolific reader of real-life criminal cases, she based several plots on actual poisoners, including Dr Crippen, whose tale inspired *Ordeal by Innocence*, published in 1958.

In a curious circle of influence, the pharmacist who originally trained Christie in Torquay turned up as a villain in one of her most esoteric works, *The Pale Horse*, published in 1961. This particular novel was mentioned during an Old Bailey trial in June 1962, when it was deliberated as a source of inspiration for the defendant. He denied it, but the book was important in the case nonetheless, having piqued the curiosity of a pathologist who had read *The Pale*

Horse and believed — rightly, as it turned out — that the case he was involved with featured the same unusual poison, thallium, deployed to such sinister effect in the novel. Thallium was never known to have been administered maliciously in British criminal history, but here was a young mind obsessed with it, and other poisons: the 14-year-old Neasden schoolboy, Graham Young.

6 July 1962
THE OLD BAILEY

'Thallium used to be used for depilation at one time — particularly for children with ringworm. Then it was found to be dangerous ... it's mainly used nowadays for rats, I believe. It's tasteless, soluble and easy to buy. There's only one thing, poisoning mustn't be suspected.'

Agatha Christie, *The Pale Horse* (Collins, The Crime Club, 1961)

Prologue

A CHARM OF POWERFUL TROUBLE

A pungent whiff of sulphur and smoke hung in the air outside the Old Bailey that morning. There had been heavy smog earlier in the week, alarming those who remembered the Great Smog of 1952, which claimed the lives of at least 12,000 Londoners. Despite the passing of the Clean Air Act, another 700 people would die in December 1962, when the same deadly smog shrouded the city again before further legislation was enacted. But the odour in England's capital was not the only reminder that day of how lethal chemicals could be, especially where existing laws failed or were deliberately circumvented. There was another and much more peculiar portent inside Court No. 1 of the Old Bailey.

Two hundred yards north-west of St Paul's cathedral, the Old Bailey is named after the fortified Roman wall that once stood on the site. The medieval courthouse was destroyed during the Great Fire of London in 1666; its second incarnation, alongside Newgate gaol, lasted little more than a hundred years. When court and prison were demolished, only the former was rebuilt. King Edward VII opened the new Old Bailey in 1907. Three years later, Court No. 1 hosted its first sensational trial, condemning Dr Hawley Harvey Crippen to death for the murder of his wife, Cora Henrietta.

17

Other famous and infamous names followed in his footsteps, meeting the same fate, among them Edith Thompson, John Reginald Christie and Ruth Ellis. Eager spectators would willingly spend a night or two huddled on the Newgate Street flagstones to secure a place in the public gallery. A year before our subject entered the dock, all those attending the *Lady Chatterley's Lover* trial, in which Penguin Books was acquitted of obscenity, could legitimately claim to have witnessed the beginnings of a moral and cultural revolution.

And indeed, momentous changes were afoot in the legal system itself. Campaigners for the abolition of the death penalty attracted support from all quarters, capitalising on the widespread revulsion at the 1955 execution of Ruth Ellis, a young mother who had shot dead her abusive partner. On 6 July 1962, an editorial in the *Daily Herald* highlighted the Earl of Harewood's 6,825 signature-strong petition calling for Prime Minister Harold Macmillan to end capital punishment. Reminding readers that certain categories of murder were already exempt from the death penalty sentence, the editorial declared:

Hanging fewer killers has made NO difference to the murder rate. One thing IS clear. The law as it stands in Britain is totally illogical. A poisoner escapes the rope, yet death can be the sentence for the man who in a fit of anger kills by shooting. To think of altering the law to make ALL killers liable to the death sentence would be putting the clock back. There IS a solution — to do away with the whole ghastly ritual of hanging.

The example chosen to demonstrate the arbitrary nature of the law obliquely referred to James Hanratty, hanged three months earlier. Hanratty had been found guilty of the fatal shooting of scientist Michael Gregsten, whose lover Valerie Storie had been raped and shot five times in the same incident but survived. The bloody nature of the A6 murder, from start to finish, made it one of the most controversial cases of recent times, chiefly because many people believed Hanratty to be innocent.

The shadow of Hanratty loomed large over the editorial, although he was not named. Nor was the other example identified — the one who 'escapes the rope'. But the headlines in every tabloid and broadsheet were enough, reporting on the trial that had taken place the previous day, in Court No.1 of the Old Bailey.

★ ★ ★

Three loud raps preceded the clerk's command: 'Be upstanding in court!'

A collective scraping of chairs met the directive. Moments later, a side door opened and the judge, Mr Justice Melford Stevenson, swept in, be-wigged and ermined. Born in the Cornish seaside town of Newquay in 1902, Melford Stevenson had been a high court judge since 1957. Two years earlier he had led the defence counsel for Ruth Ellis by staying virtually silent on her behalf. After the death penalty was served, he explained his ineffective approach had stemmed from his client's instructions: Ellis had told him beforehand that she wished to join her dead lover. Nonetheless, Melford Stevenson remained a controversial figure throughout his career. He was prone to dispensing tough punishments, famously putting the Kray twins behind bars for a minimum of 30 years each in 1969, and frequently delivered harsh sentences of a different kind, describing one young woman's ordeal as 'a pretty anaemic kind of rape' because she had been attacked by her former partner. On other occasions he displayed an inappropriate dry humour, telling a defendant acquitted of rape: 'I see you come from Slough. It's a terrible place — you can go back there.'

The case he was presiding over in July 1962 achieved the greater part of its notoriety in the context of later events. Once the judge was comfortably seated that summer day, assembled groups inside the courtroom sat again. Pools of sunlight spread across the public gallery, which projected out, like a theatre balcony, below the huge glass dome. The seats were filled to capacity with men in suits and open-necked shirts, and women wearing summer dresses with cardigans draped across their shoulders. Several dabbed hand-kerchiefs to their foreheads or fanned themselves using concertinaed papers.

In the front row of the gallery sat an exceptionally pretty, dark-haired young woman. The only betrayal of her emotional turmoil lay in how she clutched the hand of the matronly lady at her side. Below them, running perpendicular to the judge's bench, were the counsel's stalls, where prosecution and defence sat side by side. A dull thud accompanied each occasion when a member of counsel got to their feet; the green leather seats were like theatre chairs, flipping up to provide barristers with something to lean on while addressing defendant or witness, jury or judge.

Few members of the public would have recognised the City dignitaries or underemployed members of the Bar who occupied the benches behind counsel, but there was no mistaking the all-male press, seated either side of the dock, jotting down preliminary details in shorthand squiggles. Old hands at trial, they knew not to expect a long day in court: the jury box was empty.

For several minutes, the room was quiet, save for the low hum of central heating, an occasional creak of wood and the odd, stifled cough. But then came the sound of footsteps, faint at first, somewhere beneath the court. As the steps grew louder, a diminutive figure flanked by uniformed guards slowly emerged from the panelled stairwell inside the dock.

All those in the public gallery instinctively leaned forward. The young woman clutching the hand of the matronly lady tightened her grip. In the press benches, veteran *Daily Express* court reporter Arnold Latcham craned his neck for a clearer view, as did Peter Harris of the *Daily Mirror*. The two men were accustomed to the many tragedies, horrors and sometimes inexplicable stories that played out in the Old Bailey, day after day. Crime reporters were not easily shocked, but the copy every man turned in that day reflected the unusual nature of events relayed before them.

The defendant spoke just once. He confirmed his name and address in suburban Neasden before pleading guilty to three charges of unlawfully and maliciously administering 'a noxious thing'. He then sat near the front of the dock, which was raised to bring it almost level with the judge's bench across the court. It was impossible not to regard him as looking slightly lost, for the dock itself was vast — 16 feet by

14 feet, with reinforced glass on three sides — built to accommodate ten or more defendants in cahoots. But it was his age, too, that cast him bumpily adrift in a sea of legality: Graham Frederick Young was 14 years old.

The *Daily Mirror's* Peter Harris described him simply as 'dark-haired and pale-faced ... expressionless' throughout proceedings. Writing ten years later, Arnold Latcham remembered: 'He sat there, that summery July 5 in 1962, cross-legged and relaxed in the dock, in neat navy school blazer and grey flannels.' It was most unusual attire for those brought up from the cells beneath the Old Bailey. Graham was yet to undergo a growth spurt or two: small but lanky, he wore his black hair combed smartly to the right above an angular face, with narrow eyes that raked coolly over the judge, counsel and reporters, who unanimously labelled him the 'Boy Poisoner'. Only the public gallery escaped his impassive gaze; he kept his eyes carefully averted from the two women holding hands.

A movement on the counsel bench soon caught Graham's attention. Mr Edward James Patrick Cussen stood, smoothing down his black robes with a practised hand. Not quite 60, Limerick-born Cussen had worked during the war as legal adviser to MI5, initially from an office inside Wormwood Scrubs. In 1944, he famously interrogated P G Wodehouse regarding a number of Nazi-funded radio shows that the popular *Jeeves & Wooster* author had broadcast to the United States. Now one of six Treasury Counsel at the Old Bailey, Cussen had established himself as stern, but scrupulously fair, and was even said to receive Christmas cards from prison inmates.

Briefly summarising Graham's childhood (since there was little more to the defendant's life than that), Cussen then outlined the extraordinary circumstances which concerned the court: that the boy had, over a period of several months, administered antimony and potassium tartrate to his father and a schoolfriend in family meals and packed lunches respectively, and had laced his sister's morning cup of tea with belladonna. The motivation behind the three charges was most unusual: neither jealousy nor avarice, nor wishing his victims dead. No, Cussen explained, the boy in the dock had merely wanted to observe the effects of each substance on the three individuals. Even the prosecution felt compelled to admit that there was no real malice involved in what Graham had done, rather that he took 'a strange and dangerous interest' in poisons, having amassed a remarkably comprehensive knowledge of such things. Cussen offered a potted history of the symptoms suffered by each victim, who were all extremely fortunate to have survived. The boy's father had been left with permanent liver damage, while no one could presume to imagine the psychological trauma involved. Cussen then referred to 'Exhibit 25', extracting a typewritten sheet from the sheaf of papers before him. He read Graham's police statement in full to the court, beginning:

I have been very interested in poisons, their properties and effects since I was about 11 years old. In May last year — 1961 — I bought 25 milligrams of antimony potassium tartrate from Ries Limited chemists on Neasden Lane. Within a couple of weeks, I tried out this poison on my friend, John Williams ...

23

Two sentences hung particularly heavy in the air: 'The doses I was giving were not fatal, but I knew I was doing wrong. It grew on me like a drug habit, except that it wasn't me who was taking the drug.'

Cussen finished reading the statement. He told the court that, although Graham had referred to poisoning 'foods at home', they should be mindful that the unexpected death of his stepmother some months before had been due to natural causes, as confirmed by a post-mortem.

Cussen sat down. Miss Jean Southworth, aged 35, led Graham's defence. Born in the Lancashire town of Clitheroe, Miss Southworth had worked as a codebreaker at Bletchley Park during the war and overcame many obstacles to practise at the Criminal Bar, where some chambers refused to have a woman on the premises. She would eventually become one of the first English female judges.

Quietly spoken, Miss Southworth was compelling as she spoke of the tragic circumstances surrounding her client's formative years — which were, in truth, still forming — but defending Graham was not an easy task. There were no witnesses for the defence, and the two doctors engaged by the prosecution were formidable and damning as they delivered their professional opinions. Dr Christopher Fysh was one of two eminent psychiatrists to have interviewed Graham at length during his time on remand. Bluntly, Dr Fysh told the court that the defendant suffered from a psychopathic disorder that left him 'prepared to take the risk of killing to gratify his interest in poisons', illustrating his point with Graham's lament, 'I miss my antimony. I miss the power it gives me.' Asked for his thoughts on the boy's immediate future, Dr Fysh replied: 'In my opinion he requires care in a maximum-security hospital. There is accommodation for him at Broadmoor.'

'The boy uses the word 'obsession',' interjected Melford Stevenson. 'What do you think about that?'

Fysh reiterated: 'Poisons have tended to take an extremely prominent place in his mind because of the sense of power they gave him. He considers himself very knowledgeable about the effect of poisons.'

'Can you express a view as to the prognosis?' queried the judge.

'I feel it is bad.'

'Does that mean that this behaviour is likely to be repeated if the opportunity were available?'

The psychiatrist replied without hesitation: 'I think it is extremely likely.'

Miss Southworth rose to question the witness. Asking him to bear in mind the quantities of poison dispensed by her client, she asked, 'Dr Fysh, do you accept that Master Young knew what a fatal dose was?'

'In some cases, yes,' the psychiatrist said. 'But in others ... no.'

'Do you agree that he has not the killer instinct?'

Fysh thought for a moment before responding: 'I would say he is rather prepared to take the risk of killing.'

Miss Southworth turned to look at Graham, sitting serenely in the dock. 'Is it not possible,' she suggested, 'that normal treatment in a hospital rather less forbidding than Broadmoor might be suitable?'

Dr Fysh shook his head. 'At the request of the Ministry of Health, the boy was examined by Dr James Cameron of the Maudsley hospital. Dr Cameron came to the conclusion that he was far too dangerous to be in even that hospital.'

Miss Southworth had no further questions.

A report compiled by Dr Donald Blair, Harley Street physician and consultant psychiatrist for several institutions, was then presented. Dr Blair had interviewed Graham at length and always found him 'quiet, placid and frankly cooperative'. He described their sessions in detail, referring to the boy's 'obvious intelligence' and the manifest 'emotional satisfaction' gained from administering poison. The defendant had read 'extensively' about toxicology and was interested in literature on 'criminology appertaining to poisoning'. Contrary to the prosecution's assertion that Graham's stepmother had died of natural causes, Dr Blair pondered whether the gradual amounts of antimony dispensed in her meals 'could have been in any way responsible'.

He was unequivocal in his diagnosis:

On all the evidence available, there seems to me little doubt that, in spite of his high intelligence, he has an inherent defect in his personality, or in other words, he has a psychopathic personality. This youth is at present a very serious danger to other people. His intense, obsessive and almost exclusive interest in drugs and their poisoning effect is not likely to change and he could well repeat his cool, calm, calculating administration of these poisons at any time. He is in my estimation not suitable for care in an ordinary mental hospital and requires the special facilities available for supervision and treatment in a criminal mental hospital such as Broadmoor. The prognosis in

26

his case is dubious but, on the evidence available, seems to me at the moment to be very bad.

Detective Inspector Edward Crabb was the final witness for the prosecution. He outlined the police investigation into Graham's activities, adding that Frederick Young, the boy's father, had sold the family home and moved in with his sister. 'I think the family is apprehensive about having the boy back,' he confirmed, before stepping down.

Miss Southworth then spoke again on behalf of her client, emphasising that while Graham had possessed significant quantities of poison, he had never administered a lethal dose. Bravely, she asked the court to look upon him in the same light as 'a drug addict, to be pitied for his obsession'. Cussen then declared that pharmacists known to have sold poison to the defendant would be 'the subject of an inquiry'.

Melford Stevenson turned to Miss Southworth. He asked whether, taking into account the uncontested medical evidence, she agreed that there was 'no practical alternative to Broadmoor' for the boy. Miss Southworth reluctantly concurred.

The judge then indicated that the defendant should stand and Graham rose to his feet in the dock. Melford Stevenson cleared his throat, then committed Graham to Broadmoor under Section 66 of the 1959 Mental Health Act. He added a restriction order preventing his release before a period of 15 years without the express authority of the Home Secretary, 'because such people are always dangerous and are adept at concealing their mad compulsion which may never be wholly cured'. Graham would be the youngest patient sent to Broadmoor since 1885, when ten-year-old Bill Giles was admitted after setting fire to a haystack. Giles had passed away only three months before Graham's trial, having spent the remainder of his 87 years within Broadmoor's walls.

Graham left the dock without acknowledging his tearful sister and aunt in the public gallery. He was led through the warren of cells and corridors beneath the courts to an iron-barred enclosure where all convicted persons were held, like cattle in a pen, to await dispersion. Some wept, others fought and shouted, but the majority slumped silently, in a state of 'catatonic gloom'.

Graham stood among them, ignoring the jostles and cries. He kept his gaze locked upon an inconspicuous spot on the ceiling, privately exulting.

Because for all the combined machinations of family, school, doctors, police, forensic experts, remand centre staff, psychiatrists and the legal brains of the most famous court in England, his greatest secret remained concealed, the evidence having literally gone up in smoke.

At the age of 14, Graham Young had committed the perfect murder.

**1947—1962
NEASDEN**

'I avoided my own friends and
acquaintances, yet the loneliness of my
existence was insupportable.'

Agatha Christie, *The Pale Horse*
(Collins, The Crime Club, 1961)

1

A DEADLY SENSATION
WITHIN

'A chubby little boy — we nicknamed him Pudding,' recalls Winifred Young with an older sister's typical candour in her 1973 memoir *Obsessive Poisoner*. There were eight years between the siblings, a period which spanned the Second World War and brought about irrevocable familial change.

Their roots were primarily in London, where Winifred and Graham's paternal grandmother, Hannah, had endured a spell in Holborn workhouse as a child. A determined spirit, before the age of 20 she was head of her own home in Finsbury, where she took care of her younger brother and worked as a skilled French polisher. Hannah married jewellery-repair specialist Ralph Frederick Young on Valentine's Day 1904 and they settled in St John's Wood.

The next few years were tumultuous. Hannah bore two sons in quick succession: Ralph in 1905 and Frederick in 1906. One year later, she was widowed when her 28-year-old husband died suddenly. Shortly afterwards, she met William Davis, a delivery driver three years her senior. They married in 1909 and their daughter Winifred was born the following year.

The family unit was strong, with Hannah's second husband proving a loving father to all three children. A special bond grew between the brother and sister with such similar names, Fred and Winifred. For the rest of their lives, they stayed fiercely supportive of each other, with Winifred's compassion and practicality acting as an unassailable wall to hold back the worst of the storms her brother Fred faced in the years to come.

The young family moved to Edinburgh shortly before the First World War. William joined the army, returning safely when the conflict ended. They relocated to Aberdeen, where all three children picked up the local accent. After finishing school, Fred found work in a grocery shop and fell in love with the girl literally next door: Margaret Conboy Smith, daughter of a trawler engineer. Known to everyone as Bessie, she was a pretty, dark-haired young woman who worked as a housekeeper until her marriage. The wedding was held on 8 December 1936 at St Peter's Roman Catholic church in Aberdeen, half a mile from the street where the couple had lived as neighbours. The groom was 30, his bride 22. Three years later, Bessie gave birth to a daughter whom they named in honour of the sister they both adored: Winifred Margaret. Bessie was a devoted mother and Fred a loving, if physically unaffectionate, father.

But the world was in turmoil, and on 3 September 1939 Britain declared war on Hitler's Germany. The entire family, apart from Bessie and the baby, returned to London. Their new home was in Neasden, described by Sir John Betjeman as 'home of the gnome and average citizen' in his 1973 documentary, *Metro-land*. By the 1960s, Neasden had come to epitomise the English suburb. Relentlessly spoofed by the satirical magazine *Private Eye*, which had its origins there, the area has been described as the loneliest village in London, 'easy to loathe', with a road that swings 'like a lasso, looping wider and wider tracts of darkness'.

Thirteen miles north-west of Charing Cross, Neasden lies in the London borough of Brent, sliced in two by the North Circular Road that runs from Woolwich in the east to Chiswick in the west.

Transport shaped its fortunes and geography, first the trains, then the cars. Neasden was originally a small farming hamlet, but by the early 20th century, scores of manufacturers began relocating their factories from London's East End to the city outskirts; the ring road was built to bypass London while connecting new areas of industry and providing work for the unemployed following the First World War.

In 1924, 27 million visitors attended the British Empire Exhibition at Wembley Park. An extended celebration of colonial industry, engineering, horticulture and arts, the exhibition had a new sports ground — the original Wembley Stadium — at its centre. Visitors travelling on electric trains through the leafy suburbs found themselves longing to leave the city. 'Metro-land' fulfilled that demand: housing estates were built during the 1920s and 1930s near stations on the line out beyond Neasden. In 1933, the Metropolitan Railway linking the suburbs to central London was taken over by the London Passenger Transport Board; Neasden power station, together with Lots Road power station, continued to supply the network.

There was no more farmland, just row upon row of neat houses stretching in every direction and all along the North Circular Road as far as the eye could see. There were plenty of amenities, such as the Ritz cinema, a soaring art-deco silhouette that dominated

33

the Neasden High Road from 1935, where a year later the shopping parade opened. Yet while manufacturing boomed, communities were cut adrift by shoddy town planning. The lack of bridges over the river Brent made access between Neasden and Wembley difficult, and the ring road was a concrete moat. But employment was plentiful: Fred and Win initially found jobs at the Air Admiralty factory, where 60-year-old William worked as nightwatchman. The family lived together on Links Road for a short time, while Fred sought a home where his wife and daughter could join him.

Win became engaged to Enfield-born council worker Fred 'Jack' Jouvenat. Twelve years his fiancée's senior, Jack had grown up in Battersea with his aunt and uncle, who owned the Latchmere Hotel. His first wife had died young, nine years after their wedding. Win's family loved Jack, and her father William, as a Freemason himself, was delighted to discover that his new son-in-law was a member of the same society.

Fred swiftly found long-term work with Smith's English Clocks Ltd at their Cricklewood factory. Part of Smiths Industries, the electric clock-and-watch factory employed 8,000 people in 1939 and was the biggest employer in the area. For many years one of the local bridges bore a sign announcing: 'Cricklewood: The Home of Smiths Clocks'. During the Second World War, the company produced motor, aircraft and marine instruments, and fuses for shells. Fred was responsible for operating, setting and checking production machinery, an occupation he held until his retirement and which enabled him to take out a mortgage on a new three-bedroom terraced property with a garden at 146 Dawpool Road.

34

Bessie and the baby joined him ahead of Win and Jack's wedding in July 1940. It was the height of the Blitz: living on the outskirts of London, in an area that heaved with industry, was fraught with danger. The wailing air-raid siren was a familiar sound day and night. In August 1940, Fred and his fellow workers were lucky to avoid a bomb that fell on the main instrument repair department. Rockets descended regularly on nearby residential streets, sending people scurrying indoors to their Morrison cage shelters or running for the galvanised steel Andersons in gardens or yards.

The Youngs, Davises and Jouvenats survived the war unscathed. Close-knit as ever, they all lived within easy walking distance of each other. Fred's mother Hannah and stepfather William stayed on at 31 Links Road, while his sister and brother-in-law moved to 768 North Circular Road, where their daughter Sandra was born in July 1942. Two years after the war ended, Bessie discovered to her delight that she was pregnant again. But within weeks she had begun experiencing severe chest pains and was diagnosed with pleurisy, an inflammation of the membrane lining the lungs. Her condition worsened. She was admitted to Willesden maternity hospital on Kingsbury's Honeypot Lane. Built on the grounds of an old smallpox hospital and incorporating three pavilions, it housed women in various stages of pregnancy and their newborns.

Despite the expert care on hand, Bessie weakened. She developed tuberculosis, suffering weight loss, ragged breathing and fever. Then she began coughing up blood. In the early hours of 7 September 1947, she went into labour. 'It was a difficult birth,' her husband recalled. The baby, born barely moving and silent, was placed on antibiotics immediately because of his mother's illness. Winifred overheard her grandmother saying that he was 'rather delicate' and then 'something about him being a blue baby', although, at eight years old, neither she nor her cousin Sandra understood what that meant. The baby recovered, but his mother's condition deteriorated. It was to be a heartbreaking Christmas: on 23 December 1947, Bessie died of a spinal abscess. She was 33 years old.

'I was left with two young children on my hands and my engineering job to do,' Fred reflected 25 years later. 'Winifred went to live with my mother and Graham was taken in by my sister.' The baby, named Graham after a Scottish friend and Frederick for his father, bonded quickly with the relatives who gave him a home; he had 'a normal, loving relationship' with them. Win later described herself as Graham's 'second mother'. His sister Winifred recalled: 'Graham was very affectionate as a child. He called my aunt and uncle — Sandra's parents — Aunty Panty and Daddy Jack and I think he loved them very much.' Every weekend, Fred would walk round to Links Road and collect his daughter. 'My father used to take me round the corner to see Graham,' Winifred confirmed, 'and together we pushed him out in his pram. Number 768 was right opposite the swings in the Welsh Harp and it was pleasant to watch the sailing boats on the reservoir.'

Graham was a happy toddler, doted on by his sister and cousin. 'Sandra saw more of Graham to begin with than I did, as they lived together,' Winifred stated. 'There were no signs of jealousy between them and they managed to get up to some amusing tricks

36

as a pair.'

Graham was a very light sleeper; at 18 months old, he would pinch pens from his Uncle Jack's pocket when he and Win kissed him goodnight, then stand up in his cot to scribble on the bedroom wall while everyone else slept.

Aged two, however, he developed an illness, which caused some unusual behaviour during his early school years. What began as a simple ear infection was subsequently diagnosed as mastoiditis, an inflammation of the mastoid bone behind the ear. Although a fairly common complaint in children, Graham's problem was more serious, requiring an overnight hospital stay. Winifred recalled that when the family said goodbye to him, 'He almost screamed the place down, crying for his Aunty Panty and Daddy Jack.' A myringotomy was performed, in which the doctor made a tiny hole in Graham's eardrum to drain the fluid before putting him on a drip. When his aunt and uncle arrived to collect him, he 'beamed from ear to ear'. The experience left him terrified of any sort of medical procedure. It was also thought to account for the unusual visual symptoms and awkward limb movements he displayed until the age of eight, and later a low verbal IQ result and subsequent electro-encephalography (EEG) irregularities detected in the right frontal-parietal region.

The intense separation anxiety Graham had felt in hospital resurfaced the following year when his father, then 43, fell in love. Hampstead-born Gwendolyne Molly Petley was 28, the daughter of a British Railways police constable and his wife. Known to family and friends by her middle name, Molly, she worked at the Smiths factory alongside Fred and played the accordion at their local pub. She was bright and interested in everyone, with an open face and always wore her hair parted in the centre with two big waves on either side. Her wedding to Fred took place on 1 April 1950 at Willesden registry office and prompted change for all the family.

Determined to bring his children under one roof, Fred sold the house on Dawpool Road and bought his sister's home at 768 North Circular Road. Win and Jack, together with their daughter Sandra, then moved back to 31 Links Road to live with Hannah and William (who died the following year). Thus, Graham remained in the only home he had ever known, but with his aunt and uncle replaced by his father and new stepmother, and his sister Winifred taking over from his cousin Sandra. Molly was eager to get along with her stepchildren, but it took a while for her husband's daughter to accept her. 'Perhaps I was a bit unpleasant to her at first,' Winifred conceded. 'I suppose I didn't like her taking my mother's place — you know how it is with children. But as I grew older, we got on very well. On the other hand, Graham really loved her. Unlike me, after all, he had never known his real mother and indeed he always called Molly 'Mummy'.' Fred agreed: 'People have suggested that Graham may have nursed some grudge or resentment at being taken away from Winnie. He doted on [Molly] and she on him.'

Nonetheless, there were signs Graham was experiencing some inner turmoil. His psychiatric notes record that he regularly 'rocked himself to sleep at night and he wet the bed until ten years'. Winifred remembered this behaviour, of her brother's habit of rocking backwards and forwards in his cot: 'He would

38

do this even in his sleep, creating such a thumping sort of noise that the man next door lodged a complaint (incidentally, we saw a TV programme about deprived Vietnamese children fairly recently and they, too, rocked backwards and forwards in their cot and immediately we all thought of Graham).' Otherwise, he appeared to be 'a loving child who showed positive emotional reactions'.

Aware that her stepson was devoted to his aunt and uncle, Molly visited the Jouvenats regularly with him. The three children got along together well, and the two girls would take Graham across to play at the Welsh Harp reservoir. Apart from the busy roads, it was a pleasant area for children. Graham's peers would get into mischief, running over the North Circular Road to jump on the steam trains at Charrington's and playing on the railway land near an iron bridge later occupied by a vast Ikea outlet. Graham disliked physical activity and never joined the neighbourhood children for a weekend swim at the Willesden lido or in Gladstone Park's sloping, kidneyshaped pool. He was happy with just his sister and cousin, who had a penchant for writing and performing their own plays. Graham would take any role assigned to him even if, on one memorable occasion, it involved standing on 'stage' for half an hour, playing a Belisha beacon streetlamp.

Winifred and Sandra had already left Braintcroft primary school when Graham joined. Situated on Warren Road, half a mile from his home, it opened in 1928 as a council school. The 'chubby little boy . . . with dark brown hair, a little round face and freckles' made few friends at his new school, pointedly ignoring all playground games. He had no interest in

39

learning and even less in sports, although he was an avid reader. His fellow pupils seemed to regard him as part of the furniture; he was never bullied or deliberately excluded, but he made it clear he preferred his own company or that of a book. Photographs from a school trip to Swanage in Dorset show him as an awkward six-year-old, neat in school cap and blazer but sitting hunched among his peers, a rictus grin plastered to his face.

Fred Young remembered one bright spot during Graham's later years at Braintcroft, fostered by his recreational time with Winifred and Sandra: 'Graham was a quiet, withdrawn boy at school. He wasn't all that brilliant as a scholar. But he was a brilliant actor. I remember going to see him in a school play in which he had the part of a wicked baron. He was stupendous — he brought the house down.' Another performance — this time as an ugly sister in the Braintcroft Christmas pantomime — was likewise inspired. His family knew that he could be extremely comical in the right mood, capable of poking fun at his own fastidiousness and with a keen eye for other people's foibles.

At home, life was quiet. Fred liked to go to the pub once a week but rarely drank to excess. Molly usually joined him, leaving Graham at Links Road with his grandmother, aunt and uncle, whom he visited every day without fail. Win later questioned whether Graham's crimes were due to having 'lost two mothers by the age of three', and certainly a deep-seated unhappiness was beginning to surface. While on remand in 1962, Graham reflected: 'I am not very emotional. I used to be until I was about seven. I used to start crying when I thought of my mother dying.' He would sob himself to sleep, wondering what his life would have been like had his birth mother survived. These unhappy thoughts led to nightmares, punctuated by sleepwalking. His sister recalled: 'Once Molly, our stepmother, heard a noise during the night and ran into the living room where Graham slept on a put-u-up, just in time to catch him before he fell off the sideboard. Apparently he had clambered up at one end, walked right across it and was just about to step out into space when she caught him.' Graham told a psychiatrist who examined him years later how he would lie awake in bed at that age, experiencing 'alterations of consciousness characterised by perceiving things as exceptionally near or distant, by a pulsating and slowing of his thinking and by a feeling of 'automatism' and being outside himself'. He never mentioned it to anyone at the time.

If the premature loss of his mother caused Graham a great deal of emotional trauma as a child, then so too did his father's behaviour, according to both professionals and family members. Frank Walker — 'Uncle Frank' to Graham and his sister — had been a family friend for many years and had a lot of affection for the two children. He suspected that Fred blamed his son for Bessie's death and felt him to be an unnecessarily stern father to Graham. The relationship troubled Frank, who regarded it as strangely formal: 'His father, as far as I knew, had no time for him whatsoever. He never cherished him as he should, or anything like that.'

During his interviews with Graham in 1972, consultant psychiatrist Dr Peter Scott observed: 'The defendant did not get on well with his father, who was independently described as 'not easy to get on with'.

41

Rightly or wrongly, the defendant felt as a boy that his individuality had been 'smothered' and that he was not understood.' A staff member in Broadmoor during the mid-1960s found Fred Young was 'unable to see any point of view but his own and to be incapable of understanding anyone else's problems'. Dr Patrick McGrath, then medical superintendent at Broadmoor, surprisingly named Win as a source, albeit at a point where her sympathies lay far more with her nephew: 'Accounts by Graham's aunt suggested that the father, her brother, was a callous and selfish man, indifferent to the feelings of those around him and tended to belittle Graham because of the boy's poor mathematical ability.'

The authorities were similarly unforgiving in their assessment of Molly Young. Another Broadmoor report posthumously described her as 'domineering, house-proud and overbearing'. Dr McGrath felt that she had been 'a hoarder, almost miserly . . . over-protective', while Dr Peter Scott recorded that Graham was 'markedly ambivalent about his stepmother, defending her at some points but expressing deep resentment at others. He remembers her cane and her parsimonious and hoarding habits, her lack of friends and discouragement of allowing him to have his friends home; all these points are confirmed from independent sources.'

If Fred's feelings towards his young son were complicated, leaving him unable to express normal affection, in the years to come he conveyed both love and forgiveness where many other parents may have found it impossible. The same was also true of Molly Young. During her police interviews prior to Graham's 1962 trial, Win made no criticism of her brother or her sister-in-law, stating simply: 'My sister-in-law was a good mother to them, was very house-proud and my brother Fred was very happy.'

But the few friends Graham made at school recall that he complained Molly was too strict, kept him short of funds ('I have given him pocket money ever since he was a nipper,' Win told the police) and destroyed his collection of model aeroplanes after some minor misdemeanour. He also claimed that one of the reasons he called to see his aunt after school each day was because Molly locked him out of the house while Fred was at work, to prevent him from snacking. He also resented the fact that he wasn't allowed a dog, but Molly, who loved animals as much as the rest of the family, understandably worried about traffic on the thundering artery where they lived. She did agree to a budgie; named Lemon, the little yellow bird spent hours perched on Graham's finger. But when Molly grumbled that her stepson spoke more to Lemon than anyone else in the family and she might have the bird destroyed, Graham interpreted her words as a threat rather than an exasperated joke.

Molly's concern over the dangers of the North Circular Road was borne out in 1955 when Graham himself was knocked down by a car 'but not seriously hurt'. Apart from Dr Peter Scott's note about the accident, there are no further records available. Nonetheless, Graham's character underwent a series of changes thereafter; subtle at first, these soon became ever more pernicious.

2

POISON HATH
RESIDENCE

Ominous dark clouds heralded the perfect storm, primed to burst over the ordinary-looking house on the North Circular Road. After his accident, Graham's love of reading deepened, taking him back repeatedly to certain shelves of his local library. His interests were specific: history, the occult and pharmacy. He read volumes of biography: Julius and Tiberius Caesar, Kaiser Wilhelm II, Oliver Cromwell, Joseph Stalin and Adolf Hitler. Graham was barely nine years old. The war had ended only a decade before and was a sensitive subject, but his imagination flared at the spectacle of Nazi torchlit mass rallies and the thunder of Hitler's incandescent raging speeches. Where other boys collected stamps or stickers, he gathered clippings about Germany's war and fashioned himself a swastika armband. His family made little fuss, thinking him silly rather than sinister. Win shook her head when asked about it: 'Hitler? I think [Graham] could even tell you what he had for breakfast.'

Molly grew more worried. She visited the library, pleaded with the head librarian to keep an eye on Graham's reading materials, asking if it might be possible for them to forbid him certain books. The librarian reassured her that it was not necessarily a bad thing to read about recent history and that any obsessions were almost certainly a phase. Annoyed at her inter-

44

vention, Graham carted his books over to the Welsh Harp, reading peaceably away from Molly's watchful gaze. Fred Young said nothing about it but admitted afterwards that it was this stage when he first became aware that his son definitely seemed different to other boys: 'He did not mix well or show any interest in normal youthful activities, but spent a lot of his time reading.' Win doted on her nephew as much as ever, but realised to her consternation that although he was 'a well-behaved lad, good-mannered but withdrawn', he had developed 'morbid tastes, reading books on poisons, death, voodoo and anything horrific'.

Despite his family's attempts to nullify his interests by ignoring them, there were signs of something more serious emerging. A later psychiatric report records that at the age of ten, Graham was 'taken successively to every form in his school and made to apologise for organising an anti-Jewish movement'. The school's attitude is commendable, but they, too, were beginning to sense that he was falling out of reach; his form master described him as 'borderline Grammar School standard but underhanded, sly, frequently in trouble but slipping out of punishment'.

Graham's fascination with the occult deepened. He asked Sandra if she had read much about it. She replied that she had no interest in the subject, which prompted him to launch into an explanation of what he found so fascinating about it. He told her he had learned a lot from a chap who frequented the library; the man claimed to be part of a Willesden coven. Sandra looked at him sceptically but was alarmed when she and her mother found a tiny plasticine figure, rust-coloured with green legs and pierced through with darning needles, in one of Graham's jacket pockets.

One subject began to emerge above all else in Graham's small world. Fred had encouraged him to think about becoming an engineer, but in his last year at primary school, Graham told his father bluntly that he found it boring. He admitted to being fascinated by all things chemical, however. Sandra found him perusing the small bottles on his grandmother's dressing table in Links Road. 'He started showing an interest in queer things,' she recalled. 'He was always collecting empty perfume bottles and other odd bottles, bottles which smelled, especially nail varnish.' Her mother also noticed Graham's penchant for such things: 'He was always interested in little bottles and kept them in his pockets. We used to find them and throw them out.' They realised that he inhaled the vapours, using ether and acetone as stimulants. Sometimes he produced a bottle from his pockets and asked his sister, aunt or cousin to guess at the contents before listing the ingredients himself. He talked about the effects different poisons had on the body. Once, when Sandra encountered him near home, he stopped to tell her what happened when you ingested an aspirin on an empty stomach. Suddenly, when anyone felt a bit off-colour, Graham would question them about their symptoms as a doctor would before advising on a remedy. He referred to every ailment by its medical name and demonstrated an outstanding memory for detail.

Poison was his passion. He borrowed book after book on the subject from the library, disguising the covers with ones filched from other, less contentious books in order to avoid upsetting his stepmother. As his 11-plus exams approached, he did hardly any revision and no one was more surprised than him when he passed. As a reward, his father bought him a chemistry set.

★ ★ ★

As the 1950s came to a close, living in Neasden had its advantages. Close to 'swinging' London, it was home to Twiggy, the first supermodel, chart-toppers Johnny Kidd & the Pirates, and also boasted a thriving hub of youth culture on its doorstep in the shape of the Ace Café, which thrummed to the beat of rock 'n' roll and revving motorbikes. The pubs, most bearing mock-Tudor beams, were always busy, and there was an influx of new people as the building boom got underway again. And yet, despite its potential, Neasden slipped further into decline. The *New Statesman* cited the suburb as a prime example of what goes wrong when a large road 'both carves up and strangles an area'.

Graham had zero interest in the cultural revolution swirling about him. His head was filled with poison and its practitioners, even as he travelled into town with Molly to buy his new uniform from Myers, the outfitters on Neasden High Road. He had lost weight since leaving primary school, and when Molly took him to the barber shop on the opposite side of the street, his dark-haired reflection was all sharp angles, deep-set eyes and a narrow mouth.

Graham was one of the first pupils to attend the John Kelly secondary school on Willesden's Tanfield Avenue. Founded in 1958, it was a hulking, modern glass building with extensive playing fields and a separate school for girls, and it rose behind the residential street like a ship in harbour. Headmaster

Henry Merkel, nicknamed 'Harry' by the pupils, was a quirky but strict figure. His assembly speech, 'Box out is box out', used the metaphor of someone knocking an object from another person's grasp to remind pupils to be vigilant about their person, thoughts and possessions.

Graham established himself as a fairly mediocre student apart from in science, where teacher Geoffrey Hughes placed him in the 'A' stream for chemistry. Rather than conceal his obsession with poison, he chose to flaunt it, gaining him two nicknames: 'Acid' and the 'Mad Professor'. He remained fairly insular, but for the first time in his life found two friends who tolerated his idiosyncrasies with good humour: classmates Clive Creager and Chris Williams. 'I don't know why we were mates,' Chris reflected. 'He had no one else really and I suppose I felt sorry for him. Graham wasn't like me or like any of the boys. He was always grown up, with an adult's mentality but always warped [and] peculiar in many ways.'

All three shared an interest in chemistry. Left alone together in the school lab, Chris and Clive watched as Graham fed various substances to mice in order to study the process of death. Afterwards, he would perform elaborate post-mortems, talking his friends through the procedure as if he were a regular pathologist. He hid a mouse in his satchel, intending to carry out an autopsy in his bedroom, but when Molly discovered the dead rodent, she made him dispose of it immediately.

Enraged, Graham shut himself into his bedroom. Taking out a large sheet of paper, he drew a grave, surrounded by snakes, spiders and bats. On the headstone he wrote: 'In Hateful Memory of Molly Young,

48

Rest in Peace'. The incident might have remained no more than an unpleasant childish reaction, but in context it became something far darker. Winifred remembered Molly being terribly upset when she found the picture, where Graham had deliberately left it for her; furthermore, she believed it was around this time when her brother's mind 'began to split'.

Graham himself admitted that by then he was 'obsessed with the macabre'. Clive Creager sat next to him in the classroom and watched with disturbed amusement as Graham's pencil flew across his school-books, depicting his friends: 'I would be hanging from some gallows over a vat of acid. Graham would be holding a flame to the rope. He liked drawing people on gallows with syringes marked 'poison' sticking into them.' Similarly, when Uncle Jack made Aunt Win a clipboard for bingo, Graham covered it with doodles of skulls, monsters and bottles of poison. The original sketch of Molly's headstone was the first in a series of images: coffins engraved 'Mum' and 'Dad', nightmarish creatures, death's heads, devils and vampires. 'Uncle' Frank Walker remembered that Molly brought a couple of the sketches along to show him on a visit, asking in a troubled voice, 'What do you think of these?' Frank responded sharply, 'Well, he's your boy, isn't he?' He had little sympathy with the Youngs, believing that they had a duty to sit down with Graham and talk through the issues that led to his behaviour. At one stage, Graham tried switching from sketches to short stories, but set aside any dreams of literary stardom when the *Reader's Digest* failed to respond to his written flights of Gothic fancy.

The onset of puberty left Graham tongue-tied around the female friends of his sister and cousin. He

49

developed a habit of blurting out strange comments, either due to nerves or — as Sandra suspected — he enjoyed embarrassing people. When Jack was having treatment in Manor House hospital, Graham took the bus with Sandra. She asked the conductor for the correct fare, which included a child's ticket for her cousin, only to notice that Graham had lit a cigarette and was blowing smoke rings down the aisle. On the way home, after she pointed out a friend's boyfriend, Graham spent the rest of journey parroting the line, driving her to distraction. She reluctantly agreed to let him accompany her again to hospital and regretted it when Graham sat directly opposite a female passenger, leaning forward to glare silently at her until she moved hastily away. On another occasion when the two of them visited a café, Graham knocked a drink from the waitress' hand, triumphantly yelling Harry Merkel's line, 'Box out is box out!' The only time he behaved normally was around elderly people, whose company he seemed to find comforting. He often visited nearby Gladstone Park, where he would sit on a bench and strike up a conversation with any aged people relaxing there.

Graham's fear of undergoing any medical procedure sparked a crisis when he was sent for a check-up at the dentist. He fled the waiting room at the first opportunity and was brought home by a Harlesden police officer. Graham claimed to have been abducted by a man who drove him around Willesden before suddenly releasing him. The constable said sternly that there was no truth in the matter and Graham burst into tears, admitting he had made the story up, hoping that Molly would excuse him from his dental appointment. Sympathetic to her stepson, she arranged for him to have an orthodontal examination at hospital under anaesthetic. She also took the opportunity to make him an appointment with a psychiatrist, ostensibly because of his fears and occasional truanting, but largely to discuss his escalating 'strangeness'. The psychiatrist found 'little wrong' and instead recorded that Molly was 'rather tense, over-conscientious and over-protective'.

But Molly was right to be concerned, and particularly about her stepson's most persistent habit: smoking ether and sniffing toxic substances. When she asked him about a hole that had appeared in his school blazer, he admitted it had been caused by a small bottle of acid he had found in a bin behind the chemist shop on Neasden High Road. Molly searched his room. After discovering several similar bottles, she led Graham down to the chemist shop, warning the proprietor that she would report him if he didn't dispose of his toxic products correctly. Distraught, she spoke to both Winifred and Sandra but said nothing to her husband. 'Aunt Molly knew more about Graham's tinkering with poisons than my Uncle Fred,' Sandra states. 'She used to try and shield Graham.' Molly hated the idea of upsetting Fred; his mother Hannah died in October 1960 and he felt the loss of his beloved mother deeply.

Graham's night terrors returned with his grandmother's death. He later told Broadmoor medical superintendent Dr Patrick McGrath that he experienced 'peculiar frightening attacks' just before going to sleep, where phrases would repeat themselves and images would recede then grow in size. He spoke to no one about it but became more frequently in trouble at school. On one occasion he started a vicious

51

fight with two older boys in the playground, which Harry Merkel broke up. Graham then snapped his heels together and gave Merkel a Hitler salute. The headmaster promptly got hold of Graham's ear and marched him to his office. 'We treated it as a joke,' Clive Creager said of his friend's obsession with Hitler. 'Graham would comb his short black hair over to one side and hold the top of a comb to his upper lip. Then he'd strut about, repeating some Hitler speech in German. We all laughed.'

But Graham's behaviour was spiralling. To supplement the two-and-sixpence pocket money his father gave him, he took a weekend cleaning job at a local café for another five shillings. He spent part of it on fireworks: dismantling them in an old hut on the Welsh Harp allotments, he extracted the gunpowder, then packed it into cardboard tubes to make 'bombs'. Watched by friends, he planted the tubes on the bank of the reservoir and set them off. He was almost rumbled when one of his 'bombs' destroyed most of what was left of the hut, where he also kept poisons. Police investigating the explosion found the tubes and bottles but failed to trace them back to Graham.

Chris Williams recalled how Graham used his 'bombs' to take revenge on twin lads in Neasden whom he disliked: 'He made up some stuff — explosives with sugar and weed-killer — and blew up their garden wall.' On another occasion he put a substance on the deputy headmaster's car, which burned through the paintwork. 'He was only thirteen then,' Williams remembered. Graham had no friends among the neighbourhood teens, largely because parents disliked his habit of 'lurking' and the glare he gave those who told him to move on. He preferred being alone with his books and bottles most of the time, regardless. Winifred recalled: 'He was reading a book in particular on William Palmer, an infamous poisoner of the Victorian period. He kept drawing this book out of the library. I can remember Graham saying what a clever man he was.' Palmer was the only person Graham admired more than Hitler; he read sections from the chapter about him in *Sixty Famous Trials* to Winifred, explaining that Palmer's poison of choice was antimony. Tiring of hearing her brother describe Palmer as brilliantly clever, she retorted that he hadn't managed to avoid the hangman. Graham replied that in modern times that wouldn't be an issue. When Winifred pointed out that he would have been jailed for life nonetheless, Graham shrugged, 'That's nothing.'

True crime had been his genre of choice for some time. His favourite book appeared in 1960: *Poisoner in the Dock: Twelve Studies in Poisoning* was written by John Rowland, who made the same point regarding Palmer's fate in his introduction:

> Every convicted murderer in the past was automatically condemned to death, even though the jury might have recommended him or her to mercy; now only certain categories of murder must inevitably lead to the death sentence, and so many people who would, in a previous era, have been hanged, will not now go to the gallows ... The death penalty has been retained for those murderers who kill by the use of firearms; but it has been abolished for those who kill by the use of poison. Yet to most people it will seem that the man who discharges a revolver in a moment

of evil temper, driven well-nigh to madness, perhaps, by an unfaithful wife, is in many respects less morally guilty than the poisoner, who mixes some deadly substance with the food prepared for another member of the household. In the vast majority of cases, when murder by poison is proved, the person concerned has worked steadily and with premeditation, over a period of months or even of years; his or her purpose has been to ensure the death of someone, but to ensure that it seems due to natural causes.

It was the second chapter ('Antimony') of the book that gripped Graham most. Nineteenth-century Glasgow physician Dr Edward William Pritchard had poisoned his wife and her mother and was executed in 1865 before a 100,000-strong crowd. The chapter begins:

> It is not easy to say why arsenic has featured in so many poisoning cases and antimony in comparatively few. The two poisons are very closely related, both in chemistry and toxicology; their symptoms and their effects are much alike. Even in the realm of theoretical chemistry, arsenic and antimony are classified together. Yet for every case of poisoning by antimony, there must be a score of cases of poisoning by arsenic. And, as arsenic poisoning appears to have become less common in recent years, antimony poisoning seems to have vanished altogether from the scene ...

Over the course of 17 pages, Graham learned that antimony belongs to the same chemical family as bismuth, phosphorus and arsenic. A fragile semi-metal, odourless and colourless, it consists of crystals or granular powder, and is soluble in water or alcohol and sweet tasting. For centuries it has been used, along with other salts of antimony, in the production of cosmetics, paints, glass, rubber and medicine, but it was discontinued as a component in cough remedies due to its toxicity. A slow-working poison, antimony causes persistent vomiting, cramps and diarrhoea. Such symptoms are often mistaken for other ailments, but the regular administration of poison over a sustained period leads to muscle weakness, inability to pass water, collapse and convulsions, culminating in death. At the close of the chapter, Rowland considers what might be learned about the mind of the poisoner from the Pritchard case: 'There is, of course, the typical ruthlessness, the fact that he did not care at all whether he caused suffering — the fact, indeed, that as a doctor he must have known the suffering to this wife and mother-in-law, which was caused by the long and systematic process of poisoning which he had embarked on. There is certainly something much crueller in a slow process of this kind than when a single large dose of poison is given . . .'

Shortly after his first reading of the book, Graham told his friends that one day he would be a famous poisoner along the lines of Pritchard, Palmer or Crippen. 'We treated it as a joke,' Clive recalled.

A few days later, Graham was again involved in a playground tussle, this time provoked by his jealousy over Chris spending more time with their friend Richard Hands, who lived a few doors down from Graham. After spotting the two boys out in the neighbourhood, Graham challenged Chris to a fight at school.

55

'I'll always remember that fight,' Chris admitted. 'It was all over very quickly. Graham was much smaller than me. As he lay on the ground with me standing over him, he looked up and said to me, 'I'll kill you for that." Chris merely laughed and offered Graham a hand: 'It's the sort of thing kids say when they've lost a fight. But some time afterwards — we'd patched it all up by then — Graham said to me, 'You know, I really could kill you."

Unlike other kids, Graham meant it.

3

MY LITTLE FRIEND

In his remand interviews with Dr Donald Blair, Graham confessed to targeting Chris Williams in February 1961. Over a period of three weeks, he secretly administered five two-grain doses of sugar of lead (lead acetate) to his friend, telling Dr Blair, 'apparently with regret', that it only caused constipation. Where and how Graham obtained the substance remains unknown, but he had already amassed a lethal collection.

Following his fight with Chris, and despite their reconciliation, Graham's intentions turned truly deadly. On Friday, 28 April 1961, he visited Reis pharmacy on Neasden Lane, where he spoke to the pharmacist himself. 'I supplied him with 15 grams of antimony and potassium tartrate,' Geoffrey Reis recalled. 'The young man told me he wanted the poisons for laboratory work. I did not ask him his age, nor did he tell me, as far as I recollect.' Graham was four years below the minimum legal age for buying poison. Each sale had to be registered, and when Reis produced his ledger for detectives almost exactly a year later, it showed the sale was made to 'E Young, 768 North Circular Road, NW10'. Further sales under the same name and address were recorded the following Thursday and the Friday after, on 4 and 12 May 1961 respectively.

There were no more transactions because Molly

found out that Graham was still hiding toxic substances in his room. This time she told his father, resulting in a fierce argument between Fred and his son. 'He swore to me . . . that he had finished with all that sort of thing,' Fred confirmed. 'As a father I had forbidden him to bring home poisons. My wife used to go through his clothes. I don't know what exactly he brought home.' The row culminated in another trip to the pharmacy for Graham in his stepmother's company, as Reis recalled: 'His mother came and spoke to me and I have never supplied him with poisons since.' Graham was more careful where he stored his poisons afterwards, splitting them between the old hut by the Welsh Harp reservoir and under a hedge.

In his subsequent police statement, Graham described how 'within a couple of weeks' of buying antimony potassium tartrate he had 'tried out this poison' on Chris Williams: 'I gave him two or three grains at school. I can't remember how I caused him to take it, I think it was probably on a cream biscuit or a cake. He was sick after taking it. I gave him a second dose in May in the same way and in the following month I gave him another two doses, always two or three grains and always on food at school.'

Chris remembered vomiting at school one Monday in May after the onset of sharp, sudden stomach pains. He recovered about 6pm that night but fell ill again every Monday thereafter for at least five weeks. He later suspected that Graham had slipped the poison into a packed-lunch sandwich he insisted on swapping, or in a bottle of free school milk distributed during morning break. He recalled how Graham would 'look after me when I was ill, watching me all the time. He always wanted to know what I felt, my

58

pains and everything. It used to take me about a day to recover.' Clive Creager remembered Graham remarking to him one morning that Chris would be absent that afternoon: 'I realised that he meant that Williams would be sick and that he knew beforehand.'

Winifred knew that her brother's friend had been ill but had no idea Graham was responsible: 'He came home and said, 'Chris was very sick. They got a bucket out for him. I saw and watched.'' Following the incidents at school, Graham invited Chris to Regent's Park zoo, ostensibly to cheer his friend up. As the two boys strolled towards the enclosures, Graham expressed sympathy for Chris, then produced a large bottle of lemonade from his rucksack. He told him it would help his stomach. Chris drank from the bottle, unaware that Graham had laced it with antimony. 'I was sick straight away,' he recalled. 'We got on and off four different buses for me to be ill. I was staggering and shaking and finally we got home.'

Chris' mother had already taken him to see their local GP, Dr Wills, but he was unable to find anything wrong. After the incident at Regent's Park, Chris experienced severe headaches as well as vomiting and general pains. On Friday, 9 June, Mrs Williams took her son to Willesden general hospital, where he was seen by Dr Goldfoot, who diagnosed migraines and prescribed treatment: 'According to my case notes, he had an attack in July and one in August. These attacks were headaches with vomiting.' Goldfoot saw Chris again in October and the following February after further spells, but 'was not able to find out what was wrong with this boy ... My impression was that all these attacks were alike. I came to the conclusion that he was giving pretty typical symptoms of migraine.'

59

Unfortunately for Chris, his parents suspected him of malingering as the illnesses continued, but the doctor could find nothing wrong other than migraines. 'We thought Chris was simply playing up,' Mrs Williams recalled unhappily. 'We were told we ought to take him to a psychiatrist.' They decided not to put their son through psychological testing, however, and Chris recovered when Graham turned his attentions elsewhere. But as he and other members of their group grew more suspicious about the possibility of Graham being the cause of the illness, they felt unable to speak to an appropriate adult.

Misplaced loyalty was one reason; sharing poison was another. Chris later explained that he, like the rest of his chemistry-mad friends, had a 'laboratory' at home where he would run experiments using both 'stuff' he had bought himself from a pharmacy and the more restricted substances that Graham had given him, including digitalis, iodine, barium chloride, arcanite solution and atropine. Richard Hands, whose friendship with Chris had caused Graham's poisonous jealousy, later admitted having in his possession digitalis and antimony, which he had been given by Graham. Similarly, Clive Creager told detectives that he had at home jars and phials of phosphorus, barium chloride, morphine, lead acetate, cyanide, tartar emetic, antimony and cocaine. All were given to him by Graham, who had bought them from high-street pharmacies. 'I used some of the cyanide as a weed killer,' Clive recalled. 'I gave him back some of the lead acetate and some of the barium chloride, that was last year.'

Evidently, Graham had purchased poison from several pharmacies using different names. He told Clive that he sometimes used the surname 'Harvey' when signing the poison register. Detectives later attempted to track down all those pharmacies who had sold substances to him, but it proved impossible.

Chris found it hard to believe that Graham would administer anything toxic to his friends but admitted: 'There were some other boys at school he used to have a go at. We used to swap sandwiches and Graham would pass his over, all doped up. Then in a coffee bar on the way home, he would pass the cups around too.' Richard Hands recalled falling ill after visiting the coffee bar with Graham, but again thought it unlikely his friend was responsible for his own ailment: 'I think it was due to the bad coffee we had.'

Thus, Graham's small group of friends were all of one mind: young chemistry boffins who swapped small amounts of toxic substances in order to conduct their own experiments at home. They knew that Graham's interest in the subject was the most extreme, that he was capable of obtaining substances illegally and experimenting in some small degree on people, but they could not bring themselves to believe he would poison a friend. They knew that he was never without at least one toxic substance in his possession. Clive remembered that Graham habitually carried 'a phial of antimony potassium tartrate or some other drug' in the top left-hand pocket of his school blazer, referring to it as his 'little friend': 'He would often get it out and pass it round. 'This is my little friend,' he'd say, and chuckle over it like a gangster with his gun.'

Graham was several months into puberty. He subsequently admitted that there had been a sexual element to his passion for poison, as Broadmoor medical superintendent Dr Patrick McGrath confirmed: 'From about the age of 12 he realised that experimentation with poison stimulated him sexually. He always carried poisons, referring to the phial as his 'little friend' as he derived a sense of power and security from knowing that he had lethal doses on his person.' A global sexual revolution was on the horizon, but most British households did not discuss such matters openly as yet. Graham told Dr Peter Scott in 1972 that his stepmother's attitude towards sex had been 'Victorian' and 'puritanical', with sex itself regarded as 'disreputable and unmentionable'. He remembered 'being reprimanded by her for masturbating at six'. Curiously, Winifred remembers the puritanical one among them was Graham. A friend of her brother agreed: 'Graham always got angry over talk of sex, home life or parents. If someone told a dirty joke, he would storm off and sulk. He got so angry once in the school lab that he tried to chloroform another boy.'

Although most of his acquaintances in adult life regarded him as asexual, with little or no interest in either men or women, Graham always described himself as heterosexual. His first infatuation was at the age of nine with a girl at his primary school. Family and friends remember his first, and perhaps last, girlfriend was 'Jean', who worked at Willesden library. Fred dismissed the relationship: 'Not once in his life have I known Graham to have any interest in a girl except a girl in a library. And then only because of the books on his favourite subjects, which the library could supply.' If there was some truth to that, those closest to Graham believed he had genuine feelings for Jean, as she did for him, with Winifred recalling: 'She actually went to see him in Broadmoor a couple of times. She was a lot older than he and has since married.' Dr McGrath also referred to Jean: 'From her he got his toxicology books and also forged notes when he wanted to truant. In return he gave her small doses of tartar emetic to make her sick enough to justify a few days off work.' Chris Williams remembered more: 'We were both a bit keen on a girl called Jean at the library where he got his books. When I got tickets to a Dickie Henderson TV show at Wembley, Graham gave her something to make her sick at work, so she could get time off and come with me. He told me it was called antimony. It all seemed so innocent then.'

★ ★ ★

Fred was later unable to recall whether Graham 'started poisoning Molly or me next; maybe he started on both of us at the same time. Whichever way it was, Molly began to have these frequent attacks of sickness, diarrhoea and excruciating pains.' While on remand in 1962, Graham told Dr Blair that he began poisoning Molly first. He gave no motive, but the fact that she had twice warned local pharmacies about his poison obsession may have accounted for it.

His poisoning of Chris and Molly took place simultaneously; he started adding two or three grains of tartar emetic to his stepmother's food from June to August 1961. The doses gradually became less frequent but larger, often as much as ten grains after he realised that she was 'developing a resistance for it, just as other people develop a resistance for arsenic'. His police statement confirms that he also administered smaller quantities to his sister and father: 'I started experimenting at home, putting sometimes one,

63

sometimes three grains on prepared foods, which my mother, father and sister ate. I must have eaten some of this poisoned food occasionally because I became sick as well. I know that after eating these prepared foods my family were all sick. My mother went to our doctor about her sickness.'

That summer, Molly was not only suffering the symptoms of poisoning at the hands of her stepson, but she was also involved in a serious road accident when the bus she was on ran over an iron bar, which 'shot through the floor'. Molly was thrown from her seat and hit the ceiling. She sustained only 'two black eyes and a stiff neck', according to her sister-in-law, but any other signs of injury were almost certainly concealed by the effects of continual poisoning.

It was the latter that brought her to her doctor's surgery on the morning of 5 August 1961. Molly was referred for immediate examination at Willesden general hospital where, over the course of ten days, various tests were carried out, but, as Fred phrased it, 'they could find nothing organically wrong with her.'

Molly was due to be discharged on 16 August. Prior to that, Fred returned home from the factory at midday to prepare lunch for himself and Graham. Winifred was at work; Graham offered to help. Father and son sat down to a meal of corned beef, pineapple and tomatoes. Within half an hour of returning to work, Fred was beset by crippling stomach pains. He spent the rest of the afternoon in the staff toilets, incapacitated with sickness and diarrhoea. 'I was so ill I thought I would die,' he recalled. 'I really thought I was a goner.' When he finally arrived home, dizzy and aching all over, the trouble receded. He assumed he had contracted food poisoning, most likely from the corned beef.

Molly left hospital but there was to be no respite. 'Her first day home she was sick again,' Win recalled. 'She would not go back to the hospital. But Molly believed that Graham, who was always mucking about with poisons, had poisoned her. But I don't think she told the hospital about this.' Fred, too, was plagued by recurring bouts of illness, usually beginning after meals, none of which were prepared by Graham. 'The first time I felt ill for 24 hours,' he stated. 'I didn't feel sufficiently ill to go to see a doctor, it passed off after 24 hours. I didn't call in a doctor ... Throughout the whole of 1961 I didn't call in a doctor when I had any of these attacks. Sometimes the feeling of sickness passed off very quickly. I have suffered in the past from skin trouble. I have not suffered from anything else at all. I have never had any stomach pains before.' None of the attacks were as severe as the first, but they were still debilitating.

Months later, Fred came to realise that each bout occurred on a Monday morning, 'after I had been out for a Sunday evening pint of beer in one of the local pubs. I used to take Graham along with me because his mother was in hospital and his sister was courting. He used to sit on the pub wall outside with a soft drink and I would join him. I realise now he must have been taking any opportunity — perhaps when I went to the toilet — to slip something into my drink.'

Winifred escaped her brother's toxic attentions until the end of the summer. She was in her own happy little bubble, working as a secretary in a music publisher's office on London's Denmark Street and in a relationship with her future husband, Denis Shannon. She often ate with his family in Harlesden, saving her from the poisoned repasts at home. None-theless, one afternoon in August she was on her way to meet Denis at a cinema in Willesden, when she was overwhelmed by nausea: 'I was violently sick outside Neasden station. It probably took an hour from the time I [unknowingly] ate the poison until I began to feel the effects.' She managed to reach Denis, who was shocked by the 'terrible white shade' of her skin. Fortunately, the sickness vanished as swiftly as it had begun.

Graham turned 14 in September 1961. He later acknowledged that this was when his interest in tox-icology 'became so intense it unbalanced me'. His police statement echoes the fact that 'it had become an obsession with me and I continued giving mem-bers of my family small doses of antimony tartrate on prepared foods.' On at least one occasion he added antimony sodium tartrate to the Sunday roast, leaving his father and stepmother clutching their stomachs. All those close to the family tried to work out what was happening in the Young household, with a persis-tent virus seeming the most likely. If there were any qualms about Graham, no one said anything. Besides, Graham himself was sick on occasion, either making himself deliberately ill to deflect suspicion or acciden-tally ingesting poison.

Banned from one pharmacy on Neasden Lane, Graham visited Edgar Davies, only a few yards away. Michael Hodgetts was on duty that day, 20 Novem-ber 1961. He served the boy who, without so much as a glance around the shop, approached his desk. The subsequent entry in the poison register recorded a sale of one ounce of potassium tartrate to G Harvey. Graham called again a couple of days later, conced-

66

ing that, at 17, he was indeed small for his age, adding that he needed certain items 'to do chemical experiments'. Hodgetts sold him 1½ grams of atropine sulphate and Graham once more signed the register as 'G Harvey'.

On Monday, 29 November, Graham saw an opportunity to put one of his purchases to use. As he was getting ready for school, he spotted his sister's half-made cup of tea on the dresser and added a small quantity of belladonna to the milk. After he left for school, Molly finished making the tea and carried the cup up to her stepdaughter's room. Winifred took a few sips but abandoned it because of the bitter taste, which she mentioned to Molly, who threw away the dregs and destroyed the cup.

The poison Graham had added to his sister's morning cuppa was deadly nightshade, known by its scientific name, *Atropa belladonna* — translating in Italian as 'beautiful woman'. Used for many years as a liniment to treat neuralgia, drops from the plant are used to dilate the pupils of the eye, thereby allowing for better examination of the condition. Belladonna has been cosmetically used for the same effect, but it is also a constituent in some cough mixtures, and used as a sedative, for motion sickness, in suppositories for haemorrhoids and to counter the symptoms of opium poisoning. When administered as a toxin, belladonna causes the pupils to dilate, heart rate to increase, excessive dryness of the mouth and throat, and delirium. It can lead to paralysis, coma and, eventually, death.

Unaware of the poison she had ingested, Winifred headed to work. As the tube whistled through the tunnels on its journey below ground, she began to feel dizzy and disorientated. It was, she recalled, 'a rather extraordinary sensation. I felt absolutely unable to control my eyes. Everything was sort of coming and going and when I got out of the train, I remember bumping into people and walking into walls.' At Tottenham Court Road station, someone helped her along the platform and up the stairs. She managed to reach her office and sat down heavily at her desk, trying vainly to focus on a newspaper: 'As I stared at the paper, the print seemed to grow larger and larger. It was an extraordinarily frightening experience — the print getting larger and larger. Then, just as suddenly, it began to recede — to go back and become smaller and smaller.'

Curiously, these sensations mirrored those experienced by her brother during his pubescent night terrors, except of course he had not ingested poison.

Winifred's behaviour drew the attention of her boss. He put her into a taxi with another member of staff acting as escort and told them to head straight to the Middlesex hospital. It was 11:30am when they arrived. 'I spent the best part of the day there, undergoing several tests,' Winifred recalled. She was seen by Dr Maddocks, who confirmed: 'She came complaining of some unsteadiness; she was unable to read as she complained of dryness of the mouth. On examination, her heart rate was fast, she had widely dilated oval pupils, she was unable to accommodate, she could read perfectly at 25 feet but not at 10 inches. Those are symptoms of atropine poisoning. Atropine is a registered poison.' Dr Maddocks passed Winifred a mirror and told her to look at her eyes. 'The pupils were enormous,' she recalled, 'and almost entirely covered the irises.' He kept her under observation

68

for two hours, noting, 'The normal dose of atropine that is given is half to one milligram. This would be given for medicinal purposes by mouth. I would have thought that she received more than this, but I cannot say how much . . . Belladonna is the same as atropine.'

Winifred was aghast when Dr Maddocks gave her his diagnosis. Then she remembered the bitterness of her tea that morning, wondering if Graham had used it in one of his experiments: 'It never crossed my mind, of course, that he could possibly have done it deliberately.' By the time she arrived back at the office it was 3:30pm. Winifred was fuming. She telephoned her father, complaining that Graham had been messing about with chemicals again. Fred defended his son to Winifred, certain that he would not disobey his orders about experimenting. Nonetheless, when Graham arrived home from school, Fred and Molly asked him a few questions. Graham was indignant, insisting that it was Winifred's own fault — she had probably used the teacups for mixing her shampoo. Then he began to cry and fled to his room.

But when Winifred arrived home, Graham confronted her in a rage, telling her she was 'wicked' to suggest he would put poison in her tea. He was so distraught that she ended up apologising. He then sat and listened with his father and stepmother as Winifred described her symptoms. 'I knew that it was the effects of the belladonna,' he recounted calmly to detectives some months later. 'I was asked by my mother if I knew anything about it but I denied it. After this I gave the remaining belladonna to my friend [Chris].'

The incident soon reached the Jouvenat household, where Win was growing ever more concerned about her beloved nephew. Hoping to explain her thoughts tactfully, she called on Fred and Molly to discuss the dangers of Graham's chemistry experiments, but 'I was more or less told to mind my own business.' Unbeknown to his family, Graham had in his possession a poisoner's arsenal of atropine, antimony, arsenic, digitalis, tincture of aconite and thallium — enough, it was later said, to kill 300 people.

4

A POISON IN A SMALL DOSE IS A MEDICINE

When the Edgar Davies' shop bell rang one afternoon in December 1961, pharmacist Michael Hodgetts recognised the boy strolling towards him. It was the third time Graham had called, but Hodgetts had no intention of serving him again, having felt distinctly uncomfortable before. His resolve strengthened when Graham told him what he wanted. 'He asked me to supply him with tincture of aconite,' the pharmacist recalled. 'I did not give it to him, it is also a poison. I took steps to get some forms which have to be filled in to get such a poison. These forms have to be taken to the police station. I told him that and gave him the forms and told him he had to get them signed by the police.' Tincture of aconite was more toxic than the substances Graham had asked for previously. Although Hodgetts believed that the boy was 17 as he claimed, he felt concerned about the experiments he claimed to be conducting.

Graham left empty-handed but continued spiking the food and drinks served at home. 'We were all suffering bouts of unusual sickness,' Winifred confirmed. 'Molly suffered most of all, my father and myself. I can remember being sent home from work on several occasions. Molly suspected Graham, but I could not bring myself to believe it.' Graham's attacks of vomiting were much less frequent than the rest of the family, but enough to convince his sister that their stepmother was wrong about him.

Later, Winifred came to believe that the bouts Graham suffered were unintentional, due to his love for the dripping that Molly collected from the Sunday joint. One Sunday after lunch he called at the house on Links Road and was sick all over Win's doorstep. His aunt had already instructed her daughter Sandra not to touch any food or drink when she called on Graham and his family. She was unable to speak to her husband about it, because he defended Graham vigorously. But Win grew so worried that she even threw away a cake made by Molly's sister who worked in a bakery.

Graham's schoolfriends knew the truth but were frightened. Clive Creager recalled:

> Gradually, as he realised I could appreciate what he was doing, he began to tell me and to hint to me that he was poisoning people. And his mother was sick. Over a period of time, it became that I knew that he was doing it and he knew that I did and he didn't even try to hide it. He often used to discuss it and would tell me how ill his mother was or what poisons he was using. And towards the latter part, I remember he showed me a graph. One axis of the graph was what he said was the state of her illness and the other axis was when he was giving her poison.

Clive began avoiding Graham as much as possible: 'He was dangerous. He was evil and I was afraid of him.'

At the beginning of 1962, Molly's health deteriorated. 'It was her ill luck to be at home all the time and to have to prepare the meals and to eat with Graham,' Winifred realised. 'When he arrived home from school, Molly always had her tea with him. Then dad would arrive home and have his tea and I would get in around six-ish. Dad also used to go home from work for his dinner, which he usually ate around midday or one o'clock.' Molly's ailments saw her weight drop from 11 stone to seven; her hair fell out in clumps and she walked with a stoop due to excruciating back pain. Graham was solicitous, making Molly lie on the sofa while he looked after her. Winifred stated in bemused hindsight: 'Although he was deliberately poisoning Molly and was able to study her reactions with a callousness quite beyond the reach of a normal human being, he was at the same time concerned and worried about her. He even used to go to the chemist's to get medicine for her.'

Throughout everything, Molly's greatest concern was for her husband, who panicked when she fell ill, having lost his first wife. Nor did Molly want him to blame Graham for her sickness. Fred himself suffered three or four serious attacks of sickness and diarrhoea between January and April 1962, usually after the evening meal. Graham later admitted to giving his father five grains of tartar emetic once or twice daily; he noticed with interest that this produced a new symptom — retention of urine. In his police statement, he declared: 'Since the beginning of this year, I have on occasions put antimony tartrate solution and powder on foods at home, which both my mother and father have taken. They have become ill as the result of it. My mother lost weight all the time through it and I stopped giving it to her about February of this year. I stopped using it altogether then.' Graham may have stopped using antimony tartrate in his stepmother's food, but he did so only because he had found another poison: thallium.

* * *

'I've been looking it up. Thallium is mainly used nowadays for rats, I believe. It's tasteless, soluble and easy to buy. There's only one thing — poisoning mustn't be suspected.'

These lines are spoken by a character in Agatha Christie's *The Pale Horse*, published in Britain six months prior to Graham's procuring of thallium. Later questioned about the possibility of using the novel as inspiration, he was dismissive. Nonetheless, thallium was virtually unheard of in the UK until The Pale Horse appeared. Christie created a villain who administers thallium and victims who suffer such strange ailments that they seem to be supernaturally cursed.

Curiously, the man who discovered the element developed a keen interest in spiritualism himself. William Crookes, the 29-year-old publisher and editor of the *Chemical News*, announced in a March 1861 edition of the periodical that he had found a new element that showed as a bright green line in the spectrum of residues from a sulphuric acid plant. Using a spectrometer, he was able to demonstrate the presence of the element, which he named thallium, from the Latin *thallos*, meaning 'green shoot'. Crookes was surprised to hear, one year later, that a French physicist, 42-year-old Claude-Auguste Lamy, had discovered thallium and had isolated it in its purest form, revealing its chemical similarity to potassium. For a time, it seemed that Lamy would be credited with discovering thallium, but both men were awarded medals for their work in identifying and isolating the new element. While working on thallium, Crookes became immersed in spiritualism, largely due to the death of his beloved younger brother. Although he became one of the most well-known and respected scientists of his time, his unashamed interest in the occult brought disapprobation and scorn from his fellow scientists. He managed to repair his tattered reputation to the extent of being named president of the Royal Society but remained secretly involved in spiritualism and was a member of the Ghost Club with Charles Dickens and Arthur Conan Doyle.

Thallium remained of little interest until two very different uses for thallium acetate and thallium sulphate were found: the former could be administered orally to remove excessive body hair while the latter was developed as a pesticide. But many of those who were given thallium medically as a depilatory or for treatment of ringworm of the scalp also showed symptoms of severe thallium poisoning: joint pain, numbness in limbs, agonising sensitivity of the feet and insomnia. Accidental overdoses and mistakes in dispensation led to the phasing out of thallium acetate treatment after the Second World War. Thallium pesticides were banned in the US in 1972 but are still sold in other parts of the world.

Used maliciously or in error, thallium can also induce the sensory abnormalities of paraesthesia, polyneuritis, delirium, convulsions, muscle weakness and intense abdominal pain, leading to coma and death due to cardiac arrest or respiratory failure.

Symptoms typically appear within hours or after days or weeks, depending entirely on the amount and frequency of the dose. A teaspoon of thallium sulphate has the power to kill more than 20 people. Difficult to detect, a diagnosis requires confirmation by chemical analysis. Odourless, colourless and tasteless, it is soluble in water and alcohol. Alopecia is the most obvious symptom of chronic thallium poisoning, with complete baldness generally reached within a month. Skin also becomes dry, scaly and white, while transverse bands appear on the fingernails and toenails, usually three or four weeks after ingestion. Thallium can be excreted in urine for two months or more after its administration.

During the Second World War, thallium was used in the Netherlands as a means of killing the Nazi oppressors; in one instance, the Dutch workforce of an arms manufacturer deliberately added thallium to the water supply of the factory, killing all its German controllers. Decades later, it was used as a coating on American missiles during the Gulf War. On a much smaller scale, thallium has rarely been the poison of choice for the lone murderer, although there are a number of instances where rat poison containing thallium has been used to kill: in Australia, Yvonne Fletcher murdered two husbands via a thallium-infused pesticide, and Caroline Grills killed several members of her family with rat poison. Similarly, in Russia, Vyacheslav Solovyov used thallium as a constituent of rat poison to kill several relatives including his wife and a police investigator. More recently, Florida chemist and ardent Nazi admirer George Trepal added thallium to bottles of Coca-Cola belonging to neighbours whom he disliked; matriarch Peggy Carr died four months after being poisoned in 1988. Operating undercover, detective Susan Gorek befriended Trepal and his wife, attending the murder mystery weekends they liked to help organise. During one visit to their home, she noticed a copy of *The Pale Horse* on their coffee table. The police investigation, which took two years to complete, thereby earned itself the moniker 'Pale Horse'. George Trepal was found guilty and sentenced to death. He remains on Florida's Death Row.

In England, to date, there has been only one case of deliberate and malicious thallium poisoning pursued in the courts: Graham Young.

★ ★ ★

On Good Friday 1962, Graham spiked his stepmother's evening meal with 20 grains of thallium in its crystalline form. It was a huge dose, but Molly had endured such a relentlessly systematic campaign of poisoning that she had built up a hardy resistance. She complained of a stiff neck all week and on Saturday morning woke up with pins and needles, feeling generally unwell. Fred left for work and Winifred had arranged to help Denis decorate his mother's front room while she was on holiday.

At 10:30am, Molly called in to see Win, who worked at the Cooperative grocery on Willesden High Street. Graham was with her, but Molly looked pale and sickly. Win asked her what was wrong: 'She said to me, 'I am feeling ill. I've been to the doctor, Dr Wills in Neasden Lane. I have pins and needles in my arms. The doctor tells me I have no reflexes in my legs.' She was crying. She said, 'I am on my way to

Willesden general hospital.' I wanted to go with her, but she would not let me. Graham went with his step-mother to look after her.' The two of them travelled to the hospital by bus. When Molly was kept in, Graham returned home to collect her nightclothes and toiletries. 'Graham came back at 2pm to the shop,' Win remembered. 'He said, 'They kept Molly in the hospital. They suspect polyneuritis.' He went home.'

An apocryphal story recounts how Fred arrived home from work to find Molly in the garden, writhing on the lawn while Graham watched from his bed-room window. The story is hokum, as Fred explained: 'When I came home that afternoon, Graham was alone in the house. He said, 'Mum's in hospital.' I was just debating with myself whether to go straight along there or wait until the evening visiting hour when a policeman knocked at the door. He said I was wanted at the hospital immediately. By the time I got there, Molly was dead.'

Molly was two months past her 40th birthday, which she had been too ill to celebrate. Win recalled hearing the news after she returned home from work at 5pm: 'My brother Fred came up to our house in a taxi and informed me that Molly was dead. I believe it was about 3:30pm that day when she died.' Wini-fred was aghast when she arrived home, and Graham appeared to be distraught: 'He kept crying. Molly had a lot of musical boxes in her room and he kept going in there, opening the boxes, making them play and crying. He went with my father everywhere that week. He went with father to the funeral directors, and to get the result of the post-mortem and to make the arrangements for the cremation.'

A post-mortem was conducted by Dr Donald Teare,

the pathologist who had investigated the deaths of Timothy Evans' wife and baby at 10 Rillington Place. Teare identified 'compression of the spinal cord due to acute prolapse of the cervical disc' as the cause of death, thought to be a result of the accident Molly had been involved in the previous year. 'We all thought her death had or could have had something to do with that,' Win told detectives. 'Graham appeared to be very upset at his stepmother's death.'

Fred was in no state to plan a funeral by himself; depleted by his own illness, the loss of another young wife was almost more than he could bear. Graham helped, suggesting cremation rather than a burial for Molly, and his father agreed. Between Molly's death on Saturday and her funeral at Golders Green crematorium on Thursday, 26 April, Fred was repeatedly sick, whether from trauma or his son's 'experiments'.

The gathering after the funeral was not without incident. Molly's brother-in-law, John Miller, who lived in Fulham, attended her wake at the house on North Circular Road. Fred recalled: 'Graham's Uncle John — actually my wife's sister's husband — became violently ill after putting some mustard pickle on his ham sandwich. Fortunately, he was the only one to eat the pickle and he recovered sufficiently to drive himself home later.' When Graham was eventually taken into custody, Win received a telephone call from the police welfare service: '[She] told me not to touch the mustard pickle or Andrews Liver Salts, as they contained antimony. Graham had apparently told her. This mustard pickle was that which was on the table at the meal after Molly's funeral.'

Molly's ashes were scattered at Golders Green. 'Graham was apparently very upset,' Sandra recalled.

'He cried a lot. I can remember at Aunt Molly's funeral, he cried a lot. About a week after this my uncle Fred became seriously ill.' Before then, however, Fred asked his son and daughter to join him at the kitchen table, where he told them: 'We must all muck in and help to keep the home running. I've worked all the overtime for the past ten years to pay off the house and now it's mine. If anything happens to me, at least you will have a home. I am in a good superannuation fund and you will not be left destitute.' While Fred later surmised he had just signed his own death warrant, telling Graham he had 'something to come when I died', his daughter believed the conversation had no influence on her brother's actions.

Winifred had her last serious bout of illness the following day, Friday: 'I was quite bad, I was ill for a morning until about 2pm. I couldn't go to work. The symptoms were pretty much the same, although I wasn't sick this time.' She had drunk a cup of tea at breakfast but hadn't noticed a tang. However, Graham admitted that after Molly's death, 'I started putting antimony tartrate on foods at home and in milk and water.'

His words become more significant when read in tandem with his father's statement. The next day, Saturday, 28 April, Fred and Graham called on the Millers in Fulham. Fred's brother-in-law had recovered from his illness and Fred returned home reassured. He picked at the midday meal but felt nauseous afterwards. 'By that time I was hardly eating anything, only milk and water,' he recalled, still unaware that Graham had poisoned both substances with antimony tartrate. He forced himself to work on Monday, but on Thursday he called the doctor, despite believing his illness was due to being 'upset through losing my wife. I was upset about losing my wife. I thought it was everything coming on top of me.' He remained in bed until his appointment the following day. Dr Wills could find nothing wrong and agreed with Fred that the grieving process was still so raw that he might well be experiencing physical illness as a result.

That evening, Friday, 4 May 1962, while their father slept fitfully in bed, Winifred and Graham watched television together. Graham had already chosen a BBC programme to watch following *Dr Kildare* and *The Rag Trade*. After the news, at 9:25pm, they settled down to watch *They Hanged My Saintly Billy*, based on Robert Graves' 1957 study of the 'prince of poisons', William Palmer. Graham was rapt, apparently glued to the screen as lead actor Patrick Wymark slyly bade his fellow drinkers to 'choose your poison!'.

For a time, Win provided food for her brother and his children. 'Graham used to carry these meals to his father,' she recalled. 'Fred suffered severe vomiting, diarrhoea, loss of appetite. Every time he ate, he was sick.' On Wednesday, 9 May 1962, Fred felt so ill that he began to be fearful. He managed to reach the surgery, where Dr Lancelot Wills saw him immediately: 'He was pretty bad. He was vomiting and feeling rather distressed and giddy and I called an ambulance for him to go to hospital for further investigation.' Dr Wills was of the opinion that Fred's vomiting and diarrhoea was 'precipitated by shock following his wife's death or by peptic ulcer'.

Upon hearing that his father had been rushed to hospital, Graham tried to convince everyone that Fred had poisoned himself out of longing to be reunited with Molly. That he attempted to pass off the illness as a slow suicide was evident in his later comment to Win, 'I am not silly. Father was supposed to die from a broken heart because of her death.' His words chilled Win to the bone, leaving her reeling at the revelation that Graham had intended to kill his father.

Fred was taken to the casualty department at Willesden general hospital where his wife had died less than a fortnight before. Dr Winston Ince examined him but was unable to reach any definitive diagnosis. He suggested a diet of Benger's invalid food, which Graham promptly poisoned with antimony sodium tartrate. Watching her father trembling with pain at home that evening, Winifred felt 'frantic, completely at my wits' end as to what to do with him. I did think at one stage that he might be sick as a result of grieving over Molly's death. But as he continued to show no signs of improvement, I asked Auntie Win to go with me to our local doctor again.'

The two women visited the surgery the following day, where they were received by Dr Wills. Winifred told the GP that she believed her 14-year-old nephew was poisoning their father. Dr Wills dismissed the idea. 'He insisted my brother was only emotionally upset,' Winifred recalled. 'He would not believe me when I insisted he was being poisoned.' As a precaution, Dr Wills contacted Willesden general hospital and arrangements were made for Fred to be admitted to a ward later that day.

Win had no intention of letting her niece remain at home with Graham. She insisted that Graham should stay where she could keep an eye on him; Winifred left to stay with her boyfriend's family in Harlesden.

Win was shocked by the deterioration in Graham's behaviour. One night she opened the door to put the milk bottles out and found Graham on the doorstep, standing in silence, staring at her. Sandra had a similar experience: hearing a knock, she answered the door only to find Graham standing there in a sort of trance. He refused to speak to her and passed through the house like a ghost. He also had a habit of staring at them while they watched television and wouldn't speak at all.

Win was determined never to allow Graham to visit his father alone. On every visit, he would pull up a chair, then take notes before telling his father how his symptoms would develop. Winifred was flabbergasted by her brother's behaviour, describing it as 'completely callous and totally detached, as though he were in no way connected with the suffering figure in the bed — just watching and studying him as though he were an insect or a small animal being experimented upon by a scientist.' Family friend Frank Walker was present on another occasion when Graham began arguing with doctors, causing Fred to erupt: 'Get that boy away from me!'

On Sunday, 20 May 1962, matters began coming to a head. The London Hospital Medical College contacted Willesden general hospital: samples of Fred Young's blood and scalp hair had been examined by their Department of Forensic Medicine, whose tests revealed traces of antimony in the urine and traces of arsenic in the blood. The entire family gathered around Fred's bedside as the doctors explained the results. All eyes turned to Graham, completely oblivious and pondering aloud, 'How ridiculous, not being able to tell the difference between arsenic and antimony poisoning.' Winifred felt a sharp prickle of unease in her veins.

On the journey home, Graham kept insisting it was ridiculous that the surgeons were unable to distinguish between antimony and arsenic poisoning. He launched into a description of each, and by the time they had reached the house on Links Road, no one was in any doubt that Graham knew far more than he should. Win felt churned up, as worried for her nephew as for her brother, believing Graham to have been reckless in his experiments rather than deliberately dangerous. Finally, she asked him to be honest with her about it. Graham promised he had done nothing wrong.

But at the first opportunity, Win searched the room where Graham slept, and his clothing. They failed to check his overcoat, where he kept several phials of poison, and found only a codeine tablet and a homemade plasticine voodoo doll. When Win visited her brother again, while Graham was at school, she kept silent on the matter, even when Fred told her that the doctors had confirmed it was antimony poisoning and he had permanent liver damage. Without blaming Graham, Fred asked his sister to see that his son didn't visit again. 'I don't want him here,' he said quietly.

Win intended to consult Dr Wills before Fred was discharged, with a view to finding out what he thought about Graham. But other events took precedence. When Graham told his schoolfriends that his father was in hospital so soon after his stepmother's death, Clive Creager spoke to his parents, insisting that Graham had brought about Molly's demise and Fred's illness. At the same time, Graham's science master, Geoffrey Hughes, had been keeping him under observation since the start of the new school term, having noticed something strange in his manner. Hughes knew about the illnesses within Graham's circle and frequently spotted him poring over medical textbooks.

At the end of lessons on Monday, 21 May 1962, Hughes checked inside Graham's desk. He was astonished to find vials and small bottles of toxic substances, together with notes on infamous poisoners and macabre sketches. Hughes sought out headmaster Henry Merkel, who in turn telephoned Dr Lancelot Wills and asked him about the mysterious illnesses plaguing the Young family. The two men agreed that there was only one option.

The following day was Tuesday, 22 May 1962. After registration, Graham was sent for a careers interview with a representative from the child guidance unit. The man waiting for him was, in fact, an educational psychologist working for the police. He flattered Graham by mentioning his great gift for chemistry, adding that if he put more effort into his maths, then a university scholarship might be possible. He asked Graham if his father was likely to support a career in the pharmaceutical industry; Graham replied eagerly that he would ask him, then chattered about his love for chemistry and toxicology. Graham left the meeting convinced that he had a glittering pharmaceutical career ahead of him.

That evening Winifred joined the family at Links Road for a meal. Graham was eager to tell his sister about the supposed careers meeting. As Winifred listened, she was struck by the change in her brother's behaviour; he seemed 'more normal than he had in a long time — laughing and joking over the tea table'. His bright manner was at odds with the fact that, for the past few days, he had been steadily inhaling ether and 'the moment he entered a room, the smell emanating from him was almost overpowering'.

The educational psychologist delivered his report to Hertfordshire police the following morning, describing Graham's 'abnormal interest and knowledge of poisons and [that he] was known to possess poison'.

At 3pm, during a break in lessons, two men strolled through the gates of John Kelly secondary school. Detective Inspector Edward Crabb and Detective Sergeant Alan Burwood were both stationed at Harlesden. Harry Merkel led them into Graham's classroom, eerily silent without its children. Crabb and Burwood conducted a quick search of the place before lifting the lid of Graham's desk. They took possession of seven school-issue exercise books and one titled *Handbook of Poisoning, Diagnosis and Treatment*. Returning to their vehicle, they drove to 768 North Circular Road. Neither mentioned in their statements how entry was gained — Fred was in hospital, Winifred at work and Graham was with his schoolmates — but they collected two more books from Graham's bedroom: *Sixty Famous Trials* and *Poisoner in the Dock*. Depositing these in their car, they then drove the short distance to Links Road.

Win opened the door to the two detectives. After a moment's hesitation, she poured out all her suspicions. She then telephoned her niece to say that the police were waiting to arrest Graham. Winifred was lost for words.

Graham arrived at Links Road just after 4:30pm. He breezed past the police car and called out hello as he entered the hall. Both detectives could smell him before he appeared. Calmly taking in the scene,

Graham apologised for the smell of ether, claiming he had been sucking 'Victory V' lozenges since leaving school. DI Crabb and DS Burwood were perplexed by his confidence. Neither man had ever experienced anything quite like it.

Crabb got to his feet. 'I'm a police officer, Graham, and I'm investigating your use of poisons. I understand you carry them with you and have some at school?'

Graham met his gaze. 'I am interested in poisons but I haven't got any at the moment.'

Crabb pointed to the books they had collected: the flimsy, lined notebooks, the thick red hardback boards of *Sixty Famous Trials* with its black lettering and the smaller *Poisoner in the Dock* with the lurid blue-and-green cover. 'Are those your books?'

'Yes, they are.'

'Have you any poisons in your pocket?'

'I don't carry them about.'

Crabb stepped forward, telling Graham he intended to search him. He did so, finding two bottles containing white powder. 'What are these?' he asked.

Graham remained unflustered. 'One is thallium. I don't know about the other.'

Crabb set the bottles down on the table next to the books, then turned back to Graham: 'Last November your sister was ill and went to Middlesex hospital. She had taken belladonna — do you remember?'

Graham nodded. 'I remember her going to hospital, but I had nothing to do with it.'

'Have you ever had belladonna?'

'No, I haven't.'

'Have you ever bought antimony from a chemist in Neasden?'

87

Graham nodded again. 'Last November, from Edgar's. I got atropine as well.'

Realising that Graham was likely to answer most if not all of their questions truthfully, DI Crabb formally cautioned him, asking, 'Do you understand?'

'Yes,' said Graham.

'Atropine and belladonna are the same thing, aren't they?'

Graham repeated, 'I had nothing to do with my sister's illness, that was caused by shampoo she used in her cup the night before.'

Crabb glanced at his colleague. Apologising for the intrusion to Win, they told Graham that they were taking him in for further questioning at Harlesden police station. His aunt watched in horror as he was escorted from the house to the car and guided into the back seat. Graham kept his face turned away.

It was a two-and-a-half mile drive to the police station, a red-brick monolith that dominated the Craven Road junction. After parking at the rear, the two officers led Graham through the building to an interview room. They had no sooner sat down when he offered, 'The other bottle — it's antimony. I suppose you would have found out anyway.'

Burwood began taking notes while Crabb asked questions. 'Have you ever given any of it to your family? They have all been ill at various times and your father is ill with poisoning of some sort now.'

'No,' Graham replied. 'I have experimented with plants and that is all.'

During the course of the interview, he revealed that he kept most of his poisons in the hut near the Welsh Harp reservoir, some beneath a hedge and more squirrelled about his room. However, Graham initially denied all the allegations put to him, despite seeming completely stoic.

Early that evening, Win and Winifred arrived at the station. Both were tense and upset. Graham had already been charged with poisoning Winifred but was allowed out of his cell to see them. Win's face crumpled when she saw him, 'Oh Graham, why did you do it? Why?'

Her pale-faced nephew said nothing, not a word. Instead, he indicated to the constable at his side that he wanted to go back to his cell and was led away, pinch-nosed and silent.

5

A MEDICINE IN A LARGE DOSE IS A POISON

At 9am on Thursday, 24 May 1962, DI Crabb entered the detention room at Harlesden police station where Graham was sitting perfectly composed. The detective returned a few inconsequential items taken from him the night before. As he did so, Graham said, 'I think I will tell you all about it. It's been an obsession with me, like taking drugs —.'

Crabb raised a hand to stop him. He cautioned Graham again, then asked, 'Would you like to make a written statement? And would you like somebody with you — your aunt or sister perhaps?'

Graham shook his head. 'I'd rather tell you on your own. You can write it down.'

Crabb settled into a chair with pen and paper. He told Graham to go ahead. His statement, prompted by questions and interjections by the detective, reads starkly:

I have been very interested in poisons, their properties and effects since I was about 11 years old. In May last year 1961, I bought 25gm antimony potassium tartrate from Rees [*sic*] Ltd, chemists, Neasden Lane. Within a couple of weeks I tried out this poison on my friend, John Williams. I gave him two or three grains at school. I can't remember how I caused him to take it, I think

90

it was probably on a cream biscuit or a cake. He was sick after taking it. I gave him a second dose in May in the same way and in the following month I gave him another two doses, always two or three grains and always on food at school. After this I started experimenting at home, putting sometimes one, sometimes three grains on prepared foods, which my mother, father and sister ate. I must have eaten some of this poisoned food occasionally because I became sick as well. I know that after eating these prepared foods my family were all sick. My mother went to our doctor about her sickness. By September of last year this had become an obsession with me and I continued giving members of my family small doses of antimony tartrate on prepared foods. In November 1961 I bought two ounces, in separate ounces, of antimony tartrate and 1½ grams of belladonna from Edgar Davies, chemists, Neasden Lane.

One morning at the end of November, it was on a Wednesday, I was getting ready to go to school. I had breakfast in the kitchen and my sister's cup was on the dresser containing a small quantity of milk. I put 1/16 grain of belladonna in the milk and then I left for school. That night when I got home from school, my mother told me that my sister had been ill during the day. When my sister came home from work, she told us all the symptoms of her illness and I knew that it was the effects of the belladonna. I was asked by my mother if I knew anything about it but I denied it. After this I gave the remaining belladonna to my friend John [Chris] Williams;

he lives at 52 Layfield Road, Hendon. I think he still has it in his room at home.

When I first bought the antimony from Rees, I also bought digitalis, but I didn't use this. I gave it to a friend, Richard Hands; he is at my school and I think I gave him six ounces. I think he gave some of it to John Williams. Since the beginning of this year, I have on occasions put antimony tartrate solution and powder on foods at home, which both my mother and father have taken. They have become ill as the result of it. My mother lost weight all the time through it and I stopped giving it to her about February of this year. I stopped using it altogether then.

After my mother died on 21 April 1962, I started putting antimony tartrate on foods at home and in milk and water that my father was drinking. As the result of this, he became ill and was taken to hospital. He had only one attack of vomiting when he was at home, but this came on when he was in hospital and I then realised how ill he was.

I can't think of anyone else that I have given poison to and I know that the doses I was giving were not fatal, but I knew I was doing wrong. It grew on me like a drug habit, except that it wasn't me who was taking the drug. The two small jars you found on me yesterday contained thallium sulphate and antimony and potassium tartrate. This antimony is the one I have been using at home and I bought it from Edgar Davies in November of last year. I bought the thallium from a chemist's in Willesden, just as one enters Willesden High Road, from Dudden Hill Lane.

I have not given anyone doses of thallium. I realise how stupid I have been with these poisons. I knew this all along but I couldn't stop.

Graham then signed the statement, which was witnessed by DI Crabb. Ostensibly, it read as an honest confession, but there were untruths and a cavernous omission. Graham's passion for poison had begun much earlier than he had claimed, and he had started collecting toxic substances and sniffing ether around the age of eight or nine. He said nothing about the incident at Regent's Park with Chris Williams and played down many other instances of adding poison to food and drink. Most significant of all, he lied about never having administered thallium. This, of course, was the substance he had given in a large, final dose to his stepmother, bringing about her death. As far as his defence was concerned, the statement contained a crucial line: 'I knew I was doing wrong ... It grew on me like a drug habit, except that it wasn't me who was taking the drug.' In that, at least, he was truthful.

Thereafter Graham was charged with having 'unlawfully and maliciously' administered 'a noxious thing so as to thereby inflict bodily harm' on his sister Winifred. Formerly cautioned, he made no reply.

At 10:30am that same morning, he appeared at Willesden Magistrates' Court, where he was remanded in custody to appear again on 30 May.

Fred Young only learned of his son's arrest two days later:

Winifred and [Win] had been keeping some things from me. They suspected that Graham had been responsible for Molly's death. They knew about

93

his interest in poisons and poisoners, his books on the subject, his weird drawings and so on. They put two and two together again — and this time they came up with the right answer. They didn't tell me but reported their suspicions instead to a doctor, and finally the police were called in. The game was up for Graham. All I knew, lying there — and I really was near to death — was that a nursing sister came to my bedside and told me, as gently as she could, that Graham had been taken away by the police. Then a detective came in and was allowed to talk to me for a short while. He asked me a few questions and suddenly it all fell into place. I knew for the first time what Graham had been doing. He was a deadly poisoner. It was the most shattering blow of my life. I can't describe how I felt.

Asked if he wished to say anything further, Fred told the detective: 'I hope you put him away and lock him up where he can never do harm to anyone again.'

The police began making inquiries at every pharmacy in the district, with a view to establishing how Graham had been able to amass such a collection of toxic chemicals. They were unable to make much progress; selling poisons to a boy of Graham's age and younger, without having taken the necessary precautions, was a criminal offence. Geoffrey Reis and Edgar Davies were cooperative, but other pharmacists were either unwilling or unable to provide any information. One pharmacist on Willesden Lane admitted selling antimony 'to a schoolboy about a year ago'. However, no signature was obtained for the poisons register and the pharmacist refused to make a written statement about the sale, despite there being 'little doubt' that Graham was 'the person who bought the poison'. Harlesden police continued with other aspects of their investigation, gathering witness statements and submitting samples from Fred Young, along with Graham's vials and bottles of poison, to the Metropolitan Police Forensic Science Laboratory for analysis. These revealed the presence of antimony in the blood and urine samples, and a long list of toxic substances in the containers confiscated from Graham's bedroom.

On the morning of 30 May 1962, having applied for legal aid, Graham appeared at Willesden Juvenile Court, represented by Miss Jean Southworth, of Lincoln & Lincoln solicitors. Evidence from the police laboratory was not yet complete and the witness who had examined them was away at Bournemouth sessions. But the brief for the prosecution, compiled the following day, sheds interesting light on the court proceedings, including the defendant himself:

From observing him at the lower court, the youth does not seem to be in the least sorry for what has occurred; however, perhaps it is rather hard to judge him on his appearance. Things were not helped in the lower court by his solicitor treating him as an adult and giving him an opportunity to cross-examine people like chemists on the effects of poisons, which highly delighted the young gentleman. At the lower court the defence made no representation for the case to be tried summarily. The Clerk to the Justices also said that even had such submission been made, his Justices would not have tried the case.

Miss Southworth submitted that Graham should be committed for an offence against Section 24 of the Offences against the Person Act 1861, that is, maliciously administering poison or a noxious thing with intent to injure, aggrieve or annoy any other person. The prosecution disagreed but left the indictment to counsel, stating: 'Assuming that a 14-year-old boy, like an adult, can be deemed to intend the natural consequences of the act, this is clearly a case for Section 23.'This was the more serious charge of maliciously administering poison or a noxious thing so as to endanger life or inflict grievous bodily harm. Facing the lesser charges on three counts, Graham was bound over to appear again on 6 June 1962 for a special sitting. At that juncture, it was expected that all witnesses, including Graham himself, would be available to give evidence, and that the results of further laboratory tests would be presented.

The brief for the prosecution further noted: 'To state the obvious, this is truly a remarkable case. The only difficulties that it presents are what to do with this boy; presumably the principal person to be worried about this is the judge ...' DI Crabb's summary of the evidence of the case against Graham was included, preceded by a covering letter, which made the point that 'It is only fair to say that although Young has admitted administering poison in the form of antimony and potassium tartrate to his stepmother, there is no evidence to suggest that he was in any way responsible for her death. This has been confirmed by Dr Teare.' Crabb declared there to be 'ample evidence' in support of the existing charge in regard to Graham's poisoning of his sister, but also 'evidence to support further charges against Young of administering poison — antimony and potassium tartrate — to Christopher John Williams and to his father, Frederick Charles Young. It is proposed to further charge him with these additional offences when he next appears before the court.' Reference was made to a number of witness statements and the interview with Fred Young in Willesden general hospital, after which Crabb reiterated: 'It will be seen that there is ample evidence to support further charges against Young of administering a noxious thing to Christopher John Williams and Mr Frederick Charles Young.'

Crabb referred again to the circumstances surrounding the death of Molly Young, explaining that Graham 'has admitted administering poison to her on a number of occasions, which undoubtedly resulted in her admission to Willesden general hospital on 5 August 1961 and her stay there until 16 August 1961. However, Dr Teare is quite certain that his post-mortem findings are correct and as the body has been cremated no useful purpose would be served in delving deeper into that matter.'

Crabb then turned his attention to Graham, describing him as 'a very intelligent young man, who, it will be gathered, has developed an absorbing interest in poisons. His knowledge of them is extraordinary and, as he explains in his statement, the use of poisons on members of his family became an obsession. Young has not previously come to the notice of police and as far as it is known he has no history of mental instability. His home conditions are good and there seems no apparent reason why he should feel disposed to poison members of his family.' It remained the most pressing question of all: why a 14-year-old boy who was of above average intelligence and clearly had an attachment, if not genuine love, for his family had repeatedly felt the urge to inflict such suffering on them, along with his closest friend.

Over the course of the following month, psychiatrists would do their utmost to understand the conundrum of Graham Young. The person tasked with observing him on a daily basis was Dr Christopher Fysh, senior medical officer at Ashford Remand Centre in the Middlesex town of the same name. Graham arrived there on 3 June 1962. Three days later, he made the journey back to Harlesden police station, where he was charged with two further offences concerning his father and Chris Williams. He made no reply. At 2pm, proceedings began at the court house in Willesden. Graham was among 14 witnesses who gave evidence under cross-examination. He seemed no more perturbed than he had during the other court appearances, which brought him face to face with his family, friends, doctors, pharmacists and police in one small space.

Fred Young described his hellish experiences at the hands of his son yet was able to state that 'My son, over the last few years, has behaved reasonably well at home. Since the age of eleven there has been no difficulty between us. There is no ill-feeling between us.' Winifred echoed her father's sentiments: 'I got on pretty well with my brother as far as I am concerned.' Clive Creager, Richard Hands and even Chris Williams described themselves as 'still good friends' with the accused. Nonetheless, when Chris was later approached by a *Daily Mirror* reporter, he declared, 'A detective told my mum that I was lucky to be alive. I reckon I am.'

On Tuesday, 19 June, Harley Street doctor and

consultant psychiatrist Dr Donald Blair arrived at Ashford Remand Centre. He had an appointment with Graham, whom he was to assess for suitability to stand trial. This and a second meeting four days later consisted of 'long interviews', at which Blair 'examined him psychiatrically as thoroughly as possible'. On both occasions, Graham appeared 'quiet, placid and frankly cooperative'. A second combined opinion was sought from Dr James Cameron of the Maudsley hospital and Dr Christopher Fysh, who had been able to observe him at a more leisurely pace in Ashford Remand Centre.

Taken together, the reports provide a damning picture of a young mind at war with itself and an obsession with poison that overrode everything, including familial bonds. Dr Blair found that Graham was suffering from mental illness. His disorder was severe enough in nature and degree to warrant his detention in a secure psychiatric hospital where medical treatment should be sought. Dr Blair was of the opinion that Graham was:

> obviously highly intelligent but his emotional reactions are slow and he never exhibited the slightest distress in relating the instances of attempted poisoning of his family and friends. Indeed, he seemed to experience emotional satisfaction in doing so and particularly in revealing his intricate knowledge of the toxicology of the various drugs concerned. His attitude to the whole matter was unrealistic and he did not seem to be able to appreciate that he had indulged in acts for which he deserved any serious reprehension. He told me of his great interest in drugs and

99

their poisonous effects but was unable to reveal any reason for such an interest.

Graham had described to Dr Blair the years he had spent borrowing books from the library on criminology and poisoning in particular. Clearly pleased to have a willing listener, he listed those criminals who interested him most — Palmer, Pritchard and George Chapman, 'who between 1897 and 1903 poisoned three wives using antimony'. Dr Blair recounted:

He mentioned about a prisoner who had put cantharidin in coconut ice to induce an aphrodisiac effect on his girlfriend. However, he had not known the dosage, and when the girl and a friend of hers ate the coconut ice, they both died. The man was not had up for murder but for manslaughter. Although he has not read about them, he has also heard of Armstrong, who murdered his wife by arsenic poisoning and Mrs Merryfield who effected a murder by phosphorus.

Graham had also given Dr Blair details regarding his own instances of administering poison, outlining 'with very few inaccuracies the symptoms resulting from poisoning by the various drugs that he used'. The doctor perceptively pondered: 'He gave his mother so much antimony that I cannot help wondering whether it could have been in any way responsible for the condition of her vertebral column which led to her death, although there is no definite proof to this effect.' Prompted by Dr Blair, Graham went further back into his own toxic history, relating how he had 'perpetrated poisoning experiments on insects and once on a mouse. He admits that he purchased from chemists such drugs as digitalis, aconite, lead and morphia [morphine], as well as those already mentioned, and he seems almost to brag of doing so.' When asked about motivation, suggesting that he might have been desirous to 'satisfy himself as to accuracy or inaccuracy of the books he had read', Graham disagreed. Dr Blair noted: 'He was sure they were accurate and he simply could not give me any reason as to why he indulged in these acts but could only tell me that they caused him considerable satisfaction. He said that he had no grievance against any of his relatives or his friend and indeed thought that he loved them quite well. It just seemed that they were the nearest people at hand for his purpose.'

In Dr Blair's view, Graham did not appear to be suffering from any 'delusions or hallucinations' or 'any definite mental illness'. However, there was evidence of 'a definite schizoid and introverted temperament', particularly because Graham conceded that his emotional reactions had become 'progressively more flat' in recent years. Most chillingly, Dr Blair had been informed by one of the Ashford Remand nurses that Graham had been 'trying to indoctrinate one of the other prisoners who had attempted to murder his mother-in-law about the effects of drugs'.

The diagnosis reached was thus:

In spite of his high intelligence, he has an inherent defect in his personality, or in other words, he has a psychopathic personality. It would seem that it is this defect which renders him narcissistic and accounts for his extraordinary apathy and lack of appreciation of the social and ethical consequences of his administration of drugs to produce poisoning in relatives and friends. However, there seems also to be about him a certain detachment from reality and a progressive diminution of emotional reaction that possibly indicate an incipient schizophrenic process, although there is no other evidence of overt schizophrenia at present.

Dr Blair was at pains to point out that Graham presented 'a very serious danger to other people. His intense, obsessive and almost exclusive interest in drugs and their poisoning effect is not likely to change and he could well repeat his cool, calm, calculating administration of these poisons at any time.' He deemed Graham unsuitable for care in an ordinary psychiatric hospital and instead recommended 'the special facilities available for supervision and treatment in a criminal mental hospital such as Broadmoor. The prognosis in his case is dubious but, on the evidence available, seems to me at the moment to be very bad.' He added one final note by hand: 'In my opinion he is fit to plead and stand his trial.'

Dr Fysh had interviewed Graham 'on many occasions' during his time in Ashford. He had also interviewed Graham's Uncle Jack and had spoken to headmaster Henry Merkel and to the educational psychologist. Dr Fysh had several reports at his d isposal, including the one from Dr Blair, another from an Ashford Remand Centre psychologist and a third from an Ashford Remand Centre social worker who had visited some of Graham's relatives, including Win.

Dr Fysh's diagnosis found a dearth of morality and personal responsibility in Graham and agreed with

Dr Blair that he was suffering from a psychopathic disorder that required treatment in a suitably secure psychiatric hospital. His report is worth reading in full, giving as it does a complete clinical assessment of Graham prior to his 1962 trial:

On Examination:
He is quiet and well-mannered. His general appearance is neat and tidy. He is quietly and conventionally dressed. He converses freely and answers all questions readily and intelligently. He shows no gross defects of memory. He shows no abnormality of his thought content and there is no evidence of delusions or hallucinations. The results of intelligence testing show him to be of well above average intelligence.

He quite clearly enjoys discussing poisons and his experience of them and has no sort of reticence in giving details of the doses of poison that he has given to his relatives and friend.

As far as can be seen, he chose his relatives for his poisoning experiments because of their propinquity and he admits as much. There seems to have been no animosity towards his victims. He describes the administering of poison to them rather as an adult might describe a chemical experiment which took place in a laboratory unconnected with human victims. He describes the symptoms of his victims freely, with interest, but without emotion. His uncle tells me that he used to come back from the hospital after visiting his father, whom he had poisoned and describe his symptoms with a similar interest.

He makes it very clear that he considers himself extremely knowledgeable about the effects of poisons, the clinical symptoms and the amount which is likely to be fatal or not. He is at times almost patronising towards myself in this connection, only too ready to correct me and quite unable to accept that he might be wrong. I asked him on one occasion only about his reaction to his father's symptoms — he described them in detail, including considerable pain, and when I asked him whether this did not cause him distress or cause him to give up administering poison, he showed no sort of regret, distress or other appropriate emotional attitude. He gives a strong impression, not acknowledged, of the pleasure he has from the power he feels when administering poisons. There is no doubt that he feels a tremendous and abnormal degree of importance over his knowledge of poisons.

There is no abnormality in his emotional reactions other than an absence of real feeling towards others, including the relatives whom he poisoned. He shows a superficial emotional response towards those who have cared for him and who have been of use to him, but this is on an infantile level. As I have said, he shows no proper regret for the sufferings he has inflicted on those who have cared for him (father and stepmother) or on those with whom he has been on apparently friendly terms (sister and schoolfriend) but who were the victims of his experiments.

While he appreciates fully that his acts of poisoning were against the law and against the socially accepted code, he appears to have no moral sense whatsoever in relation to these acts.

Opinion:

This is, in my opinion, a case in which there is a failure to develop moral feeling and with this a true moral sense, together with a lack of feeling towards others. There is nothing to suggest that this condition is due to Mental Illness or to any failure of upbringing. I consider it to be a disorder of the mind resulting in seriously irresponsible conduct and so constituting a 'psychopathic disorder' within the meaning of the Mental Health Act 1959.

Disposal:

In my opinion he requires care, supervision and treatment in a suitable mental hospital. In view of the dangerous nature of his behaviour and his absence of moral sense, I can only properly recommend that this should be in a maximum-security hospital.

I am satisfied that he is fit to plead and stand his trial.

On 28 June, Dr Fysh wrote to inform the Director of Public Prosecutions that he had received confirmation that Graham and another inmate at Ashford could be accommodated at Broadmoor if the court so directed. This came after the Maudsley hospital refused Graham admission on the grounds that he was 'too dangerous'.

But while Graham was undoubtedly a danger to others, he appeared equally so to himself. He had already told DI Crabb that the bottle found on his person at the time of his arrest was his 'exit dose' if he were ever found out, and his case files record that he twice attempted suicide during his time in Ashford. The first time he used a poison he had managed to conceal from a routine police search and the second attempt involved using his tie as a noose. Sandra received a call at work from the grocery where her mother was employed; Win had collapsed after being given the news of Graham's second attempt.

Despite having twice tried to kill himself, Graham was regarded as fit to stand trial and would do so in the place where some of his murderous heroes had appeared before him: Court No.1, the Old Bailey. At the forefront of the criminal files marked *Regina v Young*, now kept in the National Archives, is a note about the defence counsel's stance: 'We are pleading guilty to all the charges. No harm was ever intended to either Williams, his father or his sister. Calls no witnesses at this court and reserves his defence.'

★ ★ ★

On top of the dome of the Old Bailey stands a 12-foot, gold-leaf statue of Lady Justice. Unlike most depictions of the figure, she is not blindfolded; the Central Criminal Court sculpture was designed to be circumspect. This vigilance was expected to inform each decision taken in the building below. Certainly, when Mr Justice Melford Stevenson passed sentence on Graham Young, his aim was to ensure that the public would be protected by him for a sufficient period in which, it was hoped, the boy could be helped and only then safely released back into society.

Graham's family did not disagree with the ruling, but as they left court on that day in July 1962, it was almost impossible to believe that 'Pudding' — their brother, nephew, cousin and son — was being sent to Broadmoor at the tender age of 14. Ten years later, Graham's father Fred recalled that moment: 'As I walked away from the Old Bailey after he had been 'sent down', I made up my mind that I was finished with the boy for good. I was convinced that if he ever got the chance he would poison again.' Still 'yellow as a canary with jaundice', Fred had an unassailable sense of life having been repeatedly ruined by his son: 'Within the space of a few months, everything I held dear had been taken away from me. Once I had a house, a wife and family. Now Molly was dead.

Graham was in Broadmoor.'

1962–1971
BROADMOOR

'There are only two things that are
wanted badly enough to risk damnation.
The love potion or the cup of poison.'

Agatha Christie, *The Pale Horse*
(Collins, The Crime Club, 1961)

6

THE FOUL PRACTICE HATH
TURN'D ITSELF ON ME

Broadmoor has a unique place in the British consciousness. Until a short time ago, it was viewed almost entirely within the context of past mistakes and the notoriety of several patients: a secretive place whose forbidding walls epitomised our vague ideas of Gothic Victorian brutality, yet to which we remained grateful for restraining present-day serial killers who probably plotted escape and the opportunity to wreak terror again.

During the 1980s especially, the tabloid press relied on inmates Charles Bronson, Robert Maudsley, Ronnie Kray and Peter Sutcliffe for column fodder. In the last ten years, when the truth erupted about the then recently deceased TV personality Jimmy Savile, the photo most used to depict his depravity was taken at Broadmoor; it showed the paedophile, who had preyed on his victims when they were at their most vulnerable, gleefully introducing boxer Frank Bruno, then visiting the institution, to the Yorkshire Ripper. But new documentaries and books, in which staff and patients alike spoke of their experiences, have lessened the mystery of Broadmoor. The public have been able to see that while some occupants have committed dreadful crimes, the majority are simply mentally ill, presenting as much of a risk to themselves as to anyone else. In 2019, new purpose-built units opened on

111

the old premises, focusing more than ever on rehabilitation and providing a safe, therapeutic environment for patients.

Nonetheless, it is fair to say that Broadmoor has had a chequered history, running in tandem with the perception and treatment of those who came before the courts while suffering from a mental illness. The issue has long and complex roots: Marcus Aurelius, the last of the 'Five Good Emperors of Rome', decreed that a man incapable of reasoning should be exempt from punishment, kept under secure conditions but treated humanely. Prior to 1800 in Britain, the law regarded everyone committing a crime as equal, with only rare exceptions made for those held to be completely and irretrievably insane. It took two attempts on the life of the reigning monarch to change legal opinion. The first, in 1786, was committed by a middle-aged woman named Margaret Nicholson who had lost her job and wanted to petition King George III for help. After attacking him with a knife and charged with high treason, she showed clear signs of mental disturbance. The King decreed that she should be treated kindly; he himself would soon be plagued by madness. Deemed unfit to stand trial, Nicholson spent the rest of her life in Bethlem lunatic asylum.

The second attempted assassination took place in 1800 when a former British soldier took a pot shot at the King during a show at Drury Lane theatre. It swiftly emerged that James Hadfield had sustained several injuries during his service in France and tried to kill his own child just a few days before visiting Drury Lane. Hadfield wanted to committed suicide, but fearing it was a sin, he intended to kill the King in the knowledge that doing so would result in execution by the state. Hadfield's defence success-fully argued that his actions were the result of his mental illness. The verdict passed by the court was not guilty by reason of insanity. Hadfield was acquit-ted but sent to Newgate prison until, just days later, the Safe Custody of Insane Persons Charged with Offences Act of 1800 was passed, allowing his trans-fer to Bethlem. Two years later, Hadfield escaped from Bethlem after killing another patient by felling him with a single blow. Recaptured, he was sent back to Newgate prison.

During the 19th century, many privately owned and local county and borough lunatic asylums were created alongside a new medical discipline, psychiatry. The 1800 Act had introduced the idea of criminal lunacy and led to intense discussions about its nature: were those deemed criminal lunatics a variant of criminals, or of lunatics, or a combination of both? Asylums were reluctant to take those deemed criminal lunatics, and as the controversy continued, in 1807 a Select Com-mittee of Parliament found that jailing offenders with mental-health problems deprived them of the care they required and created issues with other prisoners. A separate criminal lunatic asylum was recommended, but the government decided instead to build two new wings for insane criminals on to the existing Bethlem. Hadfield was returned to the new unit. Further legisla-tion in 1816 enabled those prisoners who had developed insanity during their incarceration to be transferred to asylums if necessary. In the second half of the 19th century, the overcrowding in the two criminal wings at Bethlem led to the decision to build a new hospital which would provide the exemplary care for the crimi-nally insane: Broadmoor.

Built by convict labour on moorland where highway-
men roamed the stagecoach paths through the heath,
Broadmoor opened in 1863 and was the only place of
its kind for almost half a century. Forty miles from central London and on the eastern edge of the Berkshire
village of Crowthorne, the vast red-brick institution
set in sweeping gardens comprised one female block
and five for men, along with cottages for the staff and
a school.

The very first patient was 35-year-old Mary Ann
Parr, a young woman with learning difficulties who
had grown up in abject poverty. Ten years earlier she
had suffocated her illegitimate child when she was
unable to care for it alone. Public reaction to her
death sentence resulted in Mary Ann being sent to
Bethlem instead, where she lived for 20 years before
being transferred to Broadmoor. Towards the end of
the Victorian era, 75 per cent of women in Broadmoor had been convicted of infanticide.

Another early patient was a man whose case had a
significant impact on the legal understanding of the
correlation between insanity and criminality. Glas-
wegian Daniel McNaughton travelled briefly from
Scotland to France in 1843 to escape imaginary
persecution. Unable to shake off the sense of being
followed, he returned to Glasgow, where he bought
pistols, before heading to London intending to kill
Sir Robert Peel, the Prime Minister, but instead shot
dead his private secretary, Edward Drummond, by
mistake. As a result of the medical evidence presented
at his trial, McNaughton was found not guilty by reason of insanity and committed first to the criminal

114

section of Bethlem and then to Broadmoor.

Questions had been raised in Parliament as soon as the verdict was returned. The public and press were in uproar, querying whether justice had been done, since McNaughton had known his actions were wrong, but had told the court that he had been driven to desperation by persecution. The Lord Chancellor asked judges for clarification on the relationship between criminal responsibility and insanity. Their response included the rationale that to establish a defence on the ground of insanity it must be clearly proven that, at the time of committing the act, the party accused was labouring under such a defect of reason from disease of the mind as not to know the nature and quality of the act he was performing, or if he did know it, that he was not aware that what he was doing was wrong. This came to be known as the McNaughton Rules, which thus defined what was meant legally by criminal responsibility in Britain. McNaughton himself died in Broadmoor in 1865, aged 52.

During Broadmoor's earliest years, every one of its residents had committed a crime; this included 30 admissions for attempted suicide, which remained a criminal offence until 1961. Approximately 25 per cent of patients had committed murder. The law, as it then stood, meant that a person found not guilty by reason of insanity would automatically be sent to Broadmoor, regardless of the severity or otherwise of the offence. Residents under the age of 16 were rare, but not unknown. The age of criminal responsibility had been set at seven since the 14th century and unless a child could demonstrate that they did not know right from wrong, then they were deemed criminally responsible. Seventeen boys and six girls are recorded as having been admitted to Broadmoor between its inception and the turn of the 21st century.

Initial treatments were crude by modern standards, consisting of bleeding, blistering and purging, along with sedatives. There were never straitjackets or padded cells in Broadmoor. One remedy seems particularly unusual: patients were fed 50 pounds of local rhubarb per annum because it was thought that a healthy — and regular — body led to a sound mind. The primitive nature of the treatments contrasted with the social side of life in Broadmoor, which became renowned for pantomimes and dramas, dances and educational classes. Religion was important, with all patients encouraged to attend services, and visits from the outside were actively welcomed.

But public attitudes towards the mentally ill, and especially the criminally insane, began to shift during the late Victorian era. Many writers and artists, led by the influential clinician Henry Maudsley, developed a darker vision of insanity, viewing it as hereditary and incurable. Some of the greatest novels of the era, from *Jane Eyre* to *Dr Jekyll and Mr Hyde*, brought the issue to the forefront; the latter in particular fused the concept of madman with murderer, and was adapted for the stage at a time — in 1888 — when the most infamous killer of all, Jack the Ripper, stalked London's poorest streets. This fed into other concerns about discharging patients too soon from asylums, fears that escalated when the 1890 Lunacy Act was ushered in, with its safeguards aimed at preventing civil patients from being held in lunatic asylums. The issue was debated in the British press and other publications, with the editors of the *Journal of Mental Science* fearing the new law created unnecessary difficulties in certifying insanity, leaving the public more at risk to falling victim of crimes committed by the mentally ill. To help allay these fears and ease some pressure on Broadmoor, Rampton hospital opened in 1912 to serve the north of England. More than half a century would pass before a third hospital opened along the same lines; this was Park Lane in Liverpool, later renamed Ashworth hospital.

Changes in attitudes and medical thinking evolved even more rapidly during the turn of the 20th century. The revolutionary findings of Charles Darwin were shaped into a new concept of eugenics in which people with mental and physical disabilities were viewed as less worthy of life than the able-bodied and those of sound mind. The idea that these groups were a threat to social progress took hold in the highest levels of society, with Winston Churchill, then home secretary, addressing Parliament in 1911 to suggest compulsory labour camps for those with learning difficulties. By the time Churchill was prime minister, millions of disabled and mentally ill people were being put to death in such camps by Hitler's Nazi followers.

After the war, Broadmoor continued to operate under some of the new psychiatric techniques that had come into practice years before. The greatest change in its history occurred after the founding of the National Health Service: since opening its doors in 1863, Broadmoor had come under the jurisdiction of the Home Office. Under the new National Health Service regulations, the legal distinction between 'mental deficiency' and mental illness was abandoned, resulting in non-offenders being admitted to Broadmoor and over 100 other asylums for the first time in 1949. Thus, newer treatments were introduced as psychiatry developed, including electroconvulsive therapy (ECT), which had been used for the first time in Britain in 1939. Eleven years later, when the administration changed again, Broadmoor was placed directly under Ministry of Health management as 'a special hospital for mentally disordered persons who in the opinion of the Minister require treatment under conditions of special security on account of their dangerous, violent or criminal propensities'.

By then, two escapes had given Broadmoor a bad name, with the first especially causing untold anger and horror. John Straffen had been institutionalised for much for his young life, regarded as 'feeble-minded' in the parlance of the day. In 1951, however, he killed six-year-old Brenda Goddard and nine-year-old Cecily Batstone in separate incidents. At his trial, he was found unfit to plead, with the judge remarking that it was like trying a babe in arms. He was admitted to Broadmoor but, six months later, in April 1952, he managed to scale the walls and divest himself of his hospital clothing in favour of something less distinctive. Just four hours later he had killed five-year-old Linda Bowyer. He was captured and this time at his trial was deemed fit to plead. Found guilty, Straffen was sentenced to hang but was reprieved by the Home Secretary on grounds of insanity. Straffen was imprisoned for life, having been regarded legally as insane, then sane, and finally insane again within the space of a year. An inquiry into the circumstances of Straffen's escape commented that there remained a very real possibility that patients might display stable behaviour but without any permanent psychological improvement.

The Straffen case had a huge impact on the public image of Broadmoor. It was now regarded as a place of enormous danger, filled with those who presented the worst threat imaginable to society, and solidified the idea of mental illness being something to fear and hate. New safety measures were implemented, which included a siren in case someone else escaped and which wailed every Monday morning at 10am when tested. However, it failed to sound six years later when criminal Frank Mitchell, known as the 'Mad Axeman' from his association with the Kray twins, cut through Broadmoor's iron bars with a hacksaw; by the time his escape was discovered, hospital staff saw no point in pressing the alarm, as Mitchell would have been some distance away. He was swiftly recaptured and, as a result of his absconding, an inquiry was set up into all three special hospitals. The Emery Report, submitted to Secretary of State for Health and Social Care Enoch Powell in April 1961, recommended that a patient should be admitted to one of the three hospitals 'only after all other possibilities have been examined and found unsuitable'. It was regarded as preferable for patients to be treated locally: 'For patients who present special difficulty, because of aggressive, anti-social, or criminal tendencies, diagnostic and treatment centres should be set up . . . Close liaison should be maintained between these and the remand and observation centres being set up under the penal system.'

Powell accepted the report's main recommendations but disquiet remained in the nearby village of Crowthorne concerning security at Broadmoor. During the 1960s and early 1970s, staff members anonymously related stories to the press about violence, attacks on nurses, overcrowding, drug abuse, escape attempts and rooftop protests. During this period around 65 per cent of patients had been sent to Broadmoor after being convicted of a crime, but that left 25 per cent who had been charged but deemed unfit to plead and another 10 per cent who had no criminal charge or conviction. Many of the problems were due to the Mental Health Act of 1959, which relaxed the criteria for admission to Broadmoor; a legal finding of insanity was no longer the main prerequisite, instead the doors were opened to include mentally disordered offenders or simply those who posed a significant risk to others. This included psychopaths, whether after being convicted of an offence by a court or by severely disturbed and violent behaviour during a prison sentence. Among those who came into the former category in 1962 was 14-year-old Graham Young.

* * *

The sun vanished from view as the vehicle carrying Graham approached the red-brick Victorian gatehouse with its twin towers and central green clock. Beyond the arched entryway was a quadrangle and all the various hospital buildings, the playing fields, recreation ground and gardens stood enclosed within the high perimeter walls like an entirely self-sufficient town. Graham was escorted into the building proper, where he was met by male staff wearing long black tunics with tall collars. This was standard wear at the time, and the staff themselves were then referred to as attendants, not nurses — as those in their care were known as inmates, not patients. As members of the

120

Prison Officers' Association, many of them had been recruited from the armed forces.

Graham's school shoes clicked on the parquet flooring as his details were taken and the duty medical officer examined him and asked a few questions. Once processed, he was led through cool corridors and past barred windows to the bathroom upstairs. Attendants stood nearby as Graham gingerly obeyed their instructions to undress and bathe. He then put on the nightclothes provided and was led through the corridors again to a private room, No.5, in Block 1, Admissions. His room was smaller than the average prison cell, approximately 12 feet by 6 feet, with a solid oak bed screwed to the coconut-matting on the floor. Sunlight filtered weakly through a small barred window with thick teak shutters. The one concession to Graham's unusual status as a very young inmate was the rug on the floor — a luxury that few others were permitted.

On Graham's first evening in Broadmoor, a hot beverage and food were brought to his room. The studded green door was left open deliberately to make the transition from schoolboy to Broadmoor inmate a little less overwhelming. After that, special allowances would be few, but not unheard of, and he would forever be regarded as someone with a special status and in whom the most senior staff members took a particular interest. His routine was the same as almost every other inmate, all of whom spent their first three months on the admission block, regardless of the seriousness of their crime. During that time, each individual was required to complete an IQ test, where the average result was significantly higher than in the outside world. Graham, like everyone else, was placed under observation while his case history was studied and the nature of his illness was considered. Treatment began in admissions but was a prelude to the full process. Privileges such as using the sports field or being allowed a radio in one's room would be granted only after that first period had been completed.

Forty-two inmates occupied Graham's ward. The day began at 7am, followed by breakfast in the dining hall before everyone headed to work, which was not compulsory but encouraged. Offering both structure and variety, work covered everything from art to jewellery classes, wood-working and metal-working. Other jobs were also available: Graham was naturally fairly lazy and did nothing at first, but when he learned he could earn a small wage polishing all the brass door-knobs on the ward, he agreed to that. Midday saw an exodus from the handicraft section back to the dining hall, then from 1:45pm until 4pm, inmates were once more occupied with work. After 4pm everyone was allowed to choose their own activity until bedtime, which was set at 9pm during Graham's first summer in Broadmoor. During those hours he could join fellow inmates in the ward's day room with its television, radio and daily newspapers, play billiards, bridge, table tennis, dominoes, draughts or chess in the nearby common room, and visit the sports field near Block 4 under supervision to either participate in or watch cricket, bowls and football.

By far the biggest problem at Broadmoor — and the one from which virtually all other issues stemmed — was overcrowding. At the time of Graham's arrival, the hospital population was over 700, almost double the maximum recommended for male and female patients, many of whom were long-term. Numbers had soared, despite an increase in discharged inmates. This was a particularly unhappy period in Broadmoor's history. A 1967 report on conditions at the hospital heard evidence from 168 attendant staff, only 12 of whom felt that security on site was satisfactory. Morale was severely depleted, primarily because of the intense amount of overtime needed to maintain discipline. The report made a point that was potentially significant with regards to Graham, who had spent five years in Broadmoor at that juncture: 'Gross indiscipline and violence have produced rapid discharges from Broadmoor, a premature move to better conditions in Broadmoor, or a return to prison ... Broadmoor is guilty of callous disregard for public safety when it discharges patients for the same reasons.' Conditions were said to be 'frightful'. One attendant admitted: 'We really do not do much more than a farmer would do for his animals. We are attending to their basic bodily needs, we are maintaining observation and discipline, but we are certainly not doing the job that the hospital should be doing.' Staff did their best but trained mental health nurses were few and some were barely in their 20s — far younger than most of the patients.

Among those who were in Broadmoor at the same time as Graham was Peter Thompson. Born into poverty, he helped lead an influential public inquiry into the rehabilitation of offenders, which led to major changes in treatment. But after a series of personal setbacks, his mental health suffered and he attacked three girls with a knife, injuring two. He pleaded guilty and in 1965 was sentenced to four years in Broadmoor. After his release, Thompson set up a mental-health charity called the Matthew Trust, which continues to help people today. In his memoir, Thompson outlined some of the problems caused by over-crowding and shortage of staff in Broadmoor:

> At nights, 20 patients share one commode to a dormitory. On the two or three occasions a year when 'Berkshire Belly' strikes — an outbreak of diarrhoea and vomiting — the situation can be degrading. I remember a night when 13 men were queuing to use the commode. By the time the last one used it, the thing was overflowing and the stench was appalling, and it was not even possible to open a window, for security reasons, nor wash one's hands. This kind of situation strips away one's last vestige of human dignity.

He also recalled how patients could be violent and provoked violent reactions from the staff, with frequent 'fights and rumpuses in the day room'. For Thompson, the heaviest burden in Broadmoor was the total lack of privacy: 'Except for the hours of sleep, all of one's life was open to inspection. Baths were supervised by the staff and all day long they kept an eye on us throughout the long months of the so-called 'admission' period.'

Graham was the object of intense observation during his first few months in Broadmoor. The medical superintendent, Dr Patrick McGrath, took a personal interest in him. McGrath had been in charge of the day-to-day running of Broadmoor since 1957 and would be the institution's last superintendent, retiring in 1981. He lived together with his family in a large Victorian villa near the main gate. He was regarded

124

with respect and deference by the staff; his word was final. He had a wry sense of humour, telling one reporter that half of Broadmoor's patients were probably no longer dangerous, but the problem was that they didn't know which half. His aim was to make the hospital less custodial and more therapeutic. Peter Thompson recalled McGrath in positive terms, that he told his patients to regard Broadmoor as a crutch to help them cope with a disability and once they no longer needed it, they should throw it away for someone else to use.

Graham had regular meetings with McGrath. The older man was heavily built, with rounded shoulders and a grey tinge to his black hair, and described Graham's mood on admission as 'flattened, indifferent'. He found 'no evidence of disorder of thought process or content' and recorded that Graham 'gave an account of himself which tallies in fact with the story drawn from other sources'. The only material treatment Graham received was sedatives, which changed his appearance considerably, making him pallid and prone to weight gain.

His family noticed a difference in him when they first visited at the end of July 1962. Graham was permitted seven visits per month, but for various reasons, he never received that amount. His father had been most affected by Graham's obsession with poison and was unable to face visiting for some time, but Winifred and the Jouvenats — Win, Jack and Sandra — made the then one-and-a-half-hour journey south-west to Broadmoor approximately a fortnight after Graham arrived there. As their car neared the institution, Winifred was aware that 'my feminine emotions were constantly intruding on my more rational judgements.

After all, I was his sister and I tended to recall him so clearly as my little brother [who] hadn't had such a wonderful life.' It was hard to reconcile the figure now known in the press as 'Poison Boy' with the quiet and introspective child she had known, 'alone most of the time, reading books and occasionally listening to something like pop music'. She was neither bitter nor angry with her brother, but instead felt ready to forgive him, as did the rest of the family, apart from Fred. In Winifred's eyes, Graham was 'just a child after all', who was 'sick, terribly, dreadfully sick'. She found it impossible to hate him and had never been frightened of him: 'I just felt sorry for him.'

That first visit was difficult for all of them, Graham included. Winifred could not recall afterwards how the conversation went or what was said, only that it was 'rather awkward and stiff and then very emotional by turns'. They were all stricken by the physical change in Graham and noticed the lethargy in his movements and slurred speech. Graham explained that this was due to his medication, before going on to detail its medical properties and additional side effects. He told them that he loathed taking the sedatives but had no choice; occasionally the drugs would be forcibly administered.

During that first visit, Graham suddenly made a revelation. It was Sandra who recalled most clearly how the conversation ran. Her cousin leaned forward in his seat and said quietly but without any emotion: 'I gave Molly 20 grains of thallium the night before she died. I put it on a trifle. I knew she would die the next day because I gave her so much. And I gave Daddy antimony. They're completely different poisons. One stops the kidneys from working — that's antimony.

126

The other disintegrates the bones.' He sat back again. 'That's why they didn't find out.'

For a moment no one spoke. Then his aunt asked, 'But ... how on earth did you have the nerve to go with your daddy to collect Molly's death certificate?'

Graham's response was immediate: 'Because they would never have found out. I wasn't stupid enough to give them both the same. Daddy's symptoms were different, and if he'd died, people would just have thought he'd pined away because of Molly's death.' He paused. 'I am sorry for all I've done.'

None of the family knew what to do with this appalling information, and if there were any discussions between them about speaking to the police, these came to nothing. There was a collective sense among the relatives that Graham was mentally ill, hence his incarceration in Broadmoor, and that he would only be released if he were deemed no longer a danger to anyone. Nothing could bring Molly back either, and Graham had made a private confession, having clearly had the opportunity to tell the police that he was responsible for his stepmother's death, yet chose to remain silent on the matter. The information stayed within the family unit for the time being.

Although Winifred never mentioned having been present during that conversation, she recalled her brother apologising several times for the actions that had led him to Broadmoor and felt that he was completely sincere when he said it. The fact that he expressed remorse gave her hope for the future.

Graham told at least one other patient that he had killed his stepmother. A man whom Winifred refers to in her memoir by the pseudonym 'Joseph Fuller', and with whom she spoke at length about her brother's time in Broadmoor, afterwards told her that not only had Graham admitted killing Molly, but that he had wanted people to know he was guilty in order to gain infamy. Fuller clearly remembered how Graham had delivered the information with perfect serenity before adding, 'She was my first successful murder victim by poison.'

Fuller, committed after pleading guilty to writing threatening letters, was an alcoholic in his late 50s who had been referred for psychiatric treatment and aversion therapy but received neither. He remained in Broadmoor for five years nonetheless, where he slept two doors down from Graham on the admissions block. He remembered Graham as 'a small lad, about five feet or so, tall, slim and pale, but always very smart in his Broadmoor issue sports jacket, open neck shirt and grey flannels'. They struck up a friendship of sorts, and in conversation — usually dominated by politics and poison — Fuller found Graham 'very intense', animated and mentally mature for his age. Fuller realised that Graham's reluctance to socialise was partly due to his disdain for anyone he regarded as beneath his own level of intelligence.

Within a very short time of Graham's confession to Fuller, there would be an inquiry at Broadmoor into the death of another inmate. This particular man had incurred Graham's wrath, leading many to believe that he was to be Graham's second 'successful murder victim by poison'.

7

THOU MIXTURE RANK, OF MIDNIGHT WEEDS COLLECTED

On 9 July 1962, the *Daily Express* reported that the 'Poison Boy' had been the subject of discussion at the latest meeting of the Berkshire education committee: 'Graham still has a year's schooling to do. Mr Trevor Whitfield, Berkshire education director, said yesterday, 'We have not yet been approached by the Broadmoor authorities but we feel we should be prepared to handle this case. We have visiting tutors for children who cannot attend schools — usually for health reasons — and Young would be in this category. Special facilities could be provided for him if the Broadmoor authorities believe they would be useful.''

Winifred was informed that Graham's IQ score was the second highest in Broadmoor, surpassed only by an inmate who was a former mathematics professor. Consultations with the Berkshire education committee resulted in their director of special services, Dudley Fiske, being tasked with finding a private tutor for Graham. But the few teachers deemed suitable were unwilling to take on the job and discussions regarding a solution reached the Minister of Health, Enoch Powell, whose views on race and immigration made him one of Graham's few living idols. Eventually a tutor was found: former wartime naval officer 'Taffy' Williams, described by inmate Peter Thompson as 'a tall, fuzzy-haired Welshman' who was so fervently patriotic that

129

whatever the subject he taught — even German — he would find a way to introduce his motherland into the lesson. A special 'school room' to allow other inmates to attend was set up in the admission block, but Graham was rarely there and the number of pupils tended to hover at no more than ten. Those who did attend enjoyed the classes, but one inmate recalled that, as far as Graham was concerned, the lessons were 'of little use to him — Graham had forgotten more than the Welshman could teach him.' He successfully sat his O levels as a result, however, before flatly refusing to attend any more classes. Much to the surprise of the county education officer, Graham's decision was supported by Broadmoor's senior staff, who unanimously declared their belief that he would seek out those subjects that interested him among the books in the hospital library. They were correct — but the consequences were devastating.

★　★　★

Patients were allowed to send two letters per week and could receive any number that passed the screening process. Graham wrote regularly to all his family, apart from his father, and in his earliest letters to his sister, he frequently expressed fury at the loud snoring of another patient, John Berridge.

Resident in Broadmoor since the summer of 1959, Berridge was a former member of the RAF and had been stationed in West Germany during the mid-1950s. He claimed that he had been approached there by a Communist agent, to whom he gave confidential information in exchange for money. He then returned home on leave to South Wales, where his

130

42-year-old father Leonard reacted to the news of what he had done by threatening to expose him to the government. At 6am the following morning — 25 April 1959 — John Berridge took a 12-bore shotgun into his parents' bedroom, shooting both his father and mother Irene, 38, to death. Tried at Pembrokeshire assizes, John Berridge was found guilty but insane. On 22 June 1959, aged 19 years old, he was sent to Broadmoor, where on 6 August 1962, he was discovered unconscious on his bed. A post-mortem found traces of cyanide in his stomach; Berridge must have ingested it the night before his death and the question uppermost on everyone's lips was not why but how.

Growing along the vegetable plots in the farmland surrounding Broadmoor were many laurel bushes and a person well-versed in poison would know that it was possible to distil cyanide from laurel leaves. A mere teaspoon would be enough to annihilate half of the inmates. A still was found in one of the vegetable plots and had been used by someone to make moonshine from potatoes — it could easily have been put to use for distilling cyanide instead. The authorities strongly doubted that Berridge himself had done so, hence their suspicions arose that the cyanide had been administered deliberately by another patient. Several inmates claimed to have done the deed but were clearly incapable of doing so. Following preliminary investigations, every inmate, bar the 30 men housed behind the locked double wood-and-steel doors of Block 6, the maximum-security wing, were questioned. The 70 men on Berridge's own block were examined more closely, yet without definitive proof.

When Winifred Young heard that the patient who had so irritated her brother was dead from cyanide poisoning, she wondered fearfully whether Graham was responsible. She asked him about it during her next visit and was only slightly reassured when he denied it. He did, however, admit to having distilled weak hydrocyanic acid from the Portuguese laurel that grew in Broadmoor's gardens, and a report from the hospital states that on three occasions Graham was 'caught teaching other inmates how to produce poisons by fermenting food in sealed containers'. Thirty-eight-year-old Sidney Henry, another patient and friend of Berridge, doubted that Graham was to blame. Henry was released from Broadmoor in February 1964 and told crime writer Richard Whittington-Egan that Berridge himself claimed to have received a phial of cyanide in a bag of sugar from an agent in the KGB. Whittington-Egan doubted the story and regarded Graham as a more likely suspect. In the Broadmoor archives, John Berridge's death is recorded in a single word: suicide.

* * *

Graham remained as obsessed as he had always been by poison. He made no secret of it, even to his family when they visited. His aunt Win recalled: 'On every occasion the conversation always turned to poison. His sister Winifred used to visit Graham about three times a year too, and I know that he has had several conversations with Winifred about poisons.' If he wasn't talking about poison, then he would soon mention the various ailments of his fellow inmates. 'He took a great interest in sick patients. One doctor told me, 'He had all the patients diagnosed before I even got to the ward to examine them. I had to brush up on my medical knowledge before I talked to Young.'' Graham received a small number of other visitors and they also remembered the endless loop of his conversations; even those discussions that seemed innocuous were generally found to have the same underlying theme, as Frank Walker recalled: 'He used to say to me that he wanted matches. Which, at that time, didn't ring a bell to me. But I presume that you can make poison out of matches, can't you?' And indeed, Walker subsequently discovered that phosphorus was poisonous.

During their first visits, Graham's family remembered that he had one other obsession: his trial. He pressed Win to bring him every newspaper clipping she could find in which he was mentioned, but she refused, feeling very disturbed by how proud he was of the publicity he had received. Her daughter Sandra confirms: 'He would talk about the press reports. He wanted to see them. He hadn't been allowed to read them. He kept on about this on several occasions.'

Apart from poison, and discussing the other patients, Graham's greatest interest remained Hitler and the Nazis. One of his most prized possessions was a brick from Hitler's former home at the Berchtesgaden; it was given to him by an elderly lady who became a regular visitor after reading about his trial. A former social worker, she had travelled to Austria and Bavaria, where she had acquired the brick, then parcelled it up for Graham, who was at first perplexed and then thrilled when she explained its provenance. Within a short while, he had grown a wispy moustache and swept his hair to one side in imitation of Hitler; he wore a swastika armband and on a chain around his neck hung a brass swastika that he had made himself in the workshop. He would lift the pendant to his lips and kiss it repeatedly to the disgust of most of the other inmates. His family continued to ignore his worshipping of the Nazis, with Winifred pointedly telling him that the moustache made him look more like an uptight bank clerk than the former führer.

This behaviour marked the start of Graham's most fractious period in which he refused to cooperate with the authorities in any sense and rarely interacted with the other inmates, preferring instead to listen endlessly to Wagner's music and repeatedly read Lord Russell of Liverpool's *Scourge of the Swastika* and William L Shirer's *The Rise and Fall of the Third Reich*. His grandmother Hannah had left him £50 in her will and he spent some of it on books, music and funding the National Front. He wore the Party's badge on his lapel and was a vocal supporter of Enoch Powell, leading to furious rows with his sister.

Graham refused to participate in communal activities and preferred sitting with a book in an annexe near the common room until everyone retired to their rooms for the night. He refused to accept that he was mentally ill, referring to his fellow inmates as 'goons'. His Broadmoor notes record that, for some time after his admission, he remained withdrawn, emotionally 'unmoveable' and prone to expressing paranoid ideas. He also suffered from hallucinations each night just prior to falling asleep, and these together with his other behaviours led doctors to consider the possibility of schizophrenia. Although ECT was mooted, it was never administered, and Graham's treatment was restricted to one-on-one therapy and sedatives.

His physical appearance continued to change as a

result of his emotional state and medication. Increasingly sallow-skinned and bloated, he developed a habit of rapid finger-tapping and fidgeting while his speech also became slurred and slow. He told his relatives that consultations with psychiatrists interested him and even led him to attempt self-analysis. He was fascinated by one doctor's revelation that the subconscious took over during sleep, causing a person to behave differently, because the conscious mind formed a barrier to subconscious urges during waking hours. Graham's response to the doctor was: 'But I do things when I'm awake that normal people would only do while they're asleep.' When he told the doctor that he was carrying out instructions given to him by voices in his head, the doctor explained this as his alter ego, and that his subconscious and consciousness had become one, leaving him without a moral compass. Graham explained that the voices in his head commanded him to use poison as a means of murder on a mass scale. Much later — after his release from Broadmoor — he claimed that these voices urged him to present himself as a model patient in order to gain early release to fulfil his mission.

Graham expressed remorse to his family several times. On one occasion Winifred asked him if he truly understood the wickedness of his actions, to which he replied earnestly, 'Oh yes, I do — and if I could go back and undo it, I would.' He offered an explanation that sounded very much as if it had been put to him by a doctor: that he had poisoned his immediate family because he so longed for the love he had known as a baby with his aunt and uncle. But that failed to account for his poisoning of Chris Williams, or indeed his workmates in years to come. Sandra had always been convinced that Graham had known exactly what he was doing and that if his remorse was genuine, he would no longer have any interest in poison. Most of the books he borrowed or obtained while in Broadmoor were directly about the subject, or in some way connected. Winifred was initially pleasantly surprised when he told her he had a new obsession: Roman and Italian history. But his conversation about both revolved around the myriad cases of poisoning in the Roman Empire and assassinations by the same means in early Italy.

His fixation was evident in the most mundane matters. Patients were allowed to purchase coffee, tea, sugar, biscuits and other items from the canteen to keep in screw-top jars. Fuller noticed that Graham had removed the labels from his canisters, replacing 'tea' with 'potassum cyanide', 'sugar' with 'strychnine', 'powdered milk' with 'strophanthin' and labelling others 'sulphuric acid', 'chloroform' and 'vitrol'. Rather than forbid the practice, staff teased him about it.

In addition to Dr Patrick McGrath, Graham saw several other doctors while in Broadmoor. The psychiatrist in charge of his case was Edgar Leon Udwin, who had joined the hospital staff shortly before Graham's own arrival. Born into a Jewish family in Johannesburg, South Africa, on 28 March 1918, Udwin arrived in London after the Second World War, beginning his post-university life with a six-month stint at Hammersmith graduate hospital. Following his marriage in 1949, Udwin and his bride chose to remain in England. Deciding that psychiatry was his true vocation, he joined Horton hospital, Epsom, as a registrar in 1949, when the premises were being renovated from the shell of a war hospital into a modern

136

psychiatric unit. Udwin made a vital contribution to its success and stayed in his post for 13 years until leaving for the position of consultant at Broadmoor. In his free time, he ran a clinic for children with severe learning difficulties. Like McGrath, he took a special interest in Graham, whom he regarded as particularly challenging. Udwin noted that during Graham's first weeks in Broadmoor:

> his behaviour became so deviant that he had to be moved from the Admission Ward to Monmouth House and there he remained a centre of disaffection for a very considerable time. His small size and his youth led him to foment disorder in non-violent ways in order to preserve some sort of prominence. He was always in small bits of mischief, always threatening to concoct the most horrifying poisons because he had learned that this upset patients and staff and even talked about black magic to the more impressionable patients to upset them further. He formed alliances, always with older and rather stupid men whom he could influence. For instance, at one point he participated in sending me a message regarding the ease with which nicotine could be got out of cigarettes and used as a poison. At a later stage he got amongst a group of psychopaths and had to be warned not to stir up mischief and finally he had to be removed from them but later he was tearful and asked to get back.

Graham's first case conference in Broadmoor was held in August 1962, two months after he was admitted. Dr Robert Brittain took charge, diagnosing Graham with sadism, psychopathic disorder and schizoid tendencies. In 1970, Brittain would write what was, for many years, regarded as the definitive account of this particular type of killer — *The Sadistic Murderer* — which was believed to be based on Graham Young. In it, he describes an introverted and sexually prudish man whose traits include being timid, over-controlled, reserved and inexperienced but with a vivid, sadistic and sexually deviant fantasy life and a keen interest in violence-based activities. Brittain identified the subject as egocentric but timid, whose offences were often the result of his self-esteem being belittled. His analysis of Graham at the case conference was challenged somewhat by Dr Udwin, who felt Graham was suffering a 'neurotically engendered psychopathic disorder'. Dr McGrath felt that a diagnosis of schizophrenia would be more accurate, and later recalled how entry after entry in Graham's record referred to 'his flattened effect, to the extent that a diagnosis of schizophrenia was seriously considered'.

McGrath felt that some progress was being made by September when Graham was able to show 'some grief at his stepmother's death, for which he held himself responsible as he had given her large doses of thallium and tartar emetic.' Another figure from Graham's past features in McGrath's notes at this stage: Jean, the girl from his local library, was experiencing mental health difficulties herself and had been admitted to the Maudsley. Broadmoor officials discouraged their correspondence without any explanation.

Plans were cautiously put in place to move Graham after six months to a longer-term block with better conditions, but these were delayed because of his persistent obsession with poison and habit of talking like a medical textbook. He was kept in room No.5 of Block 1 indefinitely, where he promptly began decorating his walls with photographs of prominent Nazis and emblems of fascism. He irritated staff and patients alike with his constant monopolising of the record player in order to play his beloved Wagner.

Graham's first Christmas in Broadmoor was a withdrawn affair. He refused to help with decorating the hospital or to participate in the carol service. Christmas dinner was served and the League of Friends provided a parcel for every inmate, but most were upset at being away from home and Graham seemed to be no exception. One year after his admission, attendants felt that little or no progress had been made with his case; Graham was either sullen and silent or argumentative in the extreme. 'We had a lot of trouble with him,' one staff member recalls. 'We had to put him on drugs to subdue him. That's not too unusual, as most patients suffer from depression when they first get here. But Young was different. He lived very much in a fantasy world at first and we had a lot of trouble getting through to him. All he would talk about were his poisons. And this was the very subject we wanted to get him off, to channel his thoughts and energies into something else.'

The lack of progress was further evidenced by McGrath's notes that 'in July 1963 [Graham] told a doctor that he liked [the] 'sight and sound of the pain it gave them [his victims] — you might say it was a sexual pleasure'.' Even more disturbing was Graham's admission during the same interview that 'were he to leave hospital he would again acquire and administer poisons and he could not stop himself'.

That same month, Graham penned a quite extraordinary letter to one of his first victims, Chris Williams:

> Dear Chris,
> I hope that you are keeping well. Just a few lines
> to let you know how I am getting on.
> It is not too bad a place here. The food is
> pretty good and there are things to occupy me
> some of the time. There is television to watch
> at night and the wireless to listen to during the
> day. There is also billiards and snooker, etc.
> We can go down to the cricket field every
> other night to watch the hospital playing an out-
> side (or inside) team. I don't usually go down
> though.
> How are things with you? I get occasional
> reports about you from my 'spies' in Neasden.
> Dad saw you a couple of months ago with Rich-
> ard, so he was telling me . . .

Urged by his daughter and sister, Fred Young had
indeed begun visiting his son in Broadmoor. He travelled with Winifred, who had married Denis Shannon
the previous October, and although the conversation
was stilted and lacked warmth, it was regarded as
beneficial for Graham's rehabilitation.

In August 1963, the *Daily Sketch* ran an article
with alleged quotes from Broadmoor staff who were
disturbed by Graham being allowed to wander the
grounds unsupervised. The reality was that Graham's
liberty was no more and no less than most patients,
resulting in the newspaper being forced to publish a
formal apology to Dr McGrath for doubting his professional competence. McGrath added a personal
note to the periodical report on Graham's mental

state that was issued on 15 August 1963, which recommended that he should continue to be detained in Broadmoor: 'His mental illness is manifest by a morbid preoccupation with poisons and a sadistic satisfaction from administering them to and watching their effects on other people. He is in need of care and supervision in hospital.' However, six months later, McGrath was encouraged to find Graham 'relaxed' and with insight into his own problems, to the extent that he approved a reduction in his medication.

But this promising development failed to progress any further, with McGrath writing in April 1964 that Winifred had enquired why her brother had stopped writing to family and that Graham himself 'was found to have been instructing other patients in the preparation of anaerobic cultures (meat, potatoes, Bovril, in a sealed tobacco tin)'. Two months later, nursing staff reported Graham to be tense and paranoid, and were alarmed to discover that he had offered to help another patient commit suicide 'by the injection of an air embolism with a purloined syringe and needle'. Unsurprisingly, the periodical report on his mental condition again had a personal note to the effect that Graham was 'emotionally extremely vulnerable and still shows preoccupation with harming others by paramedical means'. McGrath took an even greater interest in his case, but despite his encouragement and the positive observation that Graham was 'alert, resilient and with a façade of insight', by 1965 the lack of progress was becoming painful. In March of that year, McGrath noted that Graham's insight was 'academic and superficial' with a manner that presented in a ''hard' psychopathic way rather than in a flattened schizoid way'.

If anything, Graham's behaviour was becoming more troubled — and troublesome. McGrath observed: 'He is consistently reported by staff to be a source of annoyance and trouble, particularly as a bad influence on new patients — a whisperer in corners. I told him of these reports and said if I heard his name again, even without specific offence, the roof would fall in on him. Following this somewhat Kiplingesque approach, Graham threatened another patient with a pen should that patient report any of Graham's doings to staff.'

McGrath's warnings clearly had no effect on Graham, who shortly after the pen incident led a group of patients into regular inebriation. Alcohol was never permitted on the premises, and staff were baffled until one orderly discovered Graham deploying a press-button lighter on the end of a short, flexible pipe to ignite the gas stove used for drinks in the common room, then blowing out the flame before plunging the nozzle into patients' drinks for a minute or so. The escaping carbon monoxide in the cups of cocoa, coffee and tea caused intoxication.

This incident and several more informed Dr McGrath's letter of 12 March 1965 to the Home Office. Addressing the matter of Graham's continued detention, McGrath gave the Under Secretary of State a summary of events in Graham's life prior to his admission to Broadmoor and a further precis of his behaviour in the past three years. Although Fred had by then visited Graham, there appears to have been another breakdown in communications between father and son, which had clearly upset Win, since McGrath declared that 60-year-old Fred 'wishes no more to do with the boy.'

McGrath then went on to describe Graham's present behaviour: 'Graham now occupies himself in ward activities, but does not avail himself of educational facilities, preferring lonely study — trivial and sporadic — of anatomy, physiology and hygiene. He has been a non-contributing member of a therapeutic group and is believed to attempt to nullify the therapist's efforts outside the group. His associates are mainly intelligent, sexually deviant and psychopathic. He is at present having a small daily dose of Stelazine.' This was the brand name for trifluoperazine, a drug used to treat mood disorders and schizophrenia, leading to less anxiety and minimising the desire to hurt oneself or others.

Regarding Graham's psychometry, McGrath noted that he had been 'extensively investigated' at school, while on remand and in Broadmoor, with 'the consistent features' being 'a high verbal scale (IQ equivalent 129) and a significantly lower non-verbal (IQ equivalent 97)'. These tests also led to the detection of personality indicators of depression and neuroticism, a tendency towards anxiety, self-doubt and other negative emotions.

McGrath ultimately described Graham as 'an intelligent young man who had, and retains, an abnormal interest in poisons, from the harmful administration of which he has derived sexual pleasure. He is not, I think, psychotic, but can truthfully be said to have persistently behaved in a seriously irresponsible way, this behaviour stemming from an abnormality of mind as demonstrated by markedly abnormal emotional tone. There is as yet no evidence of maturation, or of significant change in mood or attitude.' McGrath recommended that Graham was 'the subject of

143

psychopathic disorder' and that 'for the protection of others should continue to be detained'.

McGrath's letter went some way to nullifying Graham's first attempt at parole, which was made at the end of that year. All Broadmoor patients were entitled to apply to a review tribunal for parole. Graham filed his request, after which Fred and Win drove down to Broadmoor. Fred recalled being invited to attend:

> with all expenses paid. It was Ascot Week, I remember, and I drove to Broadmoor with Win past crowds of women done up in their finery. In the tribunal room we were faced by about five people including a doctor and a parson. It didn't last more than two or three minutes. They asked us what we thought about the idea of Graham being released on parole. Win said she didn't really think he was fit to come out. I was a bit stronger. I said, 'If you do let him out, he will never live with me. And if he comes to my sister's, I'll clear off.' They gave me a long, hard look at that but they could see I meant it.

Win was then asked if she would consider having Graham to live with her. 'I informed them that I wasn't prepared to trust him,' she remembered. 'I was required to explain my feelings and informed them I would be frightened to go out of the room in case Graham put something in the tea.'

It took the tribunal panel less than a couple of minutes to deny parole.

8

POISON HAS A
CERTAIN APPEAL

Fred Young retired from his job at Smiths in 1964. Appropriately enough, he received a gold watch from the company to mark 25 years of service. He gave up work a little sooner than he had planned, prompted by his sister and brother-in-law's decision to relocate to Sheerness, on the Isle of Sheppey in north Kent. Built as a naval port in the 16th century, by the Victorian era the town's pier and promenade had made it a popular seaside resort, but in 1960 the dockyard closed, leading to the unemployment for thousands and it became something of a ghost town compared to its thriving past. Nonetheless, its sandy beaches and proximity to London (30 miles from the capital's outskirts) made it an attractive proposition for Win and Jack's approaching old age. Their decision to move was prompted by Sandra's marriage to Leslie Lynn in January 1964. She settled in Brent and her parents invited Fred to join them in Sheerness. He accepted, disliking the idea of 'going into lodgings somewhere'. Instead, he sold the house and most of the furniture, apart from a few pieces that Winifred wanted. He soon found a job as a machine inspector at Sheerness and continued to visit his son in Broadmoor 'about a dozen times or more'.

Fred admitted to being less than keen on visiting Graham:

but Winnie and her husband Jack thought it would help him if the family rallied round and kept in touch ... Besides, I had a car and could drive them all down there. The others all used to take him presents — cakes, sweets and so on. Not me. I used to feel I had to give a couple of pounds to one of the staff for him at Christmas or on birthdays though I grudged even that. I never wrote to him. I had nothing to say — to him. Even when I joined in a visit and we all sat round a table in a room at Broadmoor, we hardly ever spoke. All he could talk about was the people he had got to know in Broadmoor, the murderers and maniacs he was mixing with, and Hitler and the Nazis. I believe he used to do a brilliant take-off of Hitler but I never saw him at it. I wasn't interested.

Both Fred and Sandra ceased visiting Graham in 1965, leaving Win, Jack and Winifred to keep them informed of Graham's well-being.

And Graham did make some progress that year. Winifred recalled that the doctors began weaning her brother off sedatives and he started to look much better. But he remained argumentative with the doctors and eager to battle the authorities. On at least one occasion his behaviour resulted in him being locked in his room. Despite being encouraged to take part in group therapy, he refused, declaring that all the exhibitionists used it as a platform for showing off, leaving everyone else sitting in silence.

While a Broadmoor report described his first four years as 'singularly unproductive and unfruitful', Graham's behaviour gradually began to show signs of stability, with privileges being afforded to him, such as listening to the radio in his own room, being allowed to keep a pet budgerigar and his door remaining unlocked except at night. From 7am he was free to do whatever he wished and he chose to spend most of his time reading in his room. But another lapse saw him sent to Block 6, the restrictive maximum-security block; conversely, he appeared more sociable there and became friendier with Joseph Fuller, who was surprised to find him 'quite cheerful' and even 'quite charming'. When his period of punishment was over, he settled better into the hospital community and was even relatively pleasant to the attendants, one of whom recalls: 'If Graham didn't want to talk to you, nothing would open him up. He'd tell you he wasn't prepared to talk and then he'd just sit there, silently staring at you. No amount of questioning would draw him out. When you did get him talking, you had to be wary, as a lot of what he said would be lies.' None of the nursing staff trusted him, regardless of his new and tentative sociability. One male nurse confirmed: 'There was something about him which warned us he could be dangerous. We knew he had an obsession about poisons and several times he made the remark that one day he would go into history books as a mass murderer.'

Dr Udwin formerly took over as Graham's psychiatrist in 1966. An official record of his time in Broadmoor notes that the next 12 months were one 'long battle' between Graham and Udwin, at the end of which Graham seemed to accept Udwin as 'a father figure' and continued to make 'steady improvement'. However Graham often remained in a position where 'he felt he had to defend himself from other inmates and staff [and] he would frighten them by indicating that he would, or had, poisoned them. He also caused some commotion among inmates of limited intellect by indicating that he practised witchcraft and would harm them in this way. Contact with other inmates seems to have been mainly on a superficial level and he felt himself superior to the majority of them.' But Udwin observed that Graham's behaviour had begun changing noticeably in early 1966. Graham spoke to Udwin about wishing to apply for parole but felt it to be pointless since he was certain that 'no tribunal would discharge him'. This led to a fairly productive discussion between them about his case; Graham showed some interest in entering treatment. Udwin recalled:

He admitted to being afraid of going mad. At this point it seemed expedient to take advantage of a change of mood and transfer him to better surroundings. Shortly after his move, he once more became disturbed, felt the effort was too much apparently and wanted to get back to his psychopathic friends in high security. This, after a quarrel, reached the point where he made threats that trouble would result if he were not returned to Monmouth House in Block 6, but he was not allowed to return and at this point seemed to settle down at a rather more adult level. I noted at that time that he was showing quite a firm desire to come back repeatedly and talk about his troubles. He even showed a desire to talk about himself rather than his impossible situation in the hospital.

Electroencephalograms were carried out on 10 February 1966, 31 July 1967 and 12 September 1967.

148

Commonly known as EEGs, the procedure tests brain activity by means of small sensors attached to the scalp, picking up the electrical signals produced when brain cells send messages to each other. EEGs can be used to diagnose epilepsy, sleep disorders, brain tumours and other anomalies, but in Graham's case they did not reveal any significant abnormality. Despite his progress, when Udwin signed Graham's periodical non-statutory report regarding his continued detention, he declared him to be 'suffering from Psychopathic Disorder' and 'remains irresponsible, not matured and in need of care'. Graham seemed to follow the path of one step forward and two back, such as when he finally agreed to participate regularly in the handicrafts class only to then quarrel violently with a member of staff before walking out. Udwin tried to make use of the incident:

I felt it absolutely necessary that he learn to back down and accept a few things so I refused to allow him to 'resign'. The battle went on for five months, during which time I refused him all other employment and he refused to go back to Handicrafts. Eventually he went back and has been on the move since then. He tends to come forward far more frequently for interview, is beginning to gain an interest in having treatment. He has at times been quite aggressively tense but has not at any point got up to any sort of his old mischief.

One thing was clear: Graham was thinking about a life beyond Broadmoor, which, although the authorities failed to recognise it, revolved around his fixation

with poison. On 2 October 1967, he wrote to the Secretary of the Pharmaceutical Society, blithely unaware
of how his past and present might affect his future
aspirations of becoming a chemist. Giving his address
as 'Kent House, State Hospital, Crowthorne, Berks',
he announced:

Dear Sir,
For some considerable time, prior to my admit-
tance here, I was an ardent student of both
pharmacology and toxicology. However, due
to the stresses and strains placed on me by my
almost incessant studying of these subjects, I
became the victim of a nervous breakdown,
which necessitated my hospitalisation here.
    Now however, that my discharge is in the
foreseeable future I would be greatly obliged
if you would inform me of certain obstacles to
what was to have been my intended career, had
I not had the misfortune to place myself in my
present unenviable position.
    As the offence with which I was initially
charged was involving the misuse of certain
highly toxic drugs, am I liable to be refused university entrance with a view to resuming what
would this time be an entirely scientific interest
in pharmacology?
    My second question, and one that is to me of
far greater importance, if I succeed in obtaining
a degree in pharmacology, is the Pharmaceutical Society likely to refuse me membership, on
the grounds of my previous lapse?
    I would be greatly obliged if you would be
so kind as to inform me of these points at your

150

earliest possible convenience. Also, I wish to know whether the journal issued by the society can only be purchased by members of the same.

Hoping to hear from you soon, I remain,
Yours faithfully,
Graham Frederick Young.

Unfortunately for Graham, the Pharmaceutical Society were fully aware that he was a highly unsuitable candidate. With extreme tact, they responded that he presently lacked the entrance requirements of three A levels and three years' university study, adding that the disciplinary committee would have to inquire deeper 'into the circumstances of your conviction'. Graham knew he was beaten and made no further attempts to become a legally operational chemist.

Summer 1967 marked the end of Graham's fifth year in Broadmoor. Accordingly, he was transferred to the more relaxed conditions of Block 2 and given more freedom to wander about the hospital grounds. Later, Winifred came to realise this was the time when her brother began actively plotting what he needed to do in order to obtain his freedom without raising suspicions. He quietly borrowed psychology books from Broadmoor's library and observed how others behaved before they were permitted greater privileges and transferred to the parole ward. Within a short while, he had become the model of good behaviour and the epitome of how the hospital's treatment and care could turn a patient's life around. Transferred to semi-parole surroundings, in February 1968 his mask slipped when he was again involved in a quarrel with a nurse with whom he had clashed shortly after his admission. Udwin recounted the incident: 'He evolved a revenge which had as its basis another poison scare, which was so obvious as to be a practical joke. He was once again demoted and was considerably shaken by this to the point of settling down very rapidly.'

Graham's revenge took the form of a notorious incident that has been re-told many times with several variations on the nature of the offence. What actually happened was recounted by Joseph Fuller, who was present at the time. Fuller was part of a group of inmates given responsibility for running the dining rooms in the block; they decided to wash down the paintwork and three packets of Manger's sugar soap was provided. The group got to work on the ceiling, leaving two packets on top of a kitchen cupboard. When the first packet was empty, Fuller looked for a second but saw that the others had gone. Graham had been loitering beforehand and Fuller immediately sought him out. He found Graham in his usual hiding place: the washroom. Graham had a habit of seeking refuge in there and pulling faces at himself in the mirrors. Fuller confronted him about the soap and he denied taking it. Certain that he was lying, Fuller attacked Graham, who 'stood there and took it all without a word' before admitting he had poured both packets of sugar soap into the water boiler and kitchen tea urn. One of the other men in Fuller's group made an official complaint regarding Graham's actions, which could have resulted in the poisoning of the 97 men on the semi-parole block. Both the water boiler and tea urn had to be thoroughly scoured, but a certain nervousness remained among everyone who had to use them.

Graham was placed in isolation as a punishment. There he met criminal Roy Shaw, who remembers:

We became friends when he asked me to look after him because another inmate had threatened him. He was an interesting bloke, although I can't say I understood him. He was a mine of information and knew a thousand ways of poisoning people and talked about it openly. He had a few visitors, one of whom was his sister, the one he'd tried to poison. She used to bring him home-made cakes. When he came back to the ward, he always offered me a slice, but I always declined and he would laugh. He had a wicked sense of humour and every day when the tea urn was brought on to the ward he would chuckle and ask me, 'What's your poison, Roy?' Shortly after, Graham was moved to another part of the hospital and I never saw him again.

The incident was one of two in which Fuller remembered involving a tea urn. On another occasion Graham squirted Harpic toilet cleaner into the staff common-room tea urn and was afterwards banned from brewing tea there. Otherwise, Graham settled into life on the block, which was less regimented than in the hospital proper. Patients were woken at 7am and expected to be washed and ready within the next half an hour. Hot water was available for tea in the kitchen until 7:50am, after which there was a voluntary recreation period, with patients allowed to wander the tree-lined airing court until breakfast at 8:15am Work began at 9am and patients made their way to jobs in the gardens, shoe shops, laundry, etc. Tea break followed at 10:15am and lunch was served in the block at noon. Work continued from 2pm until 4:15pm, with another tea break at 4:30pm, after which their time was their own until bed at 8:45pm.

Although the authorities believed that Graham was showing signs of improvement, Fuller was unconvinced:

> I saw him many times walking on a straight course with eyes staring unseeingly in front of him, and woe betide any member of the staff who had the misfortune to be in his path; that unfortunate would be bowled over as [if] he never existed. He was obviously suffering from delusions of grandeur and a pseudo-superiority complex which had become progressively worse during his 'growing up' period in Broadmoor. He had also become more progressively psychotic and ambitious in his intention to destroy his fellow men.

The 'sadistic, cruel and evil streak', which Fuller recognised in Graham from their earliest encounters, had evolved into 'a rigorous self-sufficiency which silently oozed aggression'. His persistent adoration of Nazism was symptomatic of his lack of emotional responsiveness or feeling for those around him. Fuller declared that, in the six months they were together on the semi-parole block, Graham was 'the most unpopular inmate of that block because of his strange and icy aloofness and complexities of character'. Wherever Fuller happened to be, he would know Graham was nearby if he heard his distinctive hoot, 'dry, chilling laugh coming from deep within his throat, invariably followed by a smirk of utter contempt'.

In April 1969, Patrick McGrath supported Graham's parole plea on account of his having made 'so much progress'. Less than six weeks later, Graham had his parole card rescinded for several days, due to reasons unknown. But it is patently obvious that the authorities believed him to have turned over an entirely new leaf, with Udwin stating that:

> during the 18 months [Graham] has been regularly under treatment, he has continued to make progress to the point now where the staff confidently accept him as improved and where his relationship with them is entirely changed. It was noteworthy in a recent disturbance in the ward that nursing comment was emphatic that Young was actually spending hours trying to talk a disturbed patient out of further mischief. His relationships with nursing staff have changed to the point where there is now a degree of friendship possible, where he will accept rebukes and not sulk, more often than not, and where he has achieved a good working relationship with the Handicraft instructors. There is no doubt in anyone's mind that he had made vast progress ...

This was again confirmed by McGrath in July 1969, when he too recorded that Graham had made 'exceptional progress'. Both men were pleased to hear that he was now taking a keen interest in his work in the tailor's department of handicrafts, where he displayed a natural talent for needlework.

Even Joseph Fuller — who remained sceptical

about Graham's new conformity — sensed that he had grown genuinely close to Dr McGrath, who appeared to be equally eager to be seen as a father figure to the young man. Several inmates teased Graham about his status as McGrath's blue-eyed boy, which he ignored, but it was clear to everyone that both McGrath and Udwin continued to take a special interest in him and consulted each other regularly on each step forward. Graham's newfound willingness to form friendships was taken as further evidence of his progress. Although most of his relationships in Broadmoor were largely superficial, he developed an immediate and genuine bond with one newcomer: Dr Christopher Swan, who arrived not as a staff member but as a patient.

Working from his surgery in Hackney, Swan was 32 when rumours began to spread that the practice was a thriving market for drugs. It later emerged that while he had prescribed only 168 drinamyl tablets ('purple hearts') in September 1967, six months later he had 300 new patients on his books, all of whom were drug addicts, and he was dispensing more than 23,000 tablets. He and his unqualified male medical secretary, Stephen Hartford, were drugs trafficking on a large scale, with Hartford selling false prescriptions, often in other patients' names, on to addicts who, in turn, sold any surplus medications on to other addicts. Swan's income from that alone was estimated to be around £30,000 annually, in addition to his National Health register of patients and work for other large companies. Swan lived lavishly, with a beautiful home in Forest Hill and two expensive cars at his disposal. He made no attempt to hide his lifestyle, declaring himself 'the richest doctor of my age in the country'.

The deaths of four addicts on Swan's register led to a police investigation, but no charges were brought against him. When the Dangerous Drugs Act was enforced in April 1967, Swan was no longer able to prescribe heroin and cocaine, but he continued to dole out a huge amount of medication to addicts, including a drug that hadn't been banned under the new law: methedrine. In a show of defiance, he called a press conference for the re-opening of his surgery under its new moniker, the East London Addiction Centre, and dispensed more drinamyl than ever: 44,000 tablets a month. Alerted to his activities, the *Daily Express* marshalled a team of ten reporters to carry out one of the most exhaustive enquiries ever conducted by a newspaper; they interviewed a huge number of Swan's patients before confronting the doctor himself. Swan initially refused to be interviewed but was persuaded to tell his story in an exclusive article, after which the Daily Express ran their own story detailing all of their findings.

Outraged, Swan arrived at the newspaper offices with three burly men. His threats came to nothing, but Swan and his secretary Stephen Hartford were convinced that John Wall, a former receptionist at the clinic, had leaked secrets to the press. Hartford was an associate of David Gordon, doorman of the Limbo Club in Soho; he had provided him with prescriptions for purple hearts and John Wall, too, had dealt drugs there. Following Swan's insistence that Wall had blabbed to the press, Hartford arranged for Gordon to stab Wall, but the police descended and, within hours of being charged, both Swan and Hartford were held in Brixton prison. Keen to deter potential witnesses from spilling further secrets, Swan asked another inmate if he knew of a good 'chopper-man' to deal with the problem. As a result, Swan received a visit in jail from 'Sid Green', who was in fact Detective Sergeant John Vaughan, offering his services and acting in a manner that a judge later observed 'would have deserved an Oscar in another sphere'. Unbeknown to Swan, however, Vaughan was recording their conversation.

Swan's trial at the Old Bailey in January 1969 was a media sensation. It was revealed that he had flooded the London drugs market with prescriptions for over half a million purple hearts and methedrine tablets. Taking the stand, Swan complained that people imagined him to be a gangster, 'making lots of money and indulging in sexual orgies with women patients' when he was in fact simply a 'father figure' to addicts. Sir Carl Aarvold, senior judge and Recorder of London, sentenced him to 15 years' imprisonment: seven for inciting Detective Sergeant Vaughan to murder four witnesses, five for contravening the Drugs Act, two for conspiracy to assault John Wall and one for being an accessory to two abortions. Aarvold told Swan sternly: 'You used your position as a doctor not to spread health and happiness but to bring about misery and illness for your own financial gain.' Swan's co-conspirator, Stephen Hartford, was sentenced to two years in prison for his role in the affair.

Swan appealed against his sentence, insisting he had not been fit to plead. It emerged that before he had qualified as a doctor in 1961, his superiors suspected that he had schizophrenia, and evidence of his mental illness was presented at his trial but discounted. Appeal judge Lord Justice Fenton Atkinson was not persuaded either, dismissing his appeal in

December 1969 with the damning words that Swan was not ill, but simply 'a very dangerous and very evil man'. But Swan's lawyers successfully presented further evidence of their client's mental health problems and, as a result, in February 1970 Swan was sent to Broadmoor.

He and Graham hit it off immediately, with the younger man fascinated by Swan's medical background and experiences. 'Young was always a loner but he changed when Swan came here,' one inmate recalled. 'They were always reading medical books belonging to Swan. Young and Swan were inseparable.' Graham spoke frequently to his family about Swan, insisting that his trial had been a travesty of justice. When Fred had to go into hospital, Graham telephoned to speak to a nurse, who found him so knowledgeable that she was surprised to learn afterwards that he was not part of the medical profession. He had consulted Swan in order to reassure his family, as he continued to do for some time on all such matters, including his sister's Caesarean section (she gave birth to her first child, Claire, in 1970) and his Uncle Jack's gall-bladder operation in early 1971.

The friendship with Swan went some way towards a decision about Graham's future, which was being taken behind the scenes at Broadmoor. In March 1970, at Dr Udwin's request, Winifred and her husband Denis, accompanied by Win and Jack, made an otherwise unscheduled visit to the hospital. Dr Udwin asked to speak to Win alone. She was taken aback when, after enquiring about her own health and that of her family, he told her that in his opinion Graham was 'cured'. Win sat in stupefied silence as he outlined the reasoning behind his professional

159

opinion, before asking, 'What's the job situation like in Sheerness?' Win realised he was implying that Graham would wish to stay with her after his release. 'I put him off,' she recalled, 'reporting that the job situation was terrible. I felt that Graham was not in any way different from when he was admitted to Broadmoor. I was frightened at the prospect of his return. There is only one word for it: 'frightened'. I expressed my feelings to Dr Udwin, but I didn't tell him I was frightened, just that I was apprehensive.' Win's racing thoughts turned to her brother; she knew that Fred would never countenance Graham moving in with them. Then she became aware that Dr Udwin was speaking again: '[He] informed me that he was pushing for Graham's release but that it would have to go before the Home Secretary first. That he would come out on leave first.'

On the journey home, Win broke the news to the rest of the family. From Graham's earliest days in Broadmoor, they had heard a lot about the man he generally referred to as 'that fool Udwin'. Now they discussed, in nervous tones, what might happen if Edgar Udwin got his way. Winifred fails to mention in her memoir whether or not they were aware that Dr Udwin was somewhat of a controversial figure where patients and their release was concerned. Former Broadmoor patient Peter Thompson had a huge amount of respect for Dr Udwin and credits him with playing a major role in his treatment and rehabilitation. Udwin had been central to the successful release of a number of patients, but on two occasions he had incurred the vexation of the Home Office.

The first of these concerned William Thomas Doyle, who at the age of 17 had taken part in a rooftop siege at Broadmoor. Three years later, he was transferred to a psychiatric unit at Horton, Epsom but was released within a month. Udwin's report on Doyle described him as 'no longer a security hazard', declaring: 'I do not think he will be a danger to anyone at all.' Less than 12 months later he used an iron bar to murder a hospital laundry worker, robbing him to buy heroin. Doyle was returned to Broadmoor, where he was murdered four months later. The second patient, Martin Victor Frape, was transferred from Broadmoor to Parkhurst on Udwin's recommendation. While in prison, Frape assisted in leading a riot and held a guard hostage at knife point.

Broadmoor had a set procedure for discharging patients. Release was only possible through the machinations of either a 'responsible medical officer' or through a Mental Health Review Tribunal. Both responsible medical officer and patient were commonly, but not always, interviewed about the prospect. Patients whose interviews failed to go as planned could feel very depressed and aggrieved, but for most it was the first step towards leaving Broadmoor.

There was a significant spike in the numbers of patients released or transferred from Broadmoor during the 1960s and 1970s who went on to commit serious crimes. Between 1961 and 1980, 21 former patients were found guilty of homicide. One of the most notorious cases prior to that of Graham Young was Essex-born Alan Reeve, who at the age of 15 was convicted of the manslaughter of another youth, Roger Jackson, and admitted to Broadmoor with psychopathic disorder. Three years prior to the killing, Reeve had attempted to shoot his own father and was, in fact, on the run from a borstal when he encountered Jackson. Reeve beat and stabbed the boy, then hid his body in Colchester's Castle Park before sending three postcards to Jackson's parents bearing the synonym 'DOA' (dead on arrival). His treatment in Broadmoor consisted largely of psychotherapy, but he continued to show a deep interest in the occult, drawing Satanic symbols on books and announcing that he had dedicated his life to Satan. He made failed escape attempts in November and December 1965; ten months later, having ingested a number of drinamyl tablets, he managed to scale the roof of Broadmoor. In his possession were another 150 drinamyl tablets and 25 sleeping pills. He was brought down, but in 1967 confessed to the strangulation of another patient, Billy Doyle. Although the two men were known to have argued beforehand, Doyle's death was viewed by the authorities as assisted suicide, with doctors confirming that Doyle had spoken of his wish to die. Reeve retracted his confession, and another patient was recorded as having been responsible for Doyle's death. Reeve participated in a rooftop protest at Broadmoor in the 1970s and a hunger strike. He applied for parole and was recommended for release, but the Home Office vetoed the move. In 1981, Reeve escaped from Broadmoor; his girlfriend was waiting for him in a car and together they fled abroad. They settled in Amsterdam, where Reeve attempted to steal alcohol from a shop in order to celebrate a year of freedom; the gunfight that ensued saw him wound two police officers and take a woman hostage. One of the police officers died as a result of his wounds and Reeve was subsequently sentenced to 15 years in a Dutch prison. During his time behind bars, he qualified as a lawyer and was released in 1992, having served ten years. Part of the condition of his parole was that he should report regularly to a local police station, but he failed to do so and vanished abroad again. Sometime later it emerged that he was living in the Republic of Ireland, where he worked for the Women's Poetry Circle. Extradited back to the UK, Reeve was re-admitted to Broadmoor, where in fact he had never actually been discharged. Five months later, he was released and has lived in the Republic of Ireland ever since.

The Home Office raised no strong objections to Udwin's recommendation that Graham should be released. Steps were gradually implemented for his return to society.

On 16 June 1970, Graham wrote gleefully to his sister from Ward 1 of Kent House, Broadmoor:

My dearest Win,
Many apologies from your wicked, neglectful brother, for failing to write to you for such an unconscionably long time. I really haven't had anything remotely interesting to write to you, and besides, when I think back on some of the mind-bending, utterly banal monologues which I've written to you in the past, I rather think that my omission may be counted a virtue rather than a sin!

I have, however, some good news to import to you. I had an interview with the estimable Edgar last Friday, and he told me: 'Whether or not a formal recommendation has yet gone in, I have had several conversations with the Home Office about you, and I have got things moving at the end.' He also said, 'I am going to discharge you in the latter half of this year.'

As you see from my quotes, the pot is now almost boiling. Just think, Win, another few months and your friendly neighbourhood Frankenstein will be at liberty once again!!'

The following week, Dr Udwin wrote formally to the Home Office. His letter begins: 'I wish to recommend the conditional discharge of this young man. He was admitted on 5 July 1962 ...' After a relatively detailed resume of Graham's time in Broadmoor, Udwin declared:

His interest in toxicology, Black Magic and Nazism have disappeared. He is still an extreme right-wing conservative, indeed, is a member of the National Front but has abandoned the swastika as an emblem of power. It is amusing to record that the day after the elections he was most anxious to see me to find out whether a Conservative Home Secretary would be less likely to accede to a recommendation for his discharge than a Labour one. It is interesting here to note that, despite merciless teasing from Labour members of the staff, he took it all in good part after receiving my assurance that political bias would not enter into the matter of his discharge.

He observed 'from a purely clinical point of view' the 'fairly profound changes' that had taken place in Graham over the past three or four years and felt that he could now form relationships 'other than with his aunt and uncle who were, in effect, his parent substitutes'. Graham's attempts to join in social functions were still somewhat lacking due to an inherent difficulty in such matters.

Udwin had considered whether it might be wise to transfer Graham to another hospital as a starting point but decided against it on the grounds that 'his reputation would spoil a fresh start in this fashion to say nothing of the difficulties of handing over such a long-term course in mid-career as it were. I have come to the conclusion that conditional discharge is the only feasible method of handling him.' Provided the Home Office agreed in principle with discharging Graham, Udwin would begin the long task of finding a suitable hostel relatively near to Broadmoor. Graham would initially be placed there for Udwin's personal supervision with the aid of a probation officer and would seek clerical work.

The most crucial lines of Udwin's letter appear mid-page. He states that not only was Graham able to take 'a very rational view of his future' and able to discuss his illness 'with a growing degree of insight' but that he was 'no longer obsessed by thoughts of poisons, violence or mischief and is able to achieve satisfactions instead by appearing as one of the more stable and senior members of the ward'. Thus, Udwin declared with supreme confidence: 'I am convinced that he is no longer a danger to others and that under proper supervision he will remain in this state.'

With the psychiatrist's glowing recommendation in mind, by the beginning of September all those agencies involved in approving Graham's release had categorically decided that he was indeed 'no longer a danger to others' and should be returned to freedom.

9

WITHIN THE INFANT RIND OF THIS WEAK FLOWER

Dr Udwin's letter arrived at Winifred's home in early November 1970. He wished to know whether she would be willing to accommodate her brother upon his imminent release and invited her to discuss the matter with him at Broadmoor. Winifred travelled to the hospital alone, having already spoken to her husband about it. They now had a settled family life with one infant daughter; home was a two-bedroom terraced property at 23 Ritcroft Close in Hemel Hempstead, where they had lived for the past five years. The young couple wanted to find the best option for everyone concerned, including Graham. Dr Udwin told her that in his opinion her brother was rehabilitated and there was 'no danger' of him returning to poisoning people and as a result she tentatively agreed that Graham could indeed live with her upon his release. After their meeting, Winifred spent some time with her brother, who was 'thrilled' at the thought of returning to normality. Her key question to Dr Udwin had been whether her brother was 'cured' of whatever caused him to act as he had before Broadmoor. She recalled: 'I was told he was, by the psychiatrists, and I believed it. But I feel now as I did then, that he should have had more supervision.'

A Broadmoor report noted that the Secretary of State for the Home Department, Reginald Maudling, had agreed to Graham's conditional discharge, having received reassurance from the hospital that 'he is certainly no danger to anyone as far as poisons and poisoning is concerned'. The hospital felt that because Graham had been institutionalised since the age of 15, he would need 'careful and constant support to help him adjust to a way of life that must be completely foreign and alien to him'. Graham's acceptance of Dr Udwin was viewed as 'an encouraging factor and seems to point to the fact that he is not incapable of making consistent relationships'.

Plans for Graham's release were given a further boost when a period of home leave was agreed. On 13 November 1970, Winifred received a telegram: 'Permission for leave granted Graham from 21st or 22nd November for one week please confirm if convenient — E L Udwin.' She telegrammed by return; Denis then drove the two of them to collect Graham from Broadmoor. The young couple had already decided to place their trust in the authorities and to give Graham all the freedom he wanted without surreptitiously checking up on him. In her witness statement, Winifred explained: 'I was apprehensive, but after I had spoken to Dr Udwin and received his assurance that we had nothing to fear from Graham, that he was cured, I accepted this and did my best to help him and encourage him to live a normal, happy life. I wish I had been more aware of possible danger but I'm afraid I accepted that he was now quite well.'

At the end of the week, it seemed that her faith had been rewarded; Graham talked tentatively of his future plans, which comprised completing the government training scheme and then sitting an entrance exam for Sussex University, where he would study history with a view to becoming a teacher. He gave his sister and brother-in-law no cause for concern, spending most of his time listening to the Wagner records he had brought with him from Broadmoor. His conversations revolved almost exclusively around the German composer's life and operas, or about the Great War. But Winifred reasoned that if he still had that obsessive element to his personality, then at least his new passions could bring no harm to anyone.

The success of Graham's week away from Broadmoor saw him granted pre-discharge leave in Winifred's care. After consultation with the Department of Health and Social Security (DHSS), Home Secretary Reginald Maudling agreed to a second and third period of leave prior to conditional discharge. Once more, Winifred and Denis drove from Hemel Hempstead to Broadmoor on Saturday morning and brought Graham home to Ritcroft Close. Winifred's recollection of her brother's weekend with them differs from that of her aunt; she remembers him behaving 'quite normally' and talking 'a lot about going back to Neasden'. According to Win, however: 'He got drunk a couple of times and disgraced himself.' Sandra visited him that weekend: 'He seemed to me to be embarrassed. He had grown up a lot since I had last seen him.'

Whatever the truth of his sobriety, Graham received permission to spend Christmas with his sister and her family, leaving Broadmoor on 19 December. On this occasion, he was in exceptionally good spirits, feeling that release was now in sight. He talked excitedly about the training scheme in Slough and had accepted quite happily his sister's final decision that he would have to find alternative permanent accommodation. He held no grudges; on the contrary, he seemed pleased by the prospect of complete independence. While Winifred prepared a meal, Denis took Graham to their local pub, where the locals were welcoming and impressed by his intelligence. On Christmas Eve, friends visited the house and Graham was again very sociable and happy. When the visitors had gone, Graham insisted that he couldn't wait any longer to give his family their presents. Winifred unwrapped a pretty cigarette lighter, a huge box of chocolates and a leather-bound file in which to house copies of the *Radio Times*; Denis received a biography of Rommel, headed business cards and notepaper, and there were more small gifts for everyone, including his young niece, Clare, to whom he was affectionate. His quirky humour was evident in a card he presented to his sister's beagle. Winifred recalled: 'Graham loved animals, especially dogs ... he was quite mad about our beagle, Rupert, who is a bit of a nut case.' The specially printed card read:

> To whom it may concern: This is to certify that Rupert Beagle has undergone psychoanalysis and, contrary to appearances, is not suffering from hydrophobia or any other canine psychosis. Signed, Sigmund Freud.

Winifred had noticed that her brother's drinking was slightly excessive, but on Christmas Day he went to extremes and was roaring drunk by the afternoon. He woke contrite on Boxing Day and apologised repeatedly, but had caused no offence, only concern. He may have been nervous about the planned visit to

Sheerness, having spoken at length to Winifred about his hopes of rebuilding a relationship with their father, whom he had not seen for some time. The visit went incredibly well; Winifred watched tearfully as Graham made a real effort with their father, who broke down and held his son. There was an extraordinary affection towards Graham from all family members. In her memoir, Winifred writes heartfeltly: 'We all had a very happy Christmas … [Graham] just wanted to give. I do so want to say that despite the terrible things he has done and the grief he has caused, there were lots of nice things about Graham.'

Dr Udwin recorded delightedly that Graham returned to Broadmoor for his last few weeks 'in fine fettle'. On 15 January 1971, he drafted a medical certificate for Graham, which read:

This man has suffered a deep-going personality disorder which necessitated his hospitalisation throughout the whole of his adolescence. He has, however, made an extremely full recovery and is now entirely fit for discharge, his sole disability now being the need to catch up on his lost time. He is capable of undertaking any sort of work without any restrictions as to residence, travel or environment. His natural bent is towards the non-manual and clerical and in the first instance he would do extremely well training as a store-keeper. He is of above average intelligence and capable of sustained effort. He would fit in well and not draw any attention to himself in any community.

E L Udwin, Consultant Psychiatrist.

The certificate would eventually be labelled 'Exhibit 2' at Graham's second trial.

★ ★ ★

Graham visited the government training centre in Slough on 26 January 1971. He was accompanied by Broadmoor social worker Miss Rosalyn Brown, who introduced him to the man ultimately tasked with supervising him after his discharge from hospital, Robert Mynett of the Buckinghamshire Probation and After-Care Committee.

In the subsequent scramble for absolution by each authority involved in the decision to release Graham, the decisions and recall of events from this period remain contentious. Mynett later told detectives that during his first meeting with Graham, 'I was told nothing about him other than that he had been a patient at this institution. I had a brief chat with him regarding domestic matters and he then left with Miss Brown in a police car.' Mynett's witness statement does not record whether or not on that occasion he had requested further details of Graham's background and offences.

Broadmoor sent the Home Office details of Graham's discharge arrangements on 1 February. The following day, the warrant for his conditional discharge was issued. On 3 February, Dr Udwin wrote to inform Robert Mynett precisely what those conditions entitled: that upon leaving Broadmoor Graham should go immediately to Cippenham Lodge hostel, where he would reside under the supervision of a probation officer nominated by the Buckinghamshire Probation and After-Care Committee and that he must regularly attend a psychiatric outpatient clinic. Udwin included his own medical report on Graham with the letter. It stated:

Graham Young was admitted to this hospital in 1962 and suffers the severe handicap of having been out of circulation during his formative years. He suffered from a personality disorder which has responded extremely well to treatment and he is at the present time, in my view, fit to undertake any sort of work. His natural bent is towards the sedentary and the clerical, I should think; storekeeping is, at the outset, an admirable compromise. The problems he still has to deal with are those of establishing himself in the community. He will not, I think, be at ease in large groups for some time and although on a couple of periods of leave has shown himself very adaptable and flexible will, I think, still have problems generally in settling himself in a new environment. It is very hard to predict where problems may arise but I am quite sure his reaction to them will be no more than anxiety. I intend keeping very close touch with him and I am quite ready to answer phone queries regarding any problems at any time. There are no restrictions or limitations on the work that he may undertake, the distances he may travel or conditions of work.

Mynett visited Broadmoor on the day of Graham's release — Thursday, 4 February 1971 — to meet Dr Udwin and social worker Rosalyn Brown. It was standard procedure for the responsible probation officer to visit Broadmoor before the patient was

172

released in order to discuss their case with a doctor and social worker. Although the probation service was later adamant they had little or no knowledge of Graham's criminal past, the Home Office papers state that Dr Udwin had confirmed to them that during Mynett's visit to Broadmoor, he was 'shown and read the reports on the case that had been submitted to the Home Office and the doctor discussed the case fully with him. This was in accordance with the usual practice followed by Broadmoor in their arrangements for after-care; if the clinical supervision after discharge was to be undertaken by a doctor other than the Broadmoor consultant, full copies of the medical reports were sent to the doctor concerned.' This was not so in Graham's case, but Udwin had provided Mynett with a copy of his report, despite some of his colleagues disapproving of the sharing of clinical reports. Udwin also insisted that a basic medical report had been sent to the doctor at the government training centre at Slough and 'some information' was provided to the disablement resettlement officer.

In turn, Mynett stated that his visit to Broadmoor was made following several telephone conversations with Rosalyn Brown and that during the meeting:

I learned from Dr Udwin that Young had been confined in the institution for a considerable number of years for administering poison to relatives. He described him as the 'original boy poisoner'. This was the only information which Dr Udwin would supply to me. I was unable to obtain from him any of the background history which I considered necessary in order to carry out my duties. I felt that it was necessary to have this informa-

173

tion and as a result of enquiries which I made I was able to obtain certain relevant details. These are included in my record of information on this man which are now in the hands of the probation service at Hemel Hempstead.

Asked to clarify the situation further, in a letter dated March 1972, the principal probation officer of Buckinghamshire Probation and After-Care Service stated that he had consulted Mynett, who had provided him with details 'from memory', since the Record of Supervision was no longer in his possession. The first meeting with Graham and Rosalyn Brown had been 'informal and verbal, no papers were passed over to Mr Mynett and no information about background was given'. Regarding Mynett's visit to Broadmoor, Rosyln Brown had met him alone initially and gave 'brief verbal information about the offence for which Young has been in Broadmoor'. He then saw Dr Udwin for a discussion lasting five to ten minutes. During this time, Mynett was provided with 'brief factual information' and told to be vigilant for any indications that Graham was becoming dependent on alcohol.

The letter states:

Dr Udwin said he would see Young every month himself. The case was not, in Mr Mynett's view, discussed fully. Mr Mynett was particularly anxious to ascertain his powers and responsibilities as a supervisor and to obtain some documentary support for supervision. He was certainly told that, if in any difficulty, he could make immediate contact with Dr Udwin who would, if necessary, recall Young at once. Mr Mynett then saw the social worker again and requested further information. He was given the file to read but gained the impression that this was a concession reluctantly given. Mr Mynett says that it was the social worker and not the doctor who made reports available for reading. Mr Mynett feels there was a general reluctance to give information that was regarded as highly confidential. Mr Mynett's notes on the record were made from his memory of the reading of the file at the hospital. At no time was any written report or case history or copy of these given to Mr Mynett.

In the files on Graham's case in the National Archives is a letter dated 5 February 1971 — one day after Graham's release from Broadmoor. In the letter, Robert Mynett addresses Dr Udwin, making it clear that he feels the information he had been given to date was unsatisfactory:

Thank you for your letter of 3rd February. Unfortunately, the one that informs me of the Home Office authority for Young's discharge gives me no indication of the Section of an Act of Parliament under which this young man is released. This means that I have no idea of the procedure should he be in trouble and no idea of the strictures that can be placed upon him. Unofficially I assume that he has been released under Section 66 of the Mental Health Act 1959, at the discretion of the Secretary of State, but unless I am informed of this officially, either from yourself or the Home Office, I am unable to take any action under that Section.

★ ★ ★

The decision to release Graham was made after taking into consideration many factors apart from the findings of Broadmoor's psychiatric team. Chief among these was Graham's age and how young he had been at the time of his crimes. Acting under the mistaken belief that he had never killed anyone, the authorities also had to take into account the fact that others had committed graver offences yet received more lenient sentencing. The possibility that he might become institutionalised was another key factor.

The full extent of Reginald Maudling's involvement in the matter has never been revealed, and it is possible that some of the intricacies of the decision were made on his behalf. Nonetheless, the Home Secretary held the right to consult the Mental Health Review team and other medical opinions before rubber-stamping Graham's release. He chose not to exercise this option, instead accepting Dr Udwin's recommendation on its own merits. But writer Anthony Holden makes the point that there were two files at the Home Office's C3 division, which was responsible for admissions to and discharges from Broadmoor. One contained Udwin and McGrath's recommendations that Graham should be released. The other held details of his past and the reports made by Fysh and Blair, in which they expressly stated their concerns that Graham was likely to remain a danger to others in perpetuity. According to Holden, the second file was never consulted in relation to the first, and nor were two others:

one which contained all the reports compiled by the staff of Broadmoor in regard to Graham, and another which held the records of the senior nursing staff in charge of the ward where Graham was housed.

The latter included a staff member's account of an encounter with Graham, who openly boasted of his ambition to become a famous poisoner and his chilling declaration: 'When I get out, I'm going to kill one person for every year I've spent in here.'

Graham had served eight years of his recommended 15 or more in Broadmoor. In the strangest of coincidences, within a year of his release he would face exactly eight charges of poisoning.

10

POOR, VENOMOUS FOOL, BE ANGRY AND DISPATCH

'The strangest of them all,' was how Joseph Fuller described Graham in relation to the rest of Broadmoor's population at the time of their incarceration. 'He was totally insane and, in my opinion, incurable . . . To meet him in the street, you'd think of him as a nice, intelligent, if intense young man . . . but he was as mad as a hatter.' While Graham was discharged from Broadmoor on 4 February 1971, Fuller had to wait another two years before the Home Secretary authorised his release.

Graham's family had been collectively unconvinced that he would actually be released when the date came around; Winifred wrote to her father with the news that Graham was indeed home, but her letter didn't reach him in Sheerness for a couple of days. One month later, a Broadmoor official knocked on Fred Young's door to inform him that Graham was expected to be discharged from hospital imminently. A disgruntled and unimpressed Fred replied that his son had already been to stay with him. Scotland Yard had been informed before Graham's own father, and they had previously passed the news on to Thames Valley police that he was in their area of Slough.

It was Thursday when Graham left Broadmoor and he had arranged to spend the weekend with his sister in Hemel Hempstead. His course in Slough began the following Monday. 'Again I had trouble with him over his getting drunk,' Winifred recalled, justifying Dr Udwin's concern about Graham's reliance on alcohol. He had again accompanied Denis to the pub, where he held forth in eloquent if inebriated fashion on the logistics of the Great War, Hitler's leadership of Nazi Germany and the inadequacies of the British government's dealing with the situation in Ulster. Graham declared that if he were prime minister, he would instigate pogroms and utilise every ounce of force in the British Army. Heath could learn a great deal from Hitler's handling of insurgence in Warsaw: raze the place to the ground, brick by brick. True, he admitted while accepting another pint from one of Denis' friends, a lot of innocent blood would be shed but that was war, where the end justified the means, which in this case meant destroying the IRA. Denis and Winifred reluctantly agreed that their decision to suggest Graham find himself lodgings had been the correct one and on Saturday they helped him move into a hostel on Slough's Bath Road.

Affiliated to the training centre two miles away, the hostel offered single rooms with breakfast and evening meals during the week and full board at weekends. Thirty-four-year-old divorcé Trevor Sparkes was among the other residents; he had been on the storekeeping course since 8 January 1971. 'For two weeks I was the only person on this particular course,' he recalled. 'Then I was joined by a chap, Graham Young.' The two men struck up an immediate friendship, spending their days on the course at the government training centre and their evenings drinking either at the hostel or at the Grapes pub in the centre of Slough. The only time they were apart for any significant period was at the weekends, when Sparkes went home to his parents' house in Welwyn Garden City. He was a keen footballer and usually played every Saturday and Sunday before returning to the hostel.

Sparkes found Graham to be 'a very intelligent person, in fact bordering on a genius. He was very interested in war history, medicine, which he seemed to be well versed in, and politics. He used to frequently visit the public library in Slough and also at weekends, he did not go home, a library somewhere in London.' Sparkes also mentions in his witness statement that Graham made his own fireworks 'which were very effective'.

Those elements — excessive drinking, frequent trips to the library to borrow books on war and medicine, and breaking up shop-bought fireworks to make them even more explosive — indicated that Graham remained essentially unchanged. He had managed to convince the authorities otherwise and would go on doing so for some months to come, but in truth his inability and unwillingness to jettison his obsession for poison had already manifested, and did so within 48 hours of his discharge from Broadmoor.

★ ★ ★

Graham had introduced himself to Sparkes on the day he moved into the hostel: Saturday, 6 February 1971. That evening, he invited his new friend to his room, eager to discuss the routine of the hostel and the training course that lay ahead. He offered Sparkes a glass of water and they carried on chatting. But during the night, Sparkes was awoken by a violent urge to be sick and rushed to the toilet. The vomiting was accompanied by diarrhoea that lasted four days, accompanied by pain in his testicles. Sparkes left for Welwyn Garden City on Sunday morning, where he was playing in a cup match.

'I started playing the match but by half-time I developed pains in my lower abdomen,' he recalled. 'I could only think that it was a pulled muscle and I carried on in pain through the second half and finished the match. I returned to the hostel that night. I was still in pain. I continued work during the following week and the pain started shifting down into my groin.' The question of which poison Graham had used, together with when and where he obtained it, vexed Hertfordshire constabulary when they came to investigate him at the year's end; the earliest sale of poison to him they could find was on 24 April 1971, almost three months after Sparkes fell ill. On another occasion, Sparkes accepted bromide from Graham, but his recollection of that was hazy: 'One time when I was coming home for an interview, he said to me, 'You should take some bromide, it will settle your nerves,' and he mixed me up some in a tumbler and I drank it.' This time, Sparkes suffered no ill effects.

Graham began his three-month course in industrial storekeeping on Monday, 8 February. The government training centre, where he was based, was open to everyone over the age of 18 who wanted to learn a skilled trade. Graham's hours, recorded on clock card number 497 at the Buckingham Avenue plant, were 6am until 4:45pm every Monday through Thursday, while Friday was a shorter day: 8am until 3:30pm. Ernest Nicholls had been manager of the scheme since November 1966 and described Graham as 'a very good trainee . . . very keen and industrious and made satisfactory progress through-out the course, and there were no complaints regarding his conduct, either in or out of the training centre.' The course itself was run by William (Ted) James, who had direct responsibility for the trainees. Trevor Sparkes remembered that Graham also struck up a friendship with his supervisor and visited him at his home, yet James does not appear to have been interviewed by the police during their late 1971 investigation. Curiously, the Hertfordshire constabulary report on the case, dated 1971, notes that 'to many at the centre Young was known as Fred, being the usual abbreviation of his second Christian name.' He had never previously asked anyone to call him by his father's name.

Robert Mynett called on Graham at the Bath Road hostel at 9pm the following day, Tuesday, 9 February, to find out how he was settling down. They then met at weekly interviews over the coming month, with a short gap when Mynett himself was on holiday. Afterwards, their meetings continued at fortnightly intervals. He found Graham to be 'a nervous person, always cooperative and anxious to keep his appointments with me'. Well-spoken and articulate, he was also clean and tidy. Mynett largely ignored Graham's political spoutings but became concerned about the amount of 'cheap British wine' he consumed: 'I noticed that he always had at least one bottle of wine in his room. More often than not, he would have one bottle open and another standing unopened on his chest of drawers. On one occasion he offered me a drink of VP British ruby wine, this I declined. Dr Udwin had indicated to me that there might be danger of Young becoming dependent on alcohol if he

182

was allowed to frequent public houses. Accordingly, I reported his drinking to the authorities at Broadmoor.' Mynett's other concern was his choice of 'morbid' reading material, much of which gave 'graphic accounts of atrocities committed during the Second World War'.

More worryingly, during one of their meetings at the hostel where Graham knocked back several glasses of wine, he suddenly began talking about how 'comparatively simple' it was to manufacture a wide range of poisons and 'that it did not require specialist equipment'. Mynett kept a detailed record of all his findings. Dr Udwin later told the Home Office that 'in the early stages' he had kept 'in very close contact' with Mynett regarding Graham's progress. While Udwin also insisted that he saw Graham on several occasions and that he seemed 'entirely settled', the sum total of Graham's follow-up care from Broadmoor comprised three meetings and (later) two telephone conversations with Udwin, in tandem with Mynett's visits.

In another room at the hostel, Trevor Sparkes was still suffering the effects of his weekend illness and was in sufficient pain to book a doctor's visit. Like Graham, he was registered with Dr Mark Binnie, whose surgery was on the same road as the hostel. No abnormalities were detected and Sparkes was given painkillers in an effort to subdue the strained feelings in his groin. But that weekend, when he was at his parents' home, his face suddenly became swollen 'like a balloon'. His mother sent for the doctor, who prescribed antibiotics, which reduced the swelling. The pains in his groin persisted, however, and during the next weekend away he came to regret his decision to play football: 'During the course of the game I suddenly felt peculiar all over. I seemed to lose all control of my leg and thigh muscles and I had to go off.' The sensation subsided and he returned to the hostel.

Graham had also been absent from the hostel that weekend. His Uncle Jack had experienced a long period of ill health, which included suffering from jaundice and problems with his gall bladder, which necessitated an operation. Graham travelled to Sheerness, then accompanied Win to Rochester, where his uncle was recovering from his operation in Bartholomew hospital. Afterwards, he saw his cousin Sandra at the house in Sheerness. She was now a mother of two boys — five-year-old Anthony and three-year-old Andrew — who quite happily clambered all over Graham. He enjoyed their company, but Sandra recalled his main topic of conversation was a detailed analysis of her father's operation.

On Thursday, 4 March, Jack suffered a relapse when his gallbladder stitches burst. Sandra remembers Graham arriving at Sheerness that day 'in a shocking state ... ranting and raving' about the doctors' 'stupidity' and insisting that they ought to have realised a man with a history of bronchitis might burst his stitches. Graham wept copiously, much to Win and Sandra's surprise, although they too feared that Jack might not survive. He travelled with his aunt and cousin on the bus to visit the hospital again. During the 45-minute journey, Graham kept up a steady discourse on the bubonic plague, until Sandra told him to shut up because he was upsetting her mother. He piped down and was quiet and solicitous for the remainder of his time in Sheerness, returning to Slough on the Sunday evening once they were all assured that Jack had

184

made a good recovery. Normally Graham spent his weekends with Winifred in Hemel Hempstead, where for the most part he was no trouble, except for the odd occasion when he drank too much again.

Trevor Sparkes continued to suffer a number of ailments and again visited Dr Binnie in the second week of March, when Graham had returned from his stay in Sheerness. Dr Binnie diagnosed a urinary infection and a substantial growth of E. coli, for which he was prescribed antibiotics. Sparkes' health deteriorated further after an evening spent drinking VP wine with Graham. He had already been sick again on that particular afternoon, vomiting twice, before accepting his friend's invitation to take his mind off things with a chat. 'I was up most of the night with sickness and diarrhoea and eventually only got to sleep through exhaustion,' Sparkes recalled. 'I was still bad over the next four or five days, not being able to eat or keep anything in my stomach.' The hostel had its own sick bay, where Sparkes was given a bottle of milk of magnesia, but another week and a half would pass before the vomiting and diarrhoea subsided.

Trevor Sparkes may not have been the only victim of Graham's poisoning habit during his first weeks of freedom. In their report on his crimes during that year, Hertfordshire constabulary found that during his time at the training centre there was a 'high incidence' of sickness among the students and staff, although Graham denied administering poison to anyone there other than Sparkes. Further inquiries showed that five men and one woman were ill during this period with symptoms that suggested poisoning. Leonard Wickham and Charles Bull joined Graham in his room on 6 May to celebrate the fact that he would complete his course the following day. Graham opened a bottle of wine and handed the two men a glass each. Bull was fine after sipping from his glass, but Wickham almost immediately suffered vomiting and diarrhoea. He assumed that the alcohol had reacted badly with the valium he had recently been prescribed. But during the subsequent police investigation, Wickham was seen by a police surgeon, Dr Torrens, who found him to be 'suffering from loss of hair'. Laboratory samples were taken, but due to the length of time that had elapsed, no trace of poison could be found, if that indeed was the cause.

Hertfordshire constabulary's report also describes how Graham — using the name 'Fred' — had become friendly with another resident at the hostel named George Brown. A thorough medical check had been carried out on Brown just prior to his recent release from the Royal Navy; he was fit and well. Yet, after sharing a bottle of wine with Graham, he became violently ill, vomiting repeatedly and experiencing an ache so severe that it felt 'like partial paralysis'. He had no reason to suspect Graham at the time and, even after learning the truth about his friend, refused to believe he had been poisoned. Hostel resident Henry Tennant was more suspicious. Training to be a motor mechanic at the centre in Slough, he too suffered sickness and diarrhoea after spending an evening in Graham's company and pondered: 'If I'd known about Broadmoor, it might have explained all the tummy upsets I suffered at Slough. Quite a few of us went down with a mystery bug. Knowing what we all know now, it makes you wonder.'

The only potential female victim was accounts clerk Mrs Diana Sheehy. On her regular visits to the

186

stores, she became friendly with Trevor Sparkes and Graham Young. The three of them would take tea breaks together, and afterwards Sheehy often suffered severe stomach pains, leg cramp and mobility difficulties in her left arm. She consulted her doctor, who prescribed antibiotics, but the illness continued, and she lost so much weight in such a short period that she was referred to hospital for an X-ray and tests, but nothing could be found. Labourer Charles Watts also worked at the Slough stores, where he fell ill with symptoms that mirrored those of Sheehy. He had the same tests and an X-ray, but a suspected stomach ulcer failed to show. Terence Lines attended the Slough centre regularly, where he got to know Graham and suffered repeated stomach pains, vomiting and leg pains. His doctor gave him antibiotics to clear the symptoms but was unable to make a diagnosis.

Hertfordshire constabulary concluded their study of the gathered witness statements with a single line demonstrating their view, namely 'that within a very short time of his release from Broadmoor, Young would seem to have been active in poisoning people.' The question remains as to when and where he obtained the poison, if that was indeed the case.

Graham's first-known attempt to purchase poison after his release from Broadmoor is recorded as being on Saturday, 17 April 1971. He described the events leading up to this several years later to Parkhurst prison's then medical director, Dr John Hamilton. He claimed to have felt like a completely different person upon leaving Broadmoor, with no desire to buy toxic substances or to inflict them on others. That changed, he told Dr Hamilton, when he was sitting with a pint in the sun-drenched beer garden of the

Spotted Dog in Leavesden; a No.8 bus trundled by on its way to Kilburn and he knew it would pass his old haunt, Edgar's chemist shop. That same Saturday, he called at John Bell & Croyden chemists on London's Wigmore Street, where he attempted to buy antimony potassium tartrate. But pharmacist Albert Kearne refused to allow the purchase without written authority and Graham left empty-handed. This much is certain: somehow Graham already had within his possession a substantial amount of poison, which he had lost no time in using to nefarious effect. But his plan was to do something far more wide-ranging, something that would set him firmly on the road to becoming a prolific poisoner.

His first step in achieving this malevolent ambition was to find a job.

1971—1972
HADLANDS

'A lot of workers in a factory died one after the other. Their deaths were put down to astonishingly varied causes …

The symptoms vary a good deal, I understand. They may start with diarrhoea and vomiting, or there may be a stage of intoxication, again it may begin with pain in the limbs, and be put down as polyneuritis or rheumatic fever or polio — one patient was put in an iron lung. Sometimes there's pigmentation of the skin.' 'You talk like a medical dictionary!' 'Naturally, I've been looking it up. But one thing always happens sooner or later. *The hair falls out.*'

Agatha Christie, *The Pale Horse*
(Collins, The Crime Club, 1961)

11

TO SERVE THE PURPOSES
OF DARK AMBITION

Among the new posts advertised at Hemel Hempstead labour exchange in mid-April 1971 was one for
assistant storekeeper at the company of John Hadland
(Photographic Instrumentation) Ltd at Newhouse
Laboratories in Bovingdon, Hertfordshire. It caught
the attention of J R Ayles at the government training
centre in Slough; he had a suitable candidate in mind
and called the firm, suggesting to Hadlands' managing director Geoffrey Foster that he should consider
Graham Young for the position.

Graham was delighted to hear that he had been
put forward for his first post-Broadmoor job. Ayles
arranged an interview with Geoffrey Foster and Graham set to work completing one of Hadlands' standard
applications for employment. In a matter of months,
this would become 'Exhibit 1' at his trial, pored over by
government officials seeking to piece together events
that had led to the worst crisis in mental-health care
and after-care that century. The innocuous sheet of
paper outlining Graham's suitability for the position
comprised:

Present Employer: Undergoing training at Slough
GTC ...
Position held: Trainee Storekeeper on training
allowance ...

Previous Employers: No previous employment due to hospitalisation and subsequent convalescence. Now, however, fully recovered …
Education: John Kelly Boys High School, Cricklewood,
External Student of Wolsey Hall, Oxford (subjects studied: Anatomy, Physiology, Hygiene, German O Level incomplete …
Qualifications held: O level English.

Graham added a final note in his neat and stylish handwriting: 'I have privately studied chemistry (organic and inorganic), pharmacology and toxicology over the past ten years and have, therefore, some knowledge of photographic chemicals and usage.'

With this extraordinary and obfuscating application in his possession, Ayles contacted Geoffrey Foster on 22 April in writing: 'Further to our conversation of 20th April, I am forwarding herewith the placing report concerning Mr Young, who will be coming to see you on Friday next at 2:30pm. I am also enclosing some literature that will explain more fully the functions of the government training centres and their services to industry.' The enclosed placing report was drafted by Ted James, with whom Graham had become friendly during his time on the course. He described Graham as of 'above average intelligence, he is very conscientious in his work, able to work to instructions given to him as well as on his own initiative. The ability he has shown in understanding the various aspects of storekeeping will prove him an asset to any future employer. His time-keeping and general behaviour has been excellent.'

Graham arrived at Hadlands promptly for his

interview on the afternoon of Friday, 23 April. He was greeted by Geoffrey Foster, then in his mid-30s, a genial and intelligent man who had almost 15 years' experience at Hadlands. Foster conducted the interview with George Janouch, who worked in the company's stores. He recounts: 'I started the interview on general terms, then asked Mr Young what had caused his hospitalisation. He replied, 'My mother died in very tragic circumstances whilst I was in my late teens. This caused me to have a mental breakdown and I have been in hospital ever since.' He did not say what kind of hospital he had been in and I did not ask him. I knew that his hospitalisation had been due to his mental condition and not anything physical. He appeared to be very intelligent and that he would make an excellent assistant storeman. I asked him where he lived and he said, 'With my sister in Hemel Hempstead.' I asked if he had his own car and he replied, 'I won't have any difficulty getting here in the mornings.' I was satisfied with Young, having previously had him highly recommended to me by the government training centre at Slough.'

At the conclusion of the interview, Foster suggested that Janouch should show Graham the store where he would be spending most of his time. Janouch gave him a short tour of the premises and introduced him to the staff there, all of whom were friendly, if curious about the slim young man with the intense gaze. The two men then returned to Foster's office where Graham was told the wages and conditions of payment. Foster smiled at him as they said goodbye and confirmed that he would be in touch.

The following Monday, Ayles received a request from Foster for further information about Graham's hospitalisation. After some thought, he decided to send Foster a copy of Dr Udwin's report, which made no reference to Graham's crimes, but stated that he had suffered 'a deep-going personality disorder which necessitated his hospitalisation throughout his adolescence' and that he had made 'an extremely full recovery and is now entirely fit for discharge'. Ayles added his own, extremely brief covering letter: 'In response to your request I am forwarding a copy of Dr Udwin's report on Mr Young. I am sure you will find this satisfactory.'

Foster later confirmed: 'Satisfactory assurances were given in writing on his abilities and the completeness of his recovery. It was never suggested that he might need extra supervision or in any way be treated differently to other staff members.' He confirmed that there had been no mention of Broadmoor: 'I had no idea he had been an inmate there, much less the reason why.'

When the Home Office began examining the procedure that had led to Graham's placement at Hadlands, the application form he had completed raised two immediate concerns: first, the plain glossing over of the six years he had spent in Broadmoor and second, the audacity of his acknowledging an abiding interest in poison. Officials contacted the training centre in Slough, where Ayles could only tell them his basic recollections of the process he had gone through with Graham, citing the length of time that had passed since as the reason for any confusion. He started by acknowledging that it had indeed been necessary to explain Graham's 'lost' years, but this had been done primarily in regard to his absence of previous employment rather than clarifying where he

194

had been and why. Thus, Ayles had, with Graham's agreement, referred obliquely to this period as one in which he had been hospitalised. This in turn had caused Geoffrey Foster at Hadlands to ask for more detail. Ayles felt that Dr Udwin's report should suffice, particularly since this demonstrated that Graham had made a 'total recovery according to expert opinion'. He admitted that this also informed the decision not to refer specifically to Broadmoor, which was taken deliberately: 'There was no reason possibly to imperil his chance of resettlement by indicating the institution from which he came.'

Officials then queried the copy of Udwin's report which Ayles had sent to Hadlands, noting that it differed from the original report in their files, missing the heading 'Broadmoor' and being 'slightly different' in layout with a name misspelt. Ayles was unable to shed any light on these disparities, insisting that he had either received the reference from Broadmoor or copied the report in the government training office, although there was no photocopier on the premises. One thing was certain, however: 'The firm could not be told that Graham Young was a poisoner by Mr Ayles as he did not know. The nearest he got to the actual offence was the report by the social worker which refers to 'causing harm to his parents'.'The Home Office decision was that Ayles had acted in good faith, being 'a mature and experienced man who has in the past worked as an assistant disablement resettlement officer and before this had 20 years' service in the Royal Army Medical Corps'.

The Home Office also consulted Dr Udwin on the matter. He told them 'that in this situation the employer would invariably be informed that the person he was being asked to employ was a Broadmoor patient. He would not, however, be given any details of the offence, except possibly in the broadest terms, e.g. 'an offence of violence'.' Udwin recalled that Graham had telephoned him to discuss the job interview; he had told Graham that it was up to him whether or not he told his prospective employer that he was a former Broadmoor patient. Udwin also checked his files for any record of having written directly to Hadlands but could find nothing. He added that it was not an impossibility, however, and stressed that any such letter would be in the nature of a reference, intended to encourage the employer to give the patient the opportunity of a job, and 'was not designed to warn the employer against the patient'.

As a result, Foster decided to offer Graham the job at Hadlands. Graham was ecstatic when he was given the news. But what no one else knew was that during the weekend — between his interview and Foster's request for more information from Ayles — he had, in fact, already purchased the poison he would use to such cruel and deadly effect on his unsuspecting new colleagues.

* * *

Graham had returned to John Bell & Croyden chemists on Saturday, 24 April 1971. He took with him a handwritten note on Bedford College, London University notepaper, requesting 25 grams of antimony potassium tartrate. On a previous visit, pharmacist Albert Kearne had refused to sell him the poison without written authorisation; Kearne later described Graham as 'a man aged about 22 to 23 years, 5'8"

196

tall, respectably dressed, well-spoken, dark hair, dark eyes with sallow complexion. He was very plausible.' Graham handed the pharmacist a printed letter which stated that 'M E Evans', a student, was authorised to purchase 25 grams of antimony potassium tartrate. Evans was the name Graham had used to illegally obtain poison prior to his 1962 arrest. He gave a false address — 23 Denzil Road, Willesden, NW10 — then left with his precious poison.

Graham wrote to Geoffrey Foster four days later to accept the job offer. Legitimately using the training centre as his address, he announced:

Dear Mr Foster,
Thank you for your letter of the 26th inst., in which you offer me the post of assist. Store-keeper.

I am pleased to accept your offer, and the conditions attached thereto, and shall, therefore, report for work on Monday, May 10th, at 8.30am.

May I take the opportunity to express my gratitude to you for offering me this position, notwithstanding my previous infirmity as communicated to you by the Placing Officer. I shall endeavour to justify your faith in me by performing my duties in an efficient and competent manner.

Until Monday week, I am,
Yours faithfully,
Graham Young.

Dr Udwin heard that Graham had successfully applied for the position and spoke to him by telephone a few days before his work commenced. 'He was excited and happy at the prospects of taking up this job,' Udwin recalled. 'He seemed to me in an entirely fit state. The probation service in Hemel Hempstead took him over and he has without fail kept [in] touch with them weekly.' Graham's last face-to-face meeting with Mynett occurred on 6 May 1971, the day before he completed his course in Slough and therefore had to find alternative accommodation. Trevor Sparkes had finished the course one week earlier and returned to Welwyn Garden City, where his ailments continued; he was twice admitted to hospital for groin pains and muscle strain, but no formal diagnosis could be made. Sparkes began a slow recovery from autumn onwards. He never saw Graham again, which may account for his survival.

On Friday, 7 May, Graham left the training centre in Slough, having passed each element of the store-keeping course with 'flying colours'. He collected his few belongings from the hostel and headed first to his sister's home. In a newsagent's window in the Marlowes in Hemel Hempstead town centre, he spotted an advert for a room at 29 Maynard Road, a quiet residential street that ran parallel to the Marlowes. He called round, keen to secure accommodation as soon as possible. The houses were uniform, semi-detached dwellings; No.29 stood out from the rest with its bright purple front door. The owners were Mr and Mrs Mohammed Saddiq, who lived there with their children and rented out one other room to a married couple: 22-year-old Kenneth Ritch and his wife Kathleen, two years younger. Despite his former membership of the National Front and long adoration of the Nazi movement, Graham immediately liked the Saddiqs, who spoke little English, but were friendly and keen to make their lodgers feel comfortable. He paid a small rent for his room and made his own arrangements for meals, which soon developed into a routine: lunch at work during the week, evening meals in the local Wimpy and a cooked meal at his sister's home every Thursday night and Saturday afternoon, unless he was visiting his family in Sheerness, which is where he headed for the rest of that first weekend.

Shortly before leaving for Sheerness, however, Graham paid a visit to his old haunts in Neasden. Winifred was taken aback when he told her about it afterwards, feeling he had made the journey out of a peculiar combination of bravado, sentiment, curiosity and a ghoulish desire to relive the parts of his life that had caused so much injury to others. To the surprise of other teachers who remembered him, he arrived at the John Kelly school asking to see his old headmaster but found he had retired. He then called on his Uncle Frank before walking round to his old home on the North Circular Road. He stood outside for a few minutes, remembering life there, and afterwards knocked on a neighbour's door. The couple were old friends of Fred and Molly; at first they were horrified, thinking he was on the run from Broadmoor, but he explained that he had served a shorter sentence on account of the psychiatric opinion that he was 'cured' and no longer a danger to others. He ended his day with a trip to Edgar's, the pharmacy where he had bought so much of the poison that obsessed him. On this occasion, he purchased only a tube of toothpaste.

By Sunday evening, he was ensconced in his new chambers on Maynard Road. Graham's bedroom was cell-like in its dimensions: 7 feet 6 inches by 7 feet. Situated at the back of the property, it overlooked the elongated strip of concrete and unkempt lawn that ended in a communal fence and trees, which screened the local hospital premises. Graham's narrow single bed with its striped top blanket was pushed into the space under the window with its dark, floral curtains. The only other furnishings were a wardrobe that resembled a coffin, a small table and chair and a metal ashtray stand. In the ceiling over the bed lay the trap door to the attic. Once Graham had added his two suitcases, few items of clothing and books, there was barely room to move. The whole place was made smaller and more depressing by the garish wallpaper: a headache-inducing concoction of stripes and baroque shapes finished in a high sheen. But it was at least his own space, where he had nothing to fear from anyone else under the same roof and no one to check up on him.

His new circumstances and living arrangements brought him under the jurisdiction of Hertfordshire Probation and After-Care Service. Susan Vidal, a young, single senior probation officer, was put in charge of his welfare. As before, the question later arose regarding how much she had been told of her client's past when Graham was assigned to her. An internal Home Office letter dated 1972 describes Miss Vidal as having 'some background knowledge shared with Dr Udwin', although she herself stated that she had been told nothing about Graham by Broadmoor and what knowledge she did have came from Robert Mynett, Graham's previous probation officer. A second internal letter between Home Office staff declares that Dr Udwin did not 're-brief' Miss Vidal because it was not standard practice to do so; it was expected that the original supervising officer would pass on all relevant information and case papers to the succeeding supervisor. Udwin himself felt Miss Vidal's supervision of Graham was 'entirely satisfactory', given that he had not warned her to watch for signs of Graham's 'reverting to playing with poisons' because 'he did not believe there was any such risk'.

Udwin's 'special concern', which he communicated to the probation service, was that Graham might find it difficult to cope with 'the stress of life outside' Broadmoor and that this could cause 'a retrograde reaction into irresponsible behaviour'. He therefore expected the probation officer to look out for signs that Graham was struggling to cope with his new situation and there were 'no such signs'. From his own experience, Udwin thought the practice of probation officers visiting the home of discharged patients 'varied according to the circumstances', but that they would not generally visit if the patient was reporting regularly at the probation office. Udwin presumed the probation officer would also wish to guard against calling 'undue attention' to the fact of supervision by frequent home visits.

Susan Vidal recorded her interactions with Graham in some detail. He visited her once a week on a regular basis, usually for half an hour but sometimes longer. Her initial impression was that:

compared with his contemporaries, he is a rather odd young man. He always looks very neat and precise and ... will sometimes talk at great length about the somewhat macabre subjects which interest him. At times, however, he shows a surprising insight into his own personality and we have talked quite recently about his difficulty in making relationships with people on more than a superficial level, and his inability to experience joy. At other times, he has shown me that he can indeed feel very deeply about people and a few months ago he came to my office feeling extremely angry with Dr Udwin. Towards the end of this particular interview, he was able to tell me how very important Dr Udwin had been to him.

This last observation is at odds with Graham's sarcastic writings about Udwin in his letters home; almost certainly, in his conversations with Miss Vidal, he was keen to maintain the image that had secured him his freedom.

She tried to persuade him to register with a GP in Hemel Hempstead, but he was reluctant to do so, even when an unexpected bout of cystitis and indigestion laid him low. His reticence was due entirely to his fear that full details of his psychiatric history would be passed on to a surgery and that a doctor 'might then question him about it'. Clearly, he was eager to distance himself from certain aspects of his past. Superficially at least, his efforts to escape the long shadow of Broadmoor implied that he wished to start afresh. But his clandestine behaviour within days of beginning his new job at Hadlands cast him in a stark light: his attempts to conceal what had gone before were not done in order to atone but instead to enable him to embark on the career he had always desired — that of poisoner extraordinaire.

12

STRANGE AND UNKNOWN THINGS

'Welcome to Bovingdon Village' announces the laminated information board adjacent to Vicarage Lane bus stop. Erected and maintained as such things are by the local parish council, the board features five old photographs, a couple of reasonable sketches and a map explaining the area within sight. One photograph shows Rattle Cottages on the High Street decorated for the Queen's Coronation in 1953; a sketch depicts the Bobsleigh Inn and explains that its name was bestowed in honour of the British gold medal won at the Innsbruck Winter Olympics in 1964 by the owner's son, while the top three photographs on the board were taken 'near where you stand today'.

Just visible in the distance is the crossroads and 'main gateway' to the village which, we are told by the board, 'dates from the 1200s when the forest was cleared and arable farming began. Dwellings grew adjacent to the wide-spread farms, our 13th-century church is located next to one of the oldest, Bury Farm, in Church Street. You are standing on Hempstead Road, near the crossroads . . .' To the right of the junction lies Newhouse Road, and somewhat surprisingly, the history related by the board tells us that 'Further up Newhouse Road, next to the former airfield, was Hadlands Laboratories, where in the 1970s, the 'Teacup Poisoner' Graham Young, operated . . .'

It's an unusual choice of local history snippet to provide for visitors to such a picturesque and interesting spot, but his inclusion would no doubt have delighted Graham, had he known. Hadlands has long since gone, the company ceasing to trade in the 1990s, and in its place now stands a large housing estate and, behind that, a prison. Hadlands is remembered in the name of one of the new roads running through the new estate — and on the information board in relation to its notorious former employee.

The airfield that once stood next to the factory was constructed in 1941 through to 1942 as a training base for American airmen. Until then, Bovingdon had been almost exclusively agricultural, but overnight 2,000 US servicemen arrived in the village to fly out B-17 bombers across to war-ravaged Europe. The most celebrated of these was the *Memphis Belle*, whose last mission was the subject of a successful 1990 film of the same name. The village was home to many evacuee children from London, 16 of whom stayed at Newhouse Farm near the airfield. A German bomb fell directly on the farm, destroying much of it, but miraculously no one was hurt.

When the war ended, thousands of Americans returned home via Bovingdon, the base of their European Air Transport Service. Newhouse Farm was rebuilt by the War Damage Commission, but on the day in 1948 when work was completed, a local elderly man hanged himself from an apple tree in the grounds. The effect on the village was profound; people murmured about the place being cursed and no one went near the farm after that, not until 1960 when John Hadland bought the property. Together with his wife Daphne, he had been running a thriving photographic-equipment business from home and adapted the farm into a laboratory, adding prefabricated buildings for storage and production. The firm described itself as specialising in designing and manufacturing photographic instrumentation, particularly high-speed cameras for defence research. In 1966, it reached its zenith with the development of the world's fastest camera, the Imacon, which could take 60 million pictures a second and secured them a place in the *Guinness Book of Records.*

Two years later, the neighbouring airfield closed and the remaining personnel departed, buildings were destroyed and properties disposed of, mostly to former owners. Hadlands expanded further and by 1971 employed 76 people in its units at the end of Newhouse Road. The premises consisted of three blocks: administration in a Georgian-style building with a long, barn-like extension housing the canteen; a works area of some 9,000 square feet, which included the stores, and a maintenance area in a nearby barn. The works area occupied a large Banbury structure comprising five departments: camera production, processing, service, sales demonstration and general workshops, including stores. John Hadland remained at the helm as chairman, describing his function as 'deciding policy' and 'opening up new markets abroad'. He was away for much of the summer working on the latter, leaving the man who had interviewed Graham, Geoffrey Foster, in charge. As managing director, Foster ran the company on a day-to-day basis and was regarded by Hadland as having 'first-hand knowledge of all activities concerning staff and their welfare'. Of the 76 people employed by the company, 28 worked in administration and the canteen, five on maintenance and the rest in the general works area. Most staff worked from 9am until 5pm.

Graham began working at Hadlands on 10 May 1971. As assistant storekeeper, he earned £19 gross per week. The staff in stores were responsible for maintaining stock needed in manufacturing, for storing finished goods and for sending and receiving goods. The layout of their works area was simple: a long corridor ran irregularly right through the laboratory works building and off this were various sections, such as the production room and the machine room, each neatly partitioned. The stores themselves were divided into two sections, the smaller of which was called the Work in Progress store (WIP), where those materials which were needed immediately were kept and where other workers visited to obtain an issue. Adjacent to the WIP store was the main store, entered by a half-gate that resembled a stable door. At the far end of the main store, a door led into the small packing bay. This was where Graham worked most of the time; his job entailed packing goods for dispatch and unpacking raw materials as they arrived.

Supervising Graham was store manager Robert Edward Egle, who also completed most of the paperwork. Born in Norfolk in April 1912 — two days before the sinking of the RMS *Titanic* — Bob had little memory of his father, who died during the Battle of the Somme in 1917 and was himself part of the British Expeditionary Force and Allied troops evacuated from Dunkirk in 1940. He and his wife Dorothy had been married for 37 years and lived in a beautiful cottage named Orchard Glen in Whelpley Hill, less than two miles from Bovingdon. Bob had worked at Hadlands since July 1969 and was looking forward to his retirement, when he and Dorothy intended to sell their home to live near their married daughter in the small Norfolk village of Gillingham. As Graham got to know Bob, he would regularly press him for stories of his war service, eager to hear especially about Dunkirk.

Also working in the stores was 56-year-old Fred Biggs, head of the WIP department. Fred's wife Annie, to whom he had been married over 30 years, also worked at Hadlands in the clerical section; they had both joined the company in May 1970. The couple had two sons and two daughters, all married, and lived approximately five miles from Bovingdon in Chipperfield, Kings Langley, where they had run the newsagent's and general store together during the late 1950s and early 1960s. Fred was a local councillor for five years, representing Chipperfield. He and his wife worked two full days and three mornings at Hadlands.

Both Fred and Bob took a fatherly interest in their new young colleague. Equally friendly, but slightly younger and working in the stores during Graham's first few weeks, was Ron Hewitt. Aged 41, he was employed mainly as a delivery driver, but when there were neither deliveries nor collections for him to undertake, he helped out in the packing bay, getting equipment ready for dispatch. He preferred driving and had begun looking for a suitable full-time post elsewhere, but until July he often worked with Graham in the stores. Unlike the two older men, Ron was able to discuss his first impressions of their youngest colleague with detectives in the months to come. He remembered Graham as 'perfectly pleasant, if a bit baffling'. He and his fellow storemen were curious about Graham's daily poring over of medical textbooks, and one of them raised the question of why, if the subject absorbed him so much, he hadn't chosen to become a doctor or something similar. 'His reply to that question was that he was just interested in reading this type of book and did not want to take up the profession,' Ron recalled. 'If we were talking at work about anything medical, Graham would always refer to it in the proper medical terms.'

Graham's interest in all things medical drew the attention of his other colleagues, including Martin Hancock, then 18, who was employed as a technical assistant at the laboratory prior to leaving in September that year to study at Dacorum College. 'My job involved bench work in the development department but I had to visit the stores department regularly in order to carry out this work, which mainly involved calibration,' he explained.

I knew Graham Young very well during the time that I was employed. We had many long conversations either in the store, where he worked or in the department where I worked. Almost on every occasion the conversations were about medicine and pharmacy. The only time that it wasn't was when he had just finished reading the book *The Third Reich*. I was astounded by his knowledge of medicines and pharmacy. I think he said that he had been studying it for fourteen years. He knew all the Latin names for drugs and medicines. He would always refer to things by their proper name.

He found Graham 'completely emotionless, except for his rather dry sense of humour'.

When Hertfordshire constabulary came to investigate Graham's employment at Hadlands, detectives were struck by the warm, close-knit community that existed within the firm, who placed 'considerable importance on the welfare of their employees and the premises are well equipped and appointed with this in mind'. One example was the facilities offered in the cheerful canteen, where the main midday meal was cooked and served by two kindly ladies, Mrs Pested and Mrs Lawson; all beverages were supplied free of charge to members of staff, who were also encouraged to help themselves to fruit. During lunchtimes and tea breaks, Graham usually sat with Ron Hewitt and Bob Egle, both of whom had a sweet tooth and would offer round toffees from a tin kept in a bench drawer in the stores. Graham collected the morning and afternoon tea on a tray from May, as charlady Mrs Mary Bartlett was known to everyone. Her trolley was loaded with bottles of hot water for coffees and a large teapot; she added milk and sugar before Graham took round the drinks to his colleagues sitting in the store on the packing bench. Secretary Diana Smart later worked in the stores and she occasionally noticed him 'stirring the cups' as he brought the tray back, after which he would gather the teaspoons used in the stores and put them in 'his' drawer.

In time, Diana got to know Graham better than most at the company, but the men who worked with him saw nothing out of the ordinary in his behaviour. They had no reason to be vigilant, as another employee, Anthony Oldham, explains: 'When Graham arrived, it was understood that he had come from some rehabilitation as a result of a mental breakdown. He didn't strike one as exceptional. He was very dark, somewhat glum, very articulate, clearly very intelligent and obviously conveyed through one means or another knowledge of chemistry.' When Oldham asked him what he had done in the past, Graham replied, 'Well, actually, I'm a failed chemistry student.' He and other colleagues took him at his word.

Diana Smart was more curious about Graham. Forty years old, she and her husband Norman had worked at Hadlands for six years and lived on nearby Chesham Road in the village. Until mid-October 1971, she worked mostly on the laboratory side of the main Banbury building, but she also filled in for anyone who was off sick in the stores, main office, on the switchboard, in accounts or the Imacon section. She worked often in the stores, where she found Graham unlike anyone else she had ever met and sensed there was more to him than met the eye, although she could never have imagined quite what that entailed. She found everything about him slightly odd, including his appearance: short, with a little beer belly and forever rolling his own excessively thin cigarettes, which caused her to notice his hands: 'The tiniest hands, with the tiniest fingers … cold and blank-white and his longest finger was shorter than [my] smallest.' If he held a pen, his knuckles shone unnaturally white and when he smoked, as he often did, he held the cigarette not in the normal way, between the first and second fingers, but hooked inside his nicotine-stained thumb and stubby forefinger. Otherwise, he always seemed to keep one hand in his pocket, regardless of the task he was doing. Each day he brought a toothbrush and toothpaste to work in a little paper bag and would nip to the bathroom several times a day to clean his teeth. He never told anyone when he was going to the loo either, unlike everyone else. He was clean and neat, and never said a word which could be misconstrued; he had beautiful manners and was unfailingly polite, calling her 'Diana' when everybody else referred to her as 'Di'. He asked about her health, but never made any enquiries into her home life, and had an excellent memory, which came in useful at work.

Diana, like all the Hadlands staff who came into regular contact with Graham, recalled his obsessive interest in medical matters and a period when he would bring a whole heap of textbooks on the subject to work. Remembering that he had told another colleague he was a failed chemistry student, she asked which university he had attended and was surprised when he replied that he hadn't actually gone to university but had studied medicine since first discovering a predilection for it around the age of 12. When Diana mentioned that she was taking a first-aid course through St John's Ambulance Brigade, he promptly brought her a copy of Taylor's *Principles and Practice of Forensic Medicine* and another of Whitla's *A Dictionary of Treatment*, both of which were far too technical to be of use to her. She recalled how he could even pick up a tin of toilet cleaner and list its components without referring to a label. Sometimes his use of long words would exasperate her, and for much of the time he seemed 'completely unfeeling'. She tried to draw him out on more personal matters but her questions would be met with the vaguest of responses, such as when she asked him where he had worked before Hadlands and he said airily, 'Oh, I was at Slough,' before walking off. She did find out that he

211

lived alone in a single room and took all his washing to the local laundrette, then ironed everything himself in his lodgings. She felt a pang of sympathy then that made her warm to him.

'He seemed terribly lonely,' she remembered. 'There was something even a little pathetic in the sad little pride he took in his smart appearance.' He usually wore the same few items of clothing: black, pointed shoes with laces, corduroy trousers and a dark green shirt with a lighter green tie. But one day Diana was queuing in a café in Hemel Hempstead and Graham sidled up next to her, wearing a handsome military-style raincoat. 'What do you think?' he asked, patting the buttoned flaps of his jacket. 'How do you like my new coat?' 'It's lovely,' she replied, and he beamed at her. They developed something like friendship — but not quite, and she often felt uneasy around him in a way she could not describe. He told her that he visited his sister twice a week in Hemel Hempstead and was a regular at a pub he referred to as the Great Harry and also at the Halfway House on Newhouse Road corner, where he would meet a physician friend from West Hertfordshire for a pie and a pint or read a book while enjoying a beer. On occasion, she and Graham shared a genuine laugh, such as when he left the stores for a few minutes and asked her, when he returned, if she had missed him; Diana teasingly replied that he wasn't to get it into his head that she fancied him. For the first time she saw him laugh properly, but otherwise it was difficult to get on unfeigned friendly terms when she felt 'his talk was always of death, wars, spooky films, murders, etc. I found all his talk was morbid.'

Sometimes Graham bought a transistor radio into

212

the stores but tuned it into a station that seemed to play only the most solemn music, never pop or the biggest hits of the summer: 'Knock Three Times', 'Chirpy Chirpy Cheep Cheep' and 'Get It On'. He no longer wore the swastika he had fashioned himself in the handicrafts workshop in Broadmoor, instead favouring a skull-and-crossbones ring as his only piece of jewellery, but he still talked incessantly about the Nazis and their ideology. Even something as innocuous as the office Christmas party brought Hitler to the forefront of his mind when he heard it was compulsory for everyone to wear fancy dress to the Swan in Boxmoor.

'Oh, Diana,' he said excitedly, 'can you imagine me sitting in the back of the Rover bus with all my ribbons and medals on my uniform and my little Hitler's moustache, coming from the Market Square?'

She rolled her eyes: 'They'd bloody well chuck you off before you get to the Swan!'

He grinned, 'I wonder what Laurie and Eileen said if I walked in the Halfway House like that.'

He gave a rare deep chuckle and said, 'Should I come as Dracula with my two front teeth?' He mimicked fangs and a ghastly smile, then shook his head, 'No, I think I'd rather be Hitler.'

The Halfway House was one of Graham's most regular haunts, largely because of its convenience — literally at the end of the road from his workplace. One of the barmaids there, Selina Wilson, saw nothing of the face Graham showed to Diana Smart or other female colleagues; she felt that he was a misogynist because 'whenever I went to take his glass for a refill, he would ignore me and pretend he had finished drinking. But when the landlord himself appeared, he would leap up and ask for another pint.' Graham's closeness to his female relatives, especially his aunt Win, and his tenuous female friendships past and then present, ultimately belie the idea that he detested women. Undoubtedly, he had difficulties in forming anything more than a friendship with the females he met through work or in his spare time, and he never took part in the ribald camaraderie that sometimes occurred at Hadlands. In her memoir, Winifred refers to the press speculation about her brother's apparent lack of interest in women, simply feeling that he found most company — male or female — disappointing, because few people were able to keep up with his intelligence or wanted to discuss the subjects that so engrossed him. In her view, he was almost certainly heterosexual and could have enjoyed a relationship had he been able to meet a woman on his intellectual level. There were hints that he yearned for companionship; he once asked Diana if she thought he had nice eyes, and when she in turn enquired about whether or not he had a girlfriend, he told her that he had had girlfriends in the past but was now happy in his own company.

Graham's probation officer, Susan Vidal, raised the subject in her notes, musing:

> [He] quite often goes to a local pub where he sits and drinks and smokes, getting into superficial conversation with the barmaid or barman, and possibly striking up conversation with other people in the pub ... I would imagine his relationships with women on a sexual level are non-existent. This is something we have not discussed and I could imagine that he might be deeply hurt if he

214

developed a relationship with a girlfriend which then fell through. Very early in our contact he did once mention the possibility of marriage. This was in relation to a suggestion from me that he put his name on the local housing list for a batchelor [sic] flat.

A few weeks later she wrote: 'He clearly values our sessions and would, I think, like to have more of my time . . . I think it is likely that Mr Young has already become quite attached to me and I feel that we may have to work through this before I can make our contact fortnightly instead of weekly.'

Graham's frequent trips to the pub continued to concern his sister, who recalled: 'He was drinking heavily and I had a row with him about it. He used the White Horse at Leverstock Green and King Harry and the Rose and Crown in Hemel Hempstead. He used to sit in there and read whilst he had his pint. After my having a row with him about his drinking he never came back to my house again after drinking. He still visited me.' Winifred was worried, as Dr Udwin had been, that Graham used alcohol as a crutch; she thought that he might be fearful, among other things, of his colleagues discovering he had been in Broadmoor, but when she raised the matter, he led her to believe that Hadlands knew all about his past, telling her that it had come up when he first visited the factory and they asked why there were no stamps on his insurance card; he told Winifred that he had explained the Hadlands job would be his first because he had suffered a nervous breakdown after leaving school. He added that he had told them they were welcome to look into his background, that they had done so, and he had been surprised, therefore, when he was offered the job.

In her 12 May 1971 report on her meetings with Graham, Susan Vidal also referred to his increasing dependence on alcohol. On a positive note, she felt that he had 'slowly relaxed and accepted me as a person to whom he could talk', 'spoken about his offence and circumstances leading up to it' and had 'been extremely conscious not to break the conditions of his licence and has let me know whenever anything unusual has occurred'. He had made a couple of friendships through Hadlands but she judged these in less successful terms than he did, feeling them to be 'fairly transitory' and which might even have 'tended to push him back into his shell a little'. She was pessimistic about his alcohol intake and especially, 'his liking for cheap wine. I do not know to what extent he drinks VP cherry wine, but he always seems to have a bottle handy ... the danger that exists at the moment is that if left too much to his own devices the loneliness he experiences will drive him into a bottle. My colleagues in Hemel Hempstead will have a copy of this report and I assume that they will take note of what I have said.'

Miss Vidal sent a copy of her report to the other agencies involved in Graham's release. Upon reading it, Mynett noted optimistically that their client's mental health 'seems to be more relaxed than he was two and a half months ago. I have not examined him for bodily health, having no qualifications to do so. Nothing unusual in Graham Young's conduct has occurred.'

Mynett was sorely mistaken. The 'excellent health' of Graham's kindly superior in the stores, Bob Egle, had begun to falter. On 1 June 1971, he suffered sickness and diarrhoea unlike anything he had previously experienced. Because, far from relaxing into normality, Graham's mind had once again become a vortex of poisonous obsession.

13

THE MOST HEINOUS NATURE AND BLACKEST DYE

'A strong and healthy man' until the summer of 1971 was how detectives from Hertfordshire constabulary described Bob Egle in their report to the Director of Public Prosecutions. Dorothy Egle had never known her husband to be ill and told police officers that 'Bob had only been treated for a couple of bouts of influenza during the whole of the time we were married. Since then, until the time of his illness, he had no reason to consult a doctor. He was always an active man, fond of gardening and liked to be out 'doing something' in the way of physical activity.'

Coincidentally, Dorothy had been ill over that Whitsun weekend, the last in May 1971, when she suffered severe sickness and headaches. That in itself was not unusual: 'I frequently suffer with headaches and sickness,' she admitted, but it lasted for several days, during which time Bob began feeling unwell. He arrived home from work on Tuesday lunchtime complaining that he had diarrhoea and felt sick and that Ron Hewitt had been ill the week before. He was better the following morning and returned to work, but on Thursday he had stomach cramps and diarrhoea again. 'He was taking codeine tablets about this time for headaches,' Dorothy recalled, 'but he was not one for telling me how severe they were.' Bob managed to eat dinner that evening, but from then on, he no longer had lunch in the work canteen, preferring instead to eat at home.

On Friday, 4 June 1971, the family doctor called to see Dorothy, who was once more in bed with a crippling headache and nausea. Bob felt much the same, as he explained to Dr Robert Nevill when he let him into the house. The GP gave Dorothy an injection and prescribed antibiotics, telling Bob to rest and get plenty of fluids over the weekend but to call the surgery if his symptoms worsened. By Monday morning, Bob felt well enough to return to work, but by early afternoon he had another bout of diarrhoea and vomiting and told Geoffrey Foster he would have to go home until it passed.

Graham had been in good spirits in the stores that morning. On Saturday he had paid another visit to John Bell & Croyden, posing again as student M E Evans in order to purchase antimony potassium tartrate and thallium acetate, ostensibly for laboratory work. Mrs Ruby Wooding served him in the dispensary; the sale stuck in her mind because it was the only time in the two years that she had worked there when a customer had requested poison. 'A man aged between 25 years and 30 came to the counter,' she remembered, 'and asked to be supplied with three items. I can remember the two items listed in the register, antimony and thallous acetate, but I cannot remember the third item. I told him that I didn't think we had any of these, but he insisted that he had got the antimony here before.'

Working alongside Mrs Wooding that day was Thomas Hutton-Mills, who noticed she was having 'some difficulty' with a customer and went to help. 'It became apparent that [Graham] wanted some antimony tartrate and thallous acetate,' he confirmed. 'We told him that he must have authority and he said I've got it here previously.' Hutton-Mills checked the poison register and found the relevant entry: 'Seeing this, I told Mrs Wooding to get the antimony tartrate (sodium or potassium) and thallous acetate from the stockroom downstairs. Mrs Wooding brought up these two items and I dispensed them.'

Graham had asked for 25 grams of both, but Hutton-Mills explained they had only ten grams of thallous acetate in stock. He dispensed it all, along with their remaining 23 grams of antimony sodium tartrate. As Schedule 1 poisons, the sale required the authorisation of the duty pharmacist, who had to record the transaction in the poison register. Albert Kearne thus asked Graham for identification and Mrs Wooding recalled that the young man produced 'a card of some sort'. Kearne found it satisfactory and permitted the sale, after which Graham departed for home, jubilant at his success in obtaining two new poisons.

Dr Udwin remembered seeing Graham in his outpatient clinic on 8 June. The psychiatrist was pleased to learn that his former patient had settled into his new job and wished to register with a local doctor, seemingly no longer worried about his Broadmoor experience being held against him. 'During a long interview he seemed to me entirely well and surmounting the difficulties of re-establishing himself in an entirely satisfactory fashion,' Dr Udwin later told the Home Office. Graham had also informed Udwin that he had applied for his provisional driving licence. Diana Smart's husband had agreed to give him a couple of lessons, but these ended as swiftly as they began: while practicing reversing a van at Hadlands,

Graham had accelerated too quickly and crashed into the stepladder Norman had been standing on moments before. The older man was furious, while Graham could do nothing but laugh.

Bob Egle returned to the stores on 10 June. Both he and his wife felt depleted by their recent illness and decided to take a week's holiday in Great Yarmouth. They left on Saturday, 19 June, staying in a self-catered flat near the seafront. 'During this time Bob was quite fit and well and had no recurrence of his illness,' Dorothy recalled. 'The only time I recall him mentioning anything about his health was one morning he said he felt a little giddy, but this soon passed off.' The break was exactly what they needed, and when Bob arrived for work on Monday, 28 June, he was in good spirits. Dorothy was therefore surprised and concerned when he appeared at her workplace in Hemel Hempstead the following day complaining that 'his fingers were all numb at the ends'. As Bob drove them both home, he told his wife that he had been 'feeling awful' all day and that when he combed his hair 'his head felt numb'.

Dorothy cooked a meal that evening but Bob couldn't face it. He lay down on the sofa, complaining of a painful backache. At 9pm, he got up to accompany his wife to the paddock, where their daughter's horse needed to be brought into the stable for the night. 'He felt so ill and could not walk properly,' Dorothy recalled. 'He was staggering just as if he had had a lot to drink.' They had to give up their attempts to bring in the horse 'because Bob was too ill to stop and catch it'. They made their way slowly back to the house, with Dorothy propping up her husband, who could not even manage a few steps unaided. They went straight to bed. 'Bob had difficulty in undressing because he said he could not feel the buttons on his shirt and I took off his shirt and tie for him,' Dorothy recalled. 'I did not realise how ill Bob was at this time, thinking that he had just caught a germ. When I went to bed at about 11pm, Bob was groaning with his backache. He said that he had never had a pain in his back so bad. I gave him two codeine tablets and about an hour later when he was still in pain, I fetched him a hot-water bottle to place against his back.' She slept in one of the spare bedrooms that night at her husband's suggestion; he knew she would be unable to sleep lying next to him. She kept waking up nonetheless and could hear him groaning. Twice she went in to him, and asked if they ought to call out Dr Nevill, but Bob dismissed the idea, insisting it was just 'back trouble'.

At 6am, Dorothy got up again. Bob was still awake and told her he still had numbness in his hands and could not feel his feet. He felt as if there was something wrong with his legs but couldn't describe the sensation other than an ache. Dorothy was now worried enough to go against her husband's wishes and called the surgery in Kings Langley. Their doctor was on holiday, but locum Dr Peter Sparrow arrived at their home just before 7am. He found Bob to be suffering from peripheral neuritis: weakness of the legs, pain and diminished sensation of his extremities. Dr Sparrow wondered whether he was in the early stages of a post-infective polyneuritis, but he had no significant history of an infection over the previous few weeks and his temperature was normal. He gave Bob two small tablets to take, which Dorothy handed to her husband with a glass of water after the doctor had gone. She was shaken when Bob then immediately and very violently vomited 'black liquid'.

Dr Sparrow returned to the house at 8am in response to Dorothy's second call. He found Bob ominously worse and complaining of restlessness and unbearable pain everywhere. The doctor called for an ambulance and Dorothy accompanied her husband to Hemel Hempstead hospital, where he was placed in the Rutherford ward of the St Paul's wing. 'His back was troubling him much worse by this time,' she recalled. 'He was rolling from side to side of the hospital bed. The pain was so severe that he said if something was not done to cure the pain he would jump out of the window.' Frightened and distressed to see her husband in such agony, Dorothy called for a nurse. She was told to leave the side ward while her husband was settled. When she was allowed in again, she was relieved to find him much quieter. Told that Bob would sleep for some time now, she left for home around 11am that morning.

Later that day, Bob Egle was examined by Dr Anne Solomon. She found him still suffering 'obvious pain … tone flaccid in both arms and legs, grip reduced … touch and pain sensation were reduced in the palms of both hands … light touch reduced over the feet and the front of the legs … Acutely tender on the dorsal and plantar surface of the phalanges, position and vibration sense normal.' A lumber puncture revealed a blood-stained fluid. It was hoped that the results of further tests would reveal the cause of Bob's illness.

Dorothy returned to the hospital to visit her husband that evening, accompanied by their very concerned daughter, who had never seen her father incapacitated before. He was too tired to speak to them and they left

223

after a few minutes at his bedside. Dorothy spent a restless night herself at home, then headed back to the hospital when visiting hours began the next day, Thursday 1 July. She was appalled by the deterioration in his condition, which the doctors were unable to explain: 'His eyes were partially closed, he was very slurred in his speech and when I tried to give him a drink, he bit the top off the plastic drinking mug, not realising that he was biting so hard.' Dr Solomon examined Bob again and found that he had reduced sensation in his limbs, muscular pains, bilateral facial weakness and struggled to swallow. Suspecting that he might require a respirator, she arranged for him to be transferred to the intensive care unit of St Albans city hospital.

Once more, Dorothy sat beside her husband in the ambulance and remained at the hospital until late that night. When she arrived at the ICU again the following morning, she burst into tears at the sight of her husband, who could no longer speak and was unable to open his eyes. 'His condition deteriorated fairly rapidly after that,' she quietly confirmed to detectives five months later. 'He was unable to speak to me again. I do not think he even knew I was there. From then on, my husband was being treated constantly and I stayed with him when possible.'

The news of Bob Egle's sudden illness caused shockwaves at Hadlands, where he was a popular member of staff. Company secretary Mrs Mary Berrow visited different areas of the site during the course of her day and received numerous enquiries from colleagues regarding Bob's progress. She recalled:

Among those making enquiries was Graham Young, which was quite natural as he worked with

224

Mr Egle. His enquiries were fairly frequent. As a rule he would stay and chat a few minutes and pressed for all available information. At one stage Mrs Egle mentioned that the illness her husband was suffering from was polyneuritis. This meant nothing to me and I think I told Graham and he explained this illness to me, saying that it was a virus which caused inflammation of the nerve ends. His usual questions were: How was Mr Egle? Do they know what it is? Is he any better? What were the symptoms? I always gave him as much information as I could. On one occasion he mentioned that he would like to visit Mr Egle in hospital but I don't think he actually went as Mr Egle was too ill to receive visitors.

The next time Graham visited his sister, he brought up the matter with her. 'Graham said to me, 'The storeman at our place is ill.' I said, 'What's the matter with him?' Graham said, 'Some virus or other, it's a virus that's affecting his nervous system.'' Winifred murmured that it was awful and she hoped he made a good recovery. But at St Albans hospital, Dr Roger Gulin had already begun to fear the worst:

Mr Egle continued to deteriorate. Muscle weakness in the face and throat became apparent which made swallowing difficult. Shortly afterwards the muscles affecting breathing became weak and at this stage an operation was performed on his windpipe through which a small tube was inserted and connected to a breathing-assisting machine. However, his condition continued to get worse with a fall in blood pressure and an increase in his heartbeat. Mr Egle then developed pneumonia, which added to his other complications.

Shortly after 10:15pm on Wednesday, 7 July 1971, the formerly vigorously healthy veteran of Dunkirk, Bob Egle, passed away.

His wife received a telephone call from the hospital informing her that her husband of almost 40 years had died. She in turn had to pass that news on to their devastated daughter, who had looked forward to her parents living with her after their imminent retirement.

Bob's cause of death was recorded as 'Broncho Pneumonia secondary to Guillain-Barré Polyneuritis' and certified by Dr Michael Smith, casualty officer at St Thomas' hospital, London and house physician at St Albans city hospital. On Friday, 9 July, Dr Smith attended a postmortem examination conducted by Dr John Pugh at St Albans city hospital mortuary. It was deemed necessary to determine the cause of Bob's paralysis. Dr Smith recalled that 'this it failed to do because no anatomical or histological abnormalities were found in the brain, spinal cord and peripheral nerves. The examination failed to throw any light on the cause of the paralysis.' The resultant mortuary report did reveal other elements that led to Bob's death, however. The 'well-nourished, elderly man' was found to have a largely normal heart, but his main air passages were 'full of pus' with both lungs 'solid from pneumonia throughout'. His spleen was 'red, septic' and visceral changes within his body included considerable 'circulatory disturbance in liver and kidney and hypostatic bronchopneumonia'. In addition to the clinical diagnosis of Landry's paralysis, Dr Pugh's central anatomical finding was bronchopneumonia.

The news of Bob Egle's death was met with mostly shocked silence at Hadlands, where his former colleagues had been gathered together to be told of his passing. An over-used phrase, but in this case accurate, was heard repeatedly by those who knew Bob well or as an acquaintance: no one had a bad word to say about him. There were tears and disbelief among the staff. Graham's immediate response was not recorded, but Diana Smart remembered a short discussion with him about the funeral: 'He asked me if I was going. I said, 'No, but I'm sure someone from the offices will be going to represent the firm.' He said, 'Yes, but I think I'd like to go.''

Ron Hewitt was saddened, and more than a little worried, when he heard of Bob's death. His efforts to find work as a full-time driver had paid off, and his last day at Hadlands was Friday, 9 July. Despite liking everyone with whom he had worked, Ron was relieved to be leaving the company, and more so after being told that Bob had died, because he, too, had been intermittently ill in recent weeks. 'When it first started, I was at work in the stores,' he recalled. 'It was just after tea break, because we thought it might have been something in the tea. It started as a burning feeling in the back of my throat and about five or ten minutes later, I had stomach pains as if someone had got hold of my stomach and twisted it.'

He felt better after vomiting and carried on with his work. 'But during the afternoon I had pain again and felt sick, and somebody brought me home and I left my car at work,' he stated. 'I couldn't eat anything for two or three days. Every time I tried to eat, I would

227

vomit.' He made an appointment with his doctor in Hemel Hempstead, who told him he had probably picked up a bug and gave him kaolin and morphine linctus. He took regular doses during a week's sick leave and returned to Hadlands feeling better, if somewhat fragile. Mid-week, however, he had another attack of stomach pains and sickness, but not so bad as before and was able to clear it with the medicine and some antibiotics. He left Hadlands feeling certain that he had contracted something from the premises, possibly even the same virus that killed Bob Egle. There had long been talk of the 'Bovingdon Bug', which was peculiar to the area around the old aerodrome and documented in medical books as similar to gastro-enteritis — several schoolchildren had suffered from it. For the time being at least, Ron Hewitt was simply grateful to think he had survived the strange and arcane virus.

* * *

Graham visited his sister on Saturday, 10 July. He told her, 'The storeman has died.' When she asked him what had caused Bob's death, he replied, 'It was a rare virus.' He seemed unperturbed by the loss of his colleague and said no more about it.

That same day, the body of Bob Egle was collected from the mortuary at St Albans city hospital by Idris Arnold, manager of Cooks Funeral Services. He conveyed the body to their Chapel of Rest in Chesham, where it was laid out in an open coffin. On Sunday, Dorothy Egle visited her husband for the final time.

On the morning of Monday, 12 July 1971, Bob Egle's coffin was closed and sealed in preparation for his funeral that afternoon at Whelpley Hill, a hamlet behind the old airfield. The service at the small Victorian church of St Michael's and All Angels was short but moving. Graham had managed to wangle himself an invitation, sitting stiffly but alert on a pew alongside Geoffrey Foster, who was both a friend of the deceased and there to represent the firm of Hadlands. The funeral was held immediately after the service, at Chiltern crematorium.

Foster drove, with Graham fidgeting in the passenger seat; he was talkative during the 20-minute journey. It was a hot, dry afternoon. 'Do we know from what illness Bob Egle has died?' Graham enquired.

Foster nodded. 'I got a copy of the death certificate that morning. It said 'polyneuritis'.'

Graham frowned. 'Did the certificate qualify this in any way, as polyneuritis is only a general term?'

'There was some specific name, but it was in French — I can't recall,' said Foster.

'Oh, that sounds like the Guillain-Barré syndrome,' said the younger man.

Feeling a jolt of surprise, Foster glanced at him. 'Yes, that's it.'

'Guillain-Barré syndrome had only recently been identified.'

Graham then described in great detail the various treatments that were being tried for it. Foster could not understand much of what he was saying, given how technical some of the terms were. There was a moment's silence, then Graham looked out of the window at the summer hedgerows flashing by in green and white, before remarking, 'It's terribly sad that a man like Bob Egle should survive the dangers of Dunkirk only to fall victim to a strange virus at this time.' He sighed heavily and leant against the glass. Foster said nothing, but was amazed by his medical knowledge, which Graham demonstrated again on their journey back to Bovingdon when he began another discourse with the opening, 'When people suffer from nervous diseases, it very often turns to bronchopneumonia which is the actual cause of death ...'

At the crematorium, staff dealt with the final stages of the funeral, which was the only one held there that day. Bob Egle's ashes were placed in an oak casket on which an inscription plate bore the words: 'Robert Edward Egle (60 years), died 7.7.71. At Rest'.

Although no one knew it then, the cremation of this kindly, active man would lead to an important advance in British forensic history; it would also help secure Graham's conviction years after he had suggested cremating his first victim in the belief that the process would ensure he was never found out.

14

THE DARK ANGEL OF DEATH

There were many aspects of Bob Egle's death that pleased Graham, including his promotion to laboratory storeman. Winifred recalled that Graham mentioned it when he visited her shortly after the funeral. He told her that it meant an increase in his wages, then added, 'But it's sad the way it happened.' Reflecting on the conversation in the light of later knowledge, she admitted, 'I had no doubt that he sincerely meant that it was a pity a man had to die to bring about such a promotion. Yet I now realise that his conversation about Bob Egle and his death surely had a much more chilling and macabre aspect.' She felt then that he was acting out as he so often did — sailing close to the wind by talking and behaving in a way that could only draw attention to matters he should really have kept secret.

Soon after his promotion, Graham visited his sister again. This time he was annoyed, telling her, 'An older man in the stores keeps interfering in what I am doing. I've told him that I'm either running the stores or not. I'll speak to John Hadland about it.' Winifred shrugged, 'He's probably just trying to be helpful.' Graham shook his head, scowling, 'No, he's not. He's just *interfering*.' Although Winifred came to believe the man who had irritated him was Fred Biggs, one of Graham's other colleagues — student Martin Hancock — explained that she was mistaken: 'I recall him saying that he didn't like working in the stores and that people were getting on his back.' Hancock remembered that the only person Graham ever mentioned by name in regard to this was George Janouch: 'He never said why this was. It may have been because George was running the store at the time and may have been getting on to him.'

Martin had learned of Bob's death only after returning to work following his own bout of illness:

> I went into the stores on a number of occasions and noticed that Bob Egle was not at his bench. I think I asked Fred Biggs where he was and he said that he had died. I then spoke to Graham about Bob's death and he said that he had died of a nervous disease. He told me in detail all about it and said that towards the end Bob was in a great deal of pain. I got the impression that he was either there at the time Bob died or that he knew exactly what would happen to him.

In response to a question from Graham, Martin told him that he had been ill with glandular fever. Graham then described what the illness entailed using all the relevant medical terms. 'He was obviously well read on medicine,' Martin mused. 'He had all this on tap, so to speak, and had not been able to read up about my illness.'

There were other changes following the death of Bob Egle, one of which involved Fred Biggs being asked to work extra hours. This took him up to four full days a week with one half day. His wife Annie, who worked the same hours as before at Hadlands, recalled that her husband 'still did his job as storekeeper in the work-in-progress section of stores and also helped Graham Young in the main stores department'. The older man and the younger got on well together, and had several conversations that summer about insecticides and pesticides. That summer the store was plagued by wasps; Diana Smart remembered how Graham detested them, along with flies and spiders, and would leap about the place swatting madly, then collect the insects on pieces of paper to watch their death throes. She once told him off for repeatedly poking a dying spider with a pencil but he just smiled until one of the other men working nearby told him sharply to put the creature out of its misery. The wasps annoyed everyone, however, and Fred tried an old method of dealing with them: sugared water left in a bowl outside the doors to attract the wasps to the water instead of the stores. Discussing the problem, Fred mentioned that bugs of some sort were decimating the plants in his garden and Graham suggested that nicotine was an effective means of dealing with them. A couple of days later, Graham brought a tin of nicotine dust and offered it to Fred, who politely declined to try it in his garden. Graham then proposed another method: a gallon of water with 10 grams — approximately 150 grains — of thallium. He offered to provide the thallium and brought in 15 grams, warning Fred not to handle it without gloves.

Although evidence later showed that the older man had never used the substance, nor even opened the packet, it was around this time when he experienced his first serious bout of illness. In an eerie repeat of his remark about Bob Egle, managing director Geoffrey Foster described Fred as a 'vigorous, healthy person until his illness'. Annie Biggs confirmed: 'All his life Fred has been a very healthy man, never having had any serious illness.' At the age of 11, he had appendicitis and around 1965 he had a hernia operation, but those were his only hospital admissions. In spring 1971, he had a bit of trouble with indigestion but the tablets his doctor prescribed for him cleared the trouble quickly. Other than that, he enjoyed a very active life. His wife recalled: 'He was very fond of gardening and ballroom dancing. We both attended ballroom-dancing classes, once or twice a week regularly at the Irene Smythe School of Dancing in Rickmansworth. We actually won three bronze and two silver medals for our dancing together.'

Annie was unable to remember the exact date when her husband fell ill, but it was probably towards the end of August. He had been at work that morning, having risen perfectly well as usual and eaten breakfast. She gave him his packed lunch and the two of them set out for Hadlands in their car. She was very surprised when, just after she finished her shift at 1pm, Fred appeared and told her that he had asked another colleague, Peter Buck, to drive them both home in his car because he was too ill to work or drive himself. She recalled: 'When we got into our car, Fred told me he had been dreadfully sick and had some awful pains in his stomach. He was not sick on the journey and as soon as we arrived home he went straight to bed and stayed there. He was not sick anymore and he slept for most of the afternoon until about 6pm or 7pm'

Annie telephoned their dancing instructor to explain that they would not be along to train that night for their medal test, which was due in December. Shortly afterwards, Fred got up from bed and seemed much brighter, asking for a cup of Bovril. He then slept through the night and returned to work as normal the following morning. When he met her at lunchtime, he still seemed well, although he mentioned having had diarrhoea earlier. They went shopping together that afternoon and discussed their impending holiday. It would be their second that year; they had enjoyed a fortnight in the Spanish resort of Tossa de Mar shortly before Bob Egle fell ill.

Graham had booked his own holidays for September but was going no further than Kent. He left to stay with his aunt, uncle and father in Sheerness on Saturday, 4 September. Win was surprised to find him less amiable than usual:

During this holiday I found him to be extremely moody and bad-tempered. During these ten days I remember having a conversation with him in which he said, 'The man I work with has died and I have got his job.' I said, 'What did he die with?' and he said, 'Some obscure virus. He told me once jokingly that he was dying from the fingers up because he had pins and needles.' I immediately felt suspicious because it was the same as his stepmother Molly. I wanted to trust him and made the mistake of not listening to my instinct. If there wasn't anything in it, I didn't want to start things up.

Win was privately circumspect, however: 'I was never keen to let him mess about in my kitchen. I would not let him brew a cup of tea if I could help it, but I tried not to show it. None of the family really trusted him.'

Apart from Graham's poor temper, the visit passed

without incident and he returned to work on 13 September. Fred and his wife had left the day before, to spend a week touring Devon and Cornwall. But Graham's absence from Hadlands had shown that his promotion was premature: one of his colleagues in the store decided to clear out and burn all the empty boxes in the stores, which was among Graham's duties. When Graham arrived at work and saw the space created by the clearance, he remarked on how great the place looked. Nor was Graham as careful as he should have been with property; while he had been away, Norman Smart doubled his efforts in maintenance and security. Graham was responsible for putting away the expensive cameras sent in by customers for repair, and one of Norman's duties was to ensure they were locked up. He noticed that Graham had left one camera out in the stores, but when he spoke to him about it, Graham merely grinned and said that it was just a customer's camera and hardly important. Norman also grew frustrated by Graham's perpetual habit of misplacing his keys, which Norman usually found locked in the stores. When he spoke to his wife about the issues he had with Graham, Diana sympathised; among Graham's quirks was preferring to work in semi-darkness, which she disliked. There was strong fluorescent lighting in the stores, but when the natural light faded, he was loath to switch them on and would turn them off if Diana or anyone else did. He told her that it was a good thing to train your eyes to seeing in the dark instead of relying on electricity. Norman once found his wife attempting to work in the WIP section in darkness and was astonished when she told him not to switch the light on or Graham would go mad. Norman replied that she was

236

being ridiculous and put the light on for her. Graham arrived back a few moments later and asked her plaintively why she had gone against his wishes. On other occasions she found herself stumbling about the place in semidarkness because Graham insisted that the lights should remain off.

In mid-September, Dr Udwin had a long conversation with Graham over the telephone. He was keen to hear how his former patient was coping with the promotion and pleased to discover that Graham seemed 'quite well' and in no danger of relapse: 'Indeed, he seemed so settled that I was content to let him go forward with very little further interference.'

It was a cataclysmic error of judgement.

* * *

When detectives later questioned former Hadlands delivery driver Ron Hewitt about his illness, like Diana Smart he remembered that Graham had been in the habit of collecting the morning and afternoon tea for several colleagues from May Bartlett, at 11am and 3pm respectively. May was also spoken to by police and told them that she kept her tea, coffee, sugar and milk supplies in the main kitchen in the canteen. There was a tea room in the main laboratory area in Banbury 2, where she was able to brew up; she had a key to this room and only left it unlocked while she went around the premises with her trolley. She carried a biscuit tin on her trolley and put a few on a plate as she got to each department and no one else ever handled the beverages or biscuits on the trolley. She recalled that all the staff liked to have their own cups and she would try to give them the china mugs they favoured as she went round. After each tea break, she would collect the cups and take them away for washing up in her tea room, then replace the cups on the trolley. May was at pains to point out 'this is a very happy firm to work for'.

Fred Biggs had suffered no recurrence of his illness during his holiday with Annie and remained well for the first few days of his return to work. But Peter Buck — the man who had given them a lift home when Fred fell ill — was not so fortunate. Peter lived in Hemel Hempstead and, following six years working in Hadlands' import and export section, he had been promoted to manager of the department at the beginning of the year. His office was on the first floor of the main building, next to the boardroom. During the course of his day, he visited most areas of the factory, checking paperwork and supervising the packing of equipment in the stores. He had recently become directly responsible for Graham in this respect and spoke to him about reading during work hours; Graham had been poring over a library book whose title concerned humanity's apparent 'preoccupation with death'. Although Peter usually took his tea breaks in his office with George Janouch, Annie Biggs and import-and-export clerk David Tilson, lately he had sometimes drunk his cuppa in the stores with Graham.

On Monday, 20 September, Peter was in the stores during the morning tea break, working alongside David Tilson at the far end of the room. As was his wont, Graham collected three teas for them. Taking his first sip, Peter noticed that his tea had 'a foreign taste'. He drank most of it anyway, but within half an hour, his head began throbbing. A feeling of intense

238

dizziness overtook him and he sat down heavily by the door. Sharp pains shot through his stomach and he vomited. He got up and staggered to the toilets, where he vomited again. Gasping, he asked David Tilson to drive him back to Hemel Hempstead. He recalled: 'At my home I was sick on several occasions but the violent pain in my stomach subsided.' The only reason he could think of that had caused him to fall ill so suddenly was the strange-tasting tea.

Secretary Diana Smart had also been ill, suffering bouts of sickness and peculiar afflictions, including horrible-smelling feet. At first, she had been unaware of the smell, but one night in September, her husband Norman complained that he couldn't get to sleep because of it. The following night, he shook her awake and told her that she was the cause of the smell. Indignant at both being awoken and accused, she replied angrily that he was mistaken. They continued to row about it for several nights.

Then one evening, as Diana and Norman sat down to watch television with one of their young sons, she drew up her legs beneath her to get comfortable on the sofa and suddenly smelled it: a horrible stench. At first she thought her son's socks were the cause and told him to take them off. He did so but the smell lingered, and she insisted that he give his feet a quick but thorough rinse with soap and water. He did so, but the pong remained and the three of them started arguing over who was to blame. Diana suddenly bent down to smell her own feet and recoiled in disgust. 'I bloody well told you it was you,' Norman said triumphantly. She asked him to smell her feet but he refused, 'Not on your Nellie, they smell rotten.' She washed her feet and sprayed her shoes but could not get rid of the stink. She tried changing her tights two or three times a day, and kept her feet scrupulously clean, but it made no difference. The only benefit was that Norman was now sympathetic and suggested that she should visit the doctor.

Diana saw her GP, Dr Arthur Anderson, on 5 October. 'She complained of irritation and smell in her feet, being worse near the toes,' he recalled. 'This was thought to be a fungus skin infection and treated with a topical cream.' However, the cream had little effect; the stench seemed to intensify. She became depressed, feeling both embarrassed and upset because her husband could not bear to be near her. She grew short-tempered with her family and begged her doctor to find a cure. Hearing that she felt sleepy very early each evening, and had a numbness in her toes, Dr Anderson diagnosed her with diabetes. She experienced other weird ailments too, including an ability to curdle milk as soon as her lips touched the glass. An ardent coffee lover, she could no longer stomach the smell or taste of it, nor of tea either. She suffered in silence, too ashamed to pay a third visit to the doctor.

September saw longer hours at Hadlands during stock-taking fortnight. Throughout the period, after finishing her cleaning duties at 5:30pm, May Bartlett left her tea room open so that anyone working over-time could make their own drinks. On one occasion she bumped into Graham, who bade her goodnight and explained that he was rushing to catch the 7pm bus. She remembered:

I met him in the Banbury corridor a few minutes later. He came hurrying round the corridor and surprised me. I said, 'I thought you went home.' He said, 'No, I missed the bus.' I thought this was very odd as the next bus was 7:30pm and I didn't think there should have been one at 7pm. Just after that I called out to him that David Boley had offered him a lift to Hemel Hempstead. When I went to look for Graham, he was in the far end of stores, in his own department, without any lights on and it was quite dark. This seemed very strange to me, but I did not go into stores or see what he was doing. He came out when I called him and I let him and David Boley out of the building and locked up after them.

On Friday, 8 October 1971, David Tilson was among those workers putting in extra hours during stock-taking. David was one of the newer members of staff, having begun employment four months earlier. He worked mostly with Peter Buck, engaged in paperwork, but was occasionally needed to pack cameras and equipment in the stores, where he would work alongside Peter and Graham. 'There have been times when I was working in the stores when I've been offered tea and biscuits by Graham,' he recalled. 'I only used to have a few mouthfuls of the tea because Graham used to put sugar in it, which I don't like.' On this particular Friday, he had a cup of tea given to him by Graham but as usual found it had been sweetened, so left most of it.

The following morning, David found that his toes were numb and he had sharp pains in his legs. The sensations remained and four days later he visited his local surgery, where he explained to locum Dr Susan Henry that he had pains, stiffness and pins and needles in both legs and his chest felt tight. She examined him and found no abnormality in his legs but some tenderness across his sternum and prescribed two par-acetamols three times a day for the chest pains, which she thought was almost certainly 'muscular trouble'. Tilson went back to work but his legs continued to be painful, leaving him with a limp.

On Tuesday, 12 October 1971, Graham Young began keeping a diary.

15

THE DESIRED EFFECT

A Student and Officer's Case Book reads the title on the cover of the loose-leaf foolscap pad Graham kept hidden beneath his bed at Maynard Road. Bought from WHSmith's, the lined pages of the notebook's blue-backed boards reveal the workings of a young poisoner's mind: the substances and methods he employed, the choosing of his victims and the dispassionate observations with a humour blacker than coal. There could be no doubt after reading the neat handwriting that the person wielding the pen intended not only to kill but to experiment on those closest to him. He referred to the people within its pages by initials, and although he later tried to pass off the diary as the manuscript of a failed comic novel, its veracity burned through the pages like acid.

Graham's diary begins abruptly, referring to the very recent illness of David Tilson ('D') and how it had played out according to Graham's wishes. He had run the risk of being detected otherwise, especially given the similarity between David's symptoms and those of the deceased Bob Egle:

12th. My fears proved to be unfounded. D's malady was diagnosed as fibrositis, which saves me the trouble — and risk — of playing the sympathetic hospital visitor in order to finish the job. Had the illness proved sufficiently serious to demand

243

D's hospitalisation I could not have taken the chance that prolonged observation might have revealed the true cause of the trouble. Had, as was intended, the full amount been ingested, the resultant illness would have had a fatal resolution within 7—10 days, conforming in all aspects to the Guillan Barre [*sic*] syndrome and the death would have been diagnosed as such. If, however, the illness had extended into weeks — as would have been the case with so small a quantity — certain of the symptoms would present an atypical picture which may have jerked in the minds of the medico's [*sic*] — leading to a re-diagnosis. Had this been the case, it is quite likely that the similarity of the symptoms to those preceding the death of B [Bob Egle] may have been recognised and the death certificate subjected to close scrutiny. So, all in all I am quite satisfied with the situation. I now have time to reassess and decide upon my course of action.

Graham's next words make it clear that this course of action involved choosing another subject to poison and observe. There were three possibilities: storeman Fred Biggs ('F'), laboratory worker Jethro Batt ('J'), (with whom Graham was on good terms) or delivery driver John Durrant ('R'). He weighed his options as objectively as a chef deciding upon ingredients for a dish, and admonished himself to be more careful with his measures, as the diary makes plain:

I think it was probably imprudent of me to select a second subject from the same place. The similarity between the two deaths might have been commented upon. J [Jethro Batt] would be the ideal subject, living so far away [Harlow]. Access would present no problem either, but I regard him as a friend so it is out of the question.

F [Fred Biggs] would also be easy to process, but he is too closely associated with me. It would be unwise to make too many selections from my immediate circle. Also, of course, I rather like F and would be loath to inflict so cruel a fate on him. I think R [John Durrant] is the most logical choice, so it is now merely a question of opportunity. He should visit this week and a chance should occur then. This time I must restrain my tendency towards over-liberal dosage and administer the minimum necessary to achieve the desired effect. Too much and the same will happen as with D [David Tilson]. Taste will be noticeably altered and insufficient consumed — presenting the same panolopy [*sic*] of problems. Also, I shall revert to the same medium as with B. Using the crystalline form renders it far easier to guage [*sic*] the exact dosage and also safeguards against partial decomposition as I suspect may have occurred with D's solution.

Graham then returned to David Tilson's illness and muses on how he would have felt forced to act if his symptoms had given too much away:

It should be quite amusing to see D's reaction to his 'fibrositis' especially when it proves to be a most intractable ailment. Also, within 3 weeks a characteristic alopecia should occur which, to

245

a man of D's customary hironteness [hirsute-ness] should prove a trifle embarrassing. It is this very alopecia which, had he been under the eyes of the hospital authorities, would have forced me to rapidly bring about his demise, for it may well have caused them to explore avenues which would have jeapordized [sic] me. My plan for this eventuality was to visit D in the role of commis-erator [sic] and, on my first visit conspiratorially produce a Brandy miniature as a token of my sympathy for his unfortunate position. As D is a drinking man this would, I think, have been accepted and, under my direction, hastily swal-lowed; the bottle being returned to me on the grounds — entirely logical — that the nurses may otherwise discover the 'breach of hospital discipline'. A precedent having been thus estab-lished, I would, upon my second visit have produced an identical miniature to be consumed in like manner. The latter, however, would have been previously 'doctored' and would within 48 hours have brought about a deterioration of D's condition which, within a week would have ter-minated in death — astensibly [sic] from A.I.P [acute infection polyneuritis]. Had the hospital decided upon post-mortem examination, the finding would have been entirely consistent with this cause and, as the latter illness is of uncertain aetiology, certification of death would have pre-sented no problem. However, D has not been hospitalised — a happy circumstance for him — and therefore is free to live out his allotted span, for needless to say, it would be injudicious of me to focus my attentions upon him a second time.

He then decides upon his next victim, before blithely describing how interesting he found it to observe the effects poison was having on David Tilson and what could be expected next:

R [John Durrant] should suit my purpose admirably, and as there is no obvious connection between us he is a most attractive proposition. In a way it seems a shame to condemn such a likeable little man to so unpleasant an end, but I have made my decision and therefore he is doomed to premature decease.

D returned to work today and this afternoon I was able to enquire after his health. It appears that he is suffering muscular pain and stiffness from the chest downwards — of a general distribution. He has intense numbness in both feet. It would seem, therefore, that the quantity ingested was larger than I originally estimated — perhaps as much as 300mgns. The symptoms point so clearly to a polyneuritis that the competence of D's physician is questionable to say the least. It is not certain that alopecia will later develop, but it would be quite consistent with a dose of this size. If it occurs this will doubtless drive D to the doctor again but, happily, by the time hair-loss becomes sufficiently noticeable to prompt this step, excretion of the drug is likely to have ended. Of course, it is known that excretion may continue for up to three months from the time of ingestion, but this is dependent on the size of the initial dose — in this case relatively small. Another factor, which may cause D concern and possibly worry his physician, is the protracted course of the illness. The symptoms will remit only gradually — recovery in these cases is always very slow. For full sensation to return to his feet and for the muscular impairment to resolve itself may take as long as 2/3 months. For fibrositis in acute form to persist so long is unusual and ultimately a diagnosis of polyneuritis (probably viral) may well be made. We shall see. The case interests me greatly as it affords me an opportunity to observe the effects of a sub-lethal dosage.

In his next sentence, Graham appears to refer to the murder of his stepmother Molly and admits that his conversations with David Tilson gave him the chance to put his medical knowledge to the test:

My previous experience of the drug has been only of lethal doses which, in both instances led to rapid deterioration and death. D will give me an opportunity to effect a more leisurely study.

Once again I had to opportunity to engage D in conversation — this time quite lengthy. From his description of his symptoms, it seems that the damage caused by the drug is progressive. He complains of an intensification of the muscular pains and stiffness, which he describes as definitely worse than at the time of his Tuesday examination. They are, apparently, severe enough to have prevented him from sleeping last night. He also complains of feeling 'washed out' this sense of fatigue he ascribes to a sleepless night which, I think, is probably a contributing factor. However, the drug is known to produce an eunelvation [sic] and so, at least in part, the fatigue is probably due to its action. A fresh symptom has appeared — enlargement of the lympathic [*sic*] glands in the armpits and swelling of glands in the neck, accompanied by a degree of tenderness. I make, at present, no observations on this, for it is not yet certain whether this new manifestation has a toxic or bacillary/viral cause. It is most convenient, as it gives credence to the picture of 'natural' disease and will serve to obscure the true cause of illness still further. D is not satisfied with the diagnosis of fibrositis. He believes himself to have an infection — though of what nature he is unsure. He intends to apply for a fresh appointment and so a re-diagnosis might be made. It will be interesting to see the result.

★   ★   ★

Although Graham had apparently decided on delivery driver John Durrant as his next victim, and ruled out Jethro Batt due to friendship, before the week was out he had changed his mind, leaving his fellow Hadlands employee — and friend — in agony.

Batt had worked at Hadlands for five years as a self-employed prototype electronic wireman; for the past 18 months he had been employed in the Imacon test department of the laboratory. He and Graham had hit it off within a month of the younger man beginning work in the stores. Batt lived with his wife and children in Harlow but was originally from West Hendon and, as such, the two of them struck up what Batt referred to as an 'exile friendship, as none of the other workers to my knowledge came from that district of London'. From then on, they would converse on a wide range of subjects, although Graham usually turned them round to his own favourite topics: Nazi Germany, poison and true crime. 'He often spoke of people like the Acid Bath Murderer, Jack the Ripper and [John] Christie. He seemed disgusted at the stupid mistakes [Haigh, the Acid Bath Murderer] made, which enabled the police to catch him. Most of his conversations turned to the macabre.' Batt nicknamed his new friend 'the Keeper of the Black Museum' and admitted finding Graham depressing at times: 'I'd just walk away because of the macabre nature of his conversations.'

Other colleagues had similar conversations with Graham, including Eric Baxter, quality-control engineer, who described Graham as 'a compulsive talker. He was impressed by the method Christie used to murder his victims. He knew all the dates and even the number of layers of wallpaper on the kitchen walls at Christie's home in Rillington Place.' Baxter also recalled Graham's occasional habit of taking a nip from a flask at midday and asked him why he did it: 'He said it gave him confidence. When I asked him why he needed confidence, he replied, 'Ah, you don't realise.''

But of all his colleagues, Batt was the one whom Graham regarded as more than simply a co-worker with whom he got along. Batt often visited other parts of the factory, including the stores and production department, usually working until 7pm and, earlier that month, Graham had also begun to stay behind, telling Batt it was to catch up on paperwork and because his bus didn't arrive until 7:30pm. Batt would then offer to give him a lift home to Hemel

Hempstead. The only other person around at that time was May Bartlett on her cleaning duties. During the last half an hour, the two men would have coffee together and chat. Batt remembered one conversation in particular:

> He said to me something on the lines of that you could obtain this liquid and introduce it into their drink and by gradually increasing the dose it would cause a heart attack and that it would cause death. He further said that the death would seem normal and any ordinary doctor would diagnose natural causes and murder would never be suspected. I'm not sure whether he said this liquid was colourless or odourless, but the person taking it would never notice it. I remember particularly saying to him, 'You rotten bastard.' I said this more or less meaning how would he think of such a thing. I remember him gesturing with his hands and saying, 'You can read it in the books' or something like that.

Usually Batt made the coffee but, to his surprise, on Friday, 15 October, it was Graham who did it, both during the day and later in the evening when they shared their last drink together. Batt tended to make coffee for them around 6:30pm, but Graham brewed up just before 6pm. Norman Smart was on his security rounds when he spotted Graham in the small kitchen of the canteen with the tea trolley at his side. The kitchen was normally out of bounds except for the women who worked there; Norman asked him what he was doing, to which Graham replied that he was making coffee for himself and Jethro, and did Norman want one too? As Norman shook his head, Graham nodded at a picture on the wall, which showed a handsome vintage motor, much like the green racing car in the 1953 film *Genevieve*. 'Isn't that a fascinating picture up there, Norman?' he said. The older man glanced at the picture and agreed, then left Graham alone.

Batt took the cup from Graham when he returned. He had felt 'queasy' during the day and had a metallic taste in his mouth, which he described as a 'horribly bitter tang', much like the aftertaste of a filling at the dentist's. He recalled: 'I took one sip of the coffee, say just one mouthful. There was something about it, I don't know whether it was too strong or what, I remember remarking to him about it and he jokingly said, 'What, do you think I'm trying to poison you?' Within about 20 minutes I had to go outside. I wanted to vomit, but I couldn't. I tried to make myself sick, but I just couldn't. I think I mentioned something to him about feeling dodgy.'

At 7pm, they left the factory together in Batt's car. The laboratory worker felt 'bilious' all evening, with stomach pains 'just in the area of the navel' and ate a light meal. He slept well, nonetheless, but when he woke up early the next morning to take his daughter to her ballet lesson, his legs had begun to ache all over. In the afternoon he felt 'shattered' and when he joined his father in the pub, as he always did at the weekend, he could only manage one pint instead of his usual four. On Sunday, the pain in his legs was still present and he had stomach ache 'but not really severe'. He decided to walk the two-thirds of a mile to the White House pub, hoping that might help get his legs working properly again and to give himself an appetite, but he found he could only drink a couple of small beers and a tiny amount of food. In the evening, he couldn't face either food or drink.

David Tilson had similar problems that weekend. On Saturday night, he felt better than he had for a few days and went to a party where he had a few drinks and arrived home around 4am the following morning. On Sunday afternoon, he suddenly found that his legs began to stiffen, particularly around the ankles and knee joints, and his toes were still partially numb from the previous Saturday. When he woke up on Monday morning, he had chest and stomach pains and a sore throat. He managed to get an almost immediate appointment with his doctor, who told him he had a throat infection and was generally a bit run down. Dr Donald Richardson recalled his patient 'complaining of a generalised aching and pains in the neck, a state of diarrhoea was also complained of. At this stage I gave a routine examination and found an inflamed throat and slightly enlarged neck glands.' He prescribed penicillin, but Tilson was unable to sleep that night because of the pain.

Jethro Batt also visited his doctor that morning. He explained to Dr Oswald Ross that he had discomfort in his stomach, distention and wind. The doctor gave him a prescription for a medicine to ease his flatulence and Batt headed in to work, where he remained until 7pm as usual, even though he felt distinctly uncomfortable and had pains in his legs, especially when he stood up or sat down. On the journey home that evening, Graham questioned his friend about his symptoms and offered some advice before saying goodnight.

In the back bedroom of 27 Maynard Road that

night, Graham retrieved his diary from beneath the bed and reached for a pen:

October 18th. Several new developments. D's symptoms have considerably worsened over the weekend. The paraethesia [*sic*] and anaesthesia now render it difficult for him to walk at all, and apparently this morning he was unable to walk up the stairs. He was not at work of course, but telephoned in to explain his absence. Later in the morning he called back to notify P that his doctor now diagnosed a 'glandular complaint'. How much further the illness will progress is difficult to say at this stage. A second development, and one which I now regret, is that J has been afflicted. The administration was Friday night and, as only part (approximately one third) of the dose was ingested it is difficult to say how severe the resultant illness will be. The symptoms have been slower to manifest themselves than in the case of D but have been gradually appearing during the afternoon. J complains of an insidiously spreading muscular ache, accompanied by stomach pains and flatulence. The latter symptoms, however, are probably due to a mild stomach germ which seems to be currently doing the rounds.

He added: 'I have a touch of it myself.'

16

YONDER SOFT PHIAL

The mysterious spate of illnesses at Hadlands had everyone talking by mid-October. Those who were already suffering found themselves rapidly getting worse, while others also began to fall sick. David Tilson recalled struggling to get out of bed on Tuesday, 19 October, because the pain was virtually unbearable. He forced himself in to work but deteriorated further while there: 'My legs began to pain me a lot more and my concentration was going. I still had this constant pain in the stomach which later that day seemed to spread to my chest, quite shallow.' He vomited twice that night, despite only drinking water all day, bringing up bile and then retching to the point of exhaustion.

Tilson visited his GP the following morning. Dr Richardson found him 'a good deal worse. A weakness of the legs and vomiting were the general symptoms. I again examined him and found that the muscles of the legs were tender and the attempts of moving the legs were painful, although there was no joint stiffness present. The tendon reflexes were brisker than normal. There was no other neurological disturbance. In view of his poor condition, I admitted him to St Albans City Hospital with a provisional diagnosis of peripheral neuritis.'

Tilson was examined by Dr Ann Penny and later senior consultant physician Dr Edward Cowen, who listened as he described feeling numb in his feet and hands, aches in his legs, pins and needles in his extremities, loss of appetite, headache, abdominal pain, nausea, vomiting and diarrhoea. 'The diagnosis on examination was far from clear,' Dr Cowan admitted. 'He seemed to have joint trouble plus or minus peripheral neuritis and the remarkable feature was the weakness in his legs. He received treatment for relief of pain.' Despite years of training and experience with patients, none of the medical staff realised that Tilson displayed many of the symptoms of thallium poisoning.

On the day that Tilson was admitted to hospital, Jethro Batt had risen from bed feeling that his health too had deteriorated. Like Tilson, he was determined to go into work despite the pain: 'All through the day the pains were very bad, even walking was murder and I felt pretty miserable.' Batt valiantly worked his normal hours, sharing a last cup of coffee with Graham before driving them both home. Batt retired for bed almost immediately without any food: 'My appetite had gone again.' Diana Smart was also ill that day. Her husband Norman had taken poorly two days before and was off sick until 26 October. 'As he was getting better, I was getting worse,' she remembered. She was fine until the afternoon coffee break, when Graham collected the drinks for himself, Diana and Fred Biggs. 'I had to go home just after 4pm,' she recalled. 'I had been sick and vomited then again about 5:30pm. I again vomited — on and off I had this severe stomach pain which seemed to lapse after me vomiting.' She was then working entirely in the stores and WIP department, where her duties included keeping a detailed account of goods and equipment such as cameras and electrical components after Graham had received them into the store and Eric Baxter had inspected each item. She spent many hours alongside Graham and Fred, and always took her tea breaks with the two men. At lunchtime she usually headed home, since she lived nearby, but on one occasion before her husband fell ill, the couple shared a meal in the canteen with Graham and were amazed by the way he slathered salad cream over his fish and chips, adding pepper until the food appeared almost black.

Graham was the topic of a brief, quiet conversation Diana had with Fred Biggs that week. Mild-mannered Fred mentioned that he had tried to give Graham a bit of advice regarding his work, but it had fallen on deaf ears. He warned Diana that Graham might ask her for a loan. Red-faced, she replied that she had already let him borrow from her numerous times that summer. She did add that he always repaid her, but she was reluctant to lend him anymore because he seemed to spend it all in the pub. Every Friday lunchtime he would go for a drink and return fairly hyper, eager to chat between frequent trips to the toilet to empty his bladder. On one occasion she jocularly told him off for spending his wages behind a bar and gave him a little push on his tummy, saying that he was getting a beer belly. Graham took no offence. He grinned at her, then launched into a scientific list of all the ingredients he had ingested during the course of his afternoon drinking session. Diana found it hard to dislike him, however: he was always generous with his cigarettes, enquired after her health and looked after her on more than one occasion when she felt unwell. There was something peculiarly childlike about him;

257

she remembered that he was once very upset when he tried to collect his tea before everyone else and was told to wait his turn: 'I can still see him walking back into the stores with his two hands in his pockets, looking like a little kid out of school that has just been scolded. 'They won't give me my tea, Diana. May told me to go away and wait for it.' He almost looked as if he were about to cry.'

Although Graham was clearly ferociously intelligent, he could be inexplicably scatty and forgetful. Diana usually took no notice, but one afternoon when she wasn't feeling well, he irritated her by wandering about the stores chatting to everyone instead of getting on with his work. She snapped at him for it and he gave her a strange, glass-eyed glare in return. She remembered the incident because after their tea break that same day, she felt deeply nauseous: 'I was sick three times from then until I went to bed that night. This was accompanied by pains in the pit of the tummy. On that day I had had my normal drink of coffee at 11am and 3pm. This coffee I had with Graham Young and Fred Biggs in the WIP stores. Young as usual got the coffee for us from May Bartlett. He would either go outside and stand by the trolley in the corridor or collect it from her at the stores hatch.'

While Tilson remained in hospital, both Norman Smart and Jethro Batt were too ill to go into work. Batt visited his doctor on Thursday, 21 October, severely depleted by the pain, which had begun to spread, in addition to suffering backache and numbness in his toes. Dr Oswald Ross could find little wrong with him. He prescribed Calpol as pain relief and signed Batt off work for several days. Returning home, Batt headed straight to bed, where his sufferings only increased. 'I started to get these very bad hallucinations,' he recalled. 'I know I had them five nights prior to being admitted to hospital. These were so bad I'd have killed myself if I could.' His wife was terrified, feeling that she was losing her husband to 'some kind of mysterious madness'. Searching for a means of explaining the pain, Batt stated: 'I was beginning to get the feeling that someone had put on the old duelling glove — the metal glove — and had got inside my ribs and were grabbing hold of what was inside and squeezing and twisting it.' Batt's wife remembered with a shudder: 'That's when you asked me for a gun, isn't it? He got to the point of asking for a gun to shoot himself. He was in that [much] agony.' He admitted:

I don't remember much about the worst three days. But my wife does. She had a terrible time keeping me alive … If there had been a weapon beside the bed, a gun or knife, I would have killed myself. The pain was terrible, but that wasn't the reason. The depressing effect the poison gave me was dreadful. And all the time I was in agony. The soles of my feet were killing me. I used to roll around the house and throw things. I was desperate with the pain. I banged my head against the kitchen wall several times, really hard, with frustration. My wife had a rough time. When my hair started falling out and things happened to my skin and fingernails, I thought, 'What's going on? I'm falling apart.'

On the day that Batt visited his doctor, Diana too felt progressively worse and left work early, after her second cup of coffee. She had hesitated before picking up her green china mug, sniffing at it. Graham looked at her: 'What's the matter?' She asked him whether it was her coffee or his tea. 'It's all right,' he said, 'It's your coffee.' But it was too bitter for her and she left half of it in the mug before heading home to be repeatedly sick.

That evening, Graham picked up his diary and recorded:

D's condition continues to deteriorate. He was admitted to hospital this morning with paralysis of the legs. The lower peripheral neuritis is now complete. What other nerves, at present inflamed, will become subject to major disfunction is not possible to estimate at present. There is little danger to life, barring unforeseen complications. I may have to put the plan propounded in my entry for October 12th. It will be rather more difficult, however, because he is in St Albans City Hospital — somewhat impossible to me.

J has also worsened. His symptoms have developed more slowly but he is now experiencing severe pains in the feet and legs, causing difficulty in walking, and further pains in the stomach, back and chest. I feel rather ashamed of my action in harming Jeff [Blatt]. I think he's a really nice fellow and the nearest thing to a friend that I have at Hadlands. I hope, though I have no faith in it, that he will soon recover.

D [Diana Smart] irritated me intensely yesterday, so I packed her off home with an attack of sickness. I only gave her sufficient to shake her up, though I now regret I didn't give her a larger dose capable of laying her up for a few days. Needless to say the drug in question [antimony] is different in nature (though not in toxicity) from that used in the cases of D and J.

I still am not completely free of the risk of detection. If I were to be detected, I should have to follow the maxim, 'Those who live by the sword, die by the sword.'

★ ★ ★

While her husband remained at home, incapacitated by his illness, Diana struggled into work on Friday, 22 October. She felt obliged to make sure the store was clean and tidy before a new employee started the following week and told herself that she would be able to rest over the weekend. She went about her duties that morning without too much difficulty, but the afternoon tea break saw her feeling 'really ill and much worse'. She had been aware of pains in both legs above the knees; these increased in severity during the course of the day. Unable to finish her coffee, she then dashed to the bathroom: 'When I came back from the toilet to the stores, Fred Biggs remarked how awful I looked and when I was talking to Fred, Graham came up from the bottom of the stores and said, 'Are you not well, Di?' I said, 'I feel bloody awful. I feel as if I want to get some air.''

Diana walked unsteadily to the end of the stores, then leaned against the rolls of brown paper there, putting her head in her arms. Graham fetched her a paper cup of cold water and propped a chair against the back door, which was open. 'Sit here for a while,' he instructed. Diana did as she was told. He put one

261

hand on her shoulder and passed her the cup. 'Yes, you do look rough,' he said. She nodded miserably, 'I think I must have the flu coming.'

After quarter of an hour she could bear it no longer and informed Geoffrey Foster that she was going home. She recalled:

> I only live about 300 yards from the firm, but I felt as if I wasn't going to make it. I really felt rotten. I staggered in the back door, threw my bag down. I still had my coat on and I made a rush for the toilet, which is just inside the back door. I was violently sick and at the time had severe diarrhoea — I noticed that when I started the diarrhoea the pain in my stomach got really worse. I noticed the pain spread right up my stomach to under the armpits. I was in there at first for about 10 minutes — I was doubled up on the floor, I was trying to be sick in the toilet and at the same time I had violent diarrhoea — I didn't know which end of me to concentrate on.

Her sons returned home from school to find their mother weeping and groaning on her way to the bedroom. Alarmed, they ran together to Hadlands and found May Bartlett, telling her that their mother was seriously unwell. In the meantime, Diana had rushed back into the bathroom, where she collapsed on the floor with her head on the porcelain rim of the toilet before she had to get up quickly: 'I cleaned myself up a bit and then went and got a bucket from the kitchen and returned to the toilet. I was in there when May Bartlett came in. My husband in the meantime had realised I was home. He came to the toilet and he and May wondered what to do. Norman rang for the doctor, Dr Anderson, but he did not attend and he instructed I be kept on fluids as I had the 'Bovingdon Bug'.'

Diana spent the evening sitting either in or near to the toilet, making frequent trips as the 'Bovingdon Bug' took hold. Feeling as if her entire body were drained, she retired to bed that night at 10pm, but had to get up twice again to visit the bathroom. The following morning, one of her work colleagues visited to check up on her. Throughout the day, Diana remained nauseous and suffered attacks of diarrhoea. Each time a new bout began, she would be assailed by a stabbing sensation in her lower abdomen, similar to labour pains in their severity. She managed to make it to the village pharmacy, where Mr Jenkins, the chemist, sold her a mixture of kaolin and morphine, which she was unable to keep down.

In Harlow, Jethro Batt had returned to the surgery, where he was seen by Dr Merton Long, who found him to be suffering from abdominal pain, distension and wind. He gave him a repeat prescription for a medicine to stop the discomfort caused by the flatulence, and Batt headed home, wondering how much longer he would be able to manage his symptoms.

While his victims were in agony, Graham took a bus down to Sheerness to visit his family on Saturday, 23 October. 'He arrived at 6pm on that day,' Win recalled. 'His father's birthday was on Monday 25th October 1971 and he brought him down a present. I went with my husband and Graham to the Victoria Working Men's Club. I can remember Graham bringing us a drink on a tray. He went downstairs to the bar for us. I had a lemon and lime. He brought my husband a glass of Courage light ale and he had a pint of beer.' The weekend passed pleasantly, but on Monday morning Jack Jouvenat found himself feeling distinctly off colour, light-headed and nauseous. He was unable to eat that day, but by evening he had recovered.

Graham was not thought to be responsible for his uncle's brief illness, but there was no doubt his colleagues were suffering the effects of his obsession with poison. When he arrived at work on Monday morning, he found both Diana and Batt absent, but Norman Smart was once more present and reassured those who asked that his wife was starting to feel better after a distinctly horrible weekend. Graham asked secretary Mary Berrow and his workmate Peter Buck if there was any news on Tilson's condition. They both told him what little they knew from Mrs Tilson, but Buck was surprised when Graham remarked, 'I understand he's losing his hair.' The alopecia was one element of Tilson's illness that had not been mentioned generally at Hadlands. Buck replied with a puzzled frown, 'Apparently so.'

On Tuesday, 26 October, while Diana, Tilson and Batt all remained absent from the store, Fred Biggs fell ill. Annie Biggs was with her husband and Graham for most of that day, but lost sight of her husband for some time around 5pm, when another colleague informed her that Fred was in the toilet, feeling very poorly. 'He was sick and had diarrhoea and pain in his tummy,' Annie recalled. 'Fred went straight to bed as soon as we arrived home. I did not disturb him and heard no more from him until about 9pm when he came out of the bedroom and sat and watched television. He told me that he had slept. I asked him how he

264

was and he said, 'All right now.' He refused anything to eat or drink.' Fred slept well that night but visited his doctor the following morning. 'He complained of headache and tingling in his fingers,' Dr Robert Nevill confirmed. 'On examination at this time I found nothing abnormal. He appeared to be suffering from a virus infection. He was extremely worried about his condition. I felt that these symptoms could be due to anxiety. I prescribed Valium tablets.'

Jethro Batt also consulted his doctor, who ordered a blood test and an X-ray of his abdomen. Diana Smart had recovered sufficiently to return to work on Wednesday, 27 October. She continued to suffer intermittent pains in her legs and a dull headache, but other than that, was quite well. 'Graham asked me how I was,' she recalled. 'I told him that I'd had this diarrhoea and sickness all the weekend. He showed interest in this and kept asking me questions about my ailments and seemed rather surprised to think it had lasted so long and questioned to what extent the pain was.'

'Haven't you got any idea what it can be?' he asked.

She shook her head, 'No, but if it's the 'Bovingdon Bug' it's a bugger. I don't want it again. I thought I was going to die.'

He made a joke about the possibility of losing her hair. She took it in good part, responding, 'It wouldn't bloody worry me so long as I don't get the pain I had over the weekend. I can always get a wig, can't I?'

Graham laughed, 'Yes, I suppose you could. It wouldn't worry you then?'

'Not really,' she said, 'It seems to affect the older ones worse than the younger ones.'

Graham put his head on one side, as if considering

her remark. 'David Tilson's only 21, isn't he?'

Diana murmured that he was right, then left to get on with her work. Later that day, while they were discussing the various ailments going around the place, she teased him in semi-seriousness, 'I reckon you are the germ carrier.'

Graham retorted, 'So could you be if it came to that, but then if it's the 'Bovingdon Bug', I don't live in Bovingdon.'

Diana recalled: 'He didn't seem to take any offence of whatever I said to him.' But she, like others, had begun to question what was happening at the Hadland stores. And suddenly, events took an even darker turn.

17

IS THAT POISON TOO?

The man whom Graham originally intended to poison before turning his attention to Jethro Batt, Wembley-based delivery driver John Durrant, arrived on the afternoon of Thursday, 28 October for the second of his twice-weekly visits to Hadlands. Since Bob Egle's death, Durrant had dealt with Graham, although he could not recall ever asking or being told his name. He found him 'rather interesting to talk to — he appeared to be quite a knowledgeable person'. Delivering the order from his employers, Ryman's stationers in Watford, Durrant would take the boxes into the stores where Graham checked them in and signed the delivery sheet. If Durrant's arrival coincided with the Hadlands' tea break, then he would have a brew and a biscuit himself.

On this particular Thursday, Durrant accepted a cup of tea from Graham and began telling him of an incident that had occurred at home. He recalled: 'My wife put some cleaning agent down the toilet. This stuff didn't work very well so she immediately put a different one down and a gas was given off which nearly knocked her and myself out. The storekeeper then started talking about this and asked me if it was some form of salts she had been using, because if so, some of them were toxic. He intimated that he was interested in these sorts of things and that he made a study of them. I was lost by the conversation as he was using very technical terms, more like a laboratory technician.' Durrant finished his tea before he left, noticing that it had 'a tang to it, as if it was stewed'.

The following morning, Durrant woke up with 'a very bad headache. This started during the night, when I woke up with a sore head and a feeling of nausea. I took a couple of headache tablets and went back to bed, but I was unable to sleep as I still felt bad. My head was thumping, it hurt when I tried to turn it and I could not stand bright light.' On rising from his bed he felt 'a terrible aching sensation in my back, just below the left shoulder blade. It was so bad that I had to be helped to dress. This pain remained with me in a severe state for about two days and, all in, for about a week. I did not go to the doctor as I thought it was only a pulled muscle as there were no other symptoms with it.' He drove to work but the pain grew worse, and he was unable to concentrate. He returned home at 2pm and retired to bed. He remained there until the following afternoon. By Monday he was quite well again.

In the meantime, David Tilson had been discharged from hospital. Initially, he felt much improved but within 48 hours his condition began to deteriorate. Over the last weekend in October he had palpitations, difficulty breathing and sudden alopecia. Baffled and alarmed by his failing health, he called the local surgery, who dispatched Dr Richardson to his home. He found nothing noticeably wrong but advised bed rest and plenty of fluids. He was visited again the following day by Dr Richardson's partner, Dr John Porterfield, who listened to Tilson's complaints of pains everywhere, a racing heartbeat and nausea. He prescribed vitamin tablets, recalling that Tilson was 'depressed

268

on account of his hair falling out. There were large patches of baldness on his head, and he complained of pins and needles in the left arm and leg. It was difficult to make a diagnosis with his neuritis. I thought the most likely cause was a viral infection and gave him Multi-Vite to stimulate the growth of his hair.'

On Saturday, 30 October, Fred and Annie Biggs worked overtime in the WIP section to finish the stocktaking while Graham, Geoffrey Foster and George Janouch were busy in the main store. Janouch suggested a cup of tea and Graham went off to make it for everyone, having already taken possession of the key to May Bartlett's tea room. After finishing work at midday that Saturday, Annie and Fred changed into smarter clothes at home and caught a train into London, where they watched a ballroom-dancing competition at Grosvenor House in Park Lane and ate a good meal before travelling home. It would be their last carefree outing together.

The following day was Halloween and Graham penned a ghoulishly callous passage in his diary that made it clear Fred Biggs was living on borrowed time:

There is much to communicate since my last entry. Di, who I afflicted with a mild attack of gastroenteritis on October 20th, was subject to a further indisposition on the 22nd, the results of which caused violent vomiting and diarrhoea throughout the weekend. I believe she is now suitably chastened.

D though he is now discharged from hospital is still unwell, so I do not expect to see him for some time. His illness was finally diagnosed as an 'unidentified virus'. J is still off work suffering from a similarly mysterious virus. It is unlikely that the symptoms will recede with any great rapidity. I shall not expect to see him for the next week/fortnight.

F [Fred Biggs] whom I grew to like, has been the most recent subject of my attentions. I have administered a fatal dose of the 'special' [thallium] compound to him and anticipate reports of his illness on Monday (1st Nov). He should die within the week: his death being attributed to A.I.P [acute intermittent porphyria]. I gave him three separate doses, each of about 5/6grs. The total absorbed should be about 15/16grs which constitutes a lethal dose.

There could be no misinterpreting Graham's words. He had laced Fred Biggs' tea with thallium the day before, and by Sunday morning, it had begun to take effect; the senior storeman asked his wife to call out Dr Newell without explaining precisely what ailed him. Annie was reluctant because it was Sunday; to her surprise, Fred himself made an appointment, then drove out to see his GP. He returned home with antibiotics, but still would not explain his symptoms to his wife, who 'understood that he was worried and thought it best not to question him as he was so obviously trying not to frighten me. That day Fred ate no breakfast and hardly touched his lunch. He took the tablets prescribed and slept quite well that night.'

Graham had been due to see Dr Udwin at the end of October. The psychiatrist was too preoccupied with other patients prior to a holiday in Barbados and decided to postpone his meeting with Graham until his return, 'previous interviews having been so satisfactory I was entirely confident that he was doing well'. But Graham's mental state shocked his sister when he visited her that evening. She later described it as both 'heart-rending and traumatic, recalling that she mistakenly thought he had been drinking when he arrived, due to seeming 'a bit wobbly'.' He sat down and tried to make conversation for quarter of an hour, then stood up abruptly and mumbled that he was leaving. Winifred asked him what was wrong and implored him to sit down and talk over a cup of tea.

To her alarm, Graham burst into tears, crying noisily, and was unable to speak. She did her best to comfort him, but it took a long time before he managed to blurt out something that came as 'an immense revelation' to her: 'He said he was lonely and could not 'get close to people'. I attempted to break his depression by suggesting a number of conventional things that might help — such as joining a night school. He shook his head. 'No,' he said, and I shall never forget his words. 'Nothing like that can help. You see, there's a terrible coldness inside me.''

★   ★   ★

David Tilson was re-admitted to hospital on the afternoon of Monday, 1 November 1971. He was seen by Dr Ann Penny again, who found him to be suffering from severe alopecia; gently touching his scalp resulted in clumps of hair coming away from his crown. He also had the same symptoms as before, but milder with a tachycardia (fast pulse) and slight temperature. 'Treatment was given as before plus sedation,' Dr Penny recalled. 'On both occasions that Mr Tilson was in hospital no definite diagnosis was made. However, we did think that it could be viral myalgia. During both admissions, on my instructions, samples of blood, urine and hair were obtained from Mr Tilson. These samples were later handed to the police.' Jethro Batt also remained very ill. His doctor visited him at home, where his symptoms now included constipation. Dr Long prescribed him a laxative and told him that the results of his blood tests suggested a virus infection. No abnormality was revealed from the X-ray.

Graham recorded the few details he had managed to glean regarding the sufferings of Tilson and Batt:

November 1st. Some new developments: D has relapsed and has been re-admitted to hospital. A fresh, and to me, disturbing symptom has appeared. He has commenced to lose hair which, though at present only slight, is likely to progress to alopecia totalis. This may be attributed to a viral/metabolic cause, and probably will be, but it is remotely possible that one of the attendant physicians may be sufficiently familiar with the symptoms and signs of my compound that he will gain a clue of the causal factor involved. It is unlikely that excretion is still taking place as the dosage was small and over weeks have elapsed since ingestion, but I must keep myself closely informed through P [Peter Buck] and M [Mary Berrow] in order to take appropriate action if necessary.

J is apparently suffering from quite pronounced muscular weakness and finds his legs still carry him only a short way before loss of power occurs.

272

As yet he has not developed alopecia but doubtless it will occur. In his case suspicion of poison would be especially dangerous. Luckily experience of the drug is very limited in this country. Its use is strictly controlled and only a handful of doctors would have come into contact with it.

I can, as yet, report little of F. He was not at work today, and his wife telephoned to say that he had caught a 'bug' and that she was taking him to the doctor. The onset of symptoms was apparently quite sudden and seems to have occurred on Sunday when his absence from the bar was noted at the Club. As the dosage was divided into three separate quantities, spanning a period of 24 hours, the onset was likely to have been less dramatic but a quite sudden deterioration is to be expected leading to paralysis, organic brain disease and death within a week. I shall be interested to see what transpires tomorrow.

The frighteningly unemotional tone of Graham's diaries contrasted sharply with the reality of Fred's illness. He felt too ill to rise other than when he needed the toilet: after telling his wife that the ends of his toes hurt, he admitted he had pains in his chest, which was why he had wanted to consult the doctor the previous Sunday. By the morning of Tuesday, 2 November 1971, his feet were so painful that even the weight of the bedclothes caused him to writhe in agony. A neighbour called in at 10pm when she had finished her shift at a local hospital; she made a cradle to keep the blankets off Fred's legs and told Annie to call Dr Newell first thing the following morning. Annie slept in a spare bedroom in the hope that they would both be able to sleep better, but her husband was ill during the night and she kept checking in on him.

Annie rang the surgery shortly after 9am Dr Newell called in twice to check on her husband and during his second visit, at 7pm, he told her that Fred would be admitted to hospital the following morning. 'By this time, Fred's condition seemed to have deteriorated,' Annie recalled. 'He still only told me of pain in his feet, but he was quite unable to stand and he did not want anything to eat. He slept very fitfully that night.'

Graham updated his diary that evening. His entry reveals that he was beginning to fear discovery and that he had his own drastic plan if that came to pass:

November 3rd. Disturbing events. Apparently D's hair loss was almost total and the hospital authorities advanced the view that D's illness may be due 'to some kind of poisoning'. This is a very dangerous path for them to explore. Today, H spoke to D's mother and told me that the doctors are advancing all sorts of wild theories but they still seem to believe that the illness is a virus-based infection. I naturally hope that this is correct. They are running a fresh series of tests and the inescapable conclusion is that they will test for poison, possibly the compound, if only to exclude the possibility of a toxic cause. Whether or not their tests will prove negative depends upon a number of factors. 1. The skill and expertise of the analyst. 2. The quantity initially ingested. 3. The rate of excretion. If only a small quantity was ingested and I am sure that it could not have exceeded five grains, then it may have

274

been completely excreted by now. Excretion would have been going on for over three weeks and therefore may, by now, have ceased. If not, only a small quantity will be present in the urine, but even then by spectroscopy this could be detected. By chemical analysis it would quite possibly escape detection. The situation is fraught with danger and uncertainty and I must watch the situation extremely closely. If it seems inevitable that I shall be detected, then I shall have to destroy myself. There is no alternative.

F is now better. Apparently his symptoms are, at present, principally gastro-intestinal. This should extend to include neurological symptoms within a very short time now. Such symptoms normally develop within four or five days from the onset of gastro-enteric upset. His doctor apparently believes that the illness is identical to an outbreak of vomiting and diarrhoea which is presently sweeping the area. The events of the next few days will prove decisive. They will point either to my triumphal continuation of life or my destruction by my own hand.

★ ★ ★

Fred's condition deteriorated rapidly overnight. 'He seemed so ill that he did not want to talk to me,' his wife recalled. Dr Newell called round early that morning and noted a definite sensory loss and a paucity of reflexes in his legs and feet. The ambulance arrived shortly before midday. Annie accompanied her husband to Hemel Hempstead general hospital, where he was admitted to the Rutherford ward. Dr Anne

275

Solomon was on duty and noted a variety of symptoms: dry, scaly skin over his face and shoulders, a flushed complexion, a blue tinge to his nose, a dry, furred tongue, reduced strength in his right arm and loss of sensation in all limbs. Annie stayed at her husband's bedside until he was made comfortable, then returned home alone.

David Tilson was still in hospital, emaciated and 'looking like a three-quarters-plucked chicken' as Dr Cowan described him. The pattern of hair loss was 'very unusual and significant', prompting the doctors to 'think of heavy metals and the possibility of thallium poisoning'. It was the first time anyone in authority had brought up poisoning, but there were other potential causes to be considered, including the home-brewed wine made by Tilson's mother, but since she and everyone else who had tried it was fine, that too was ruled out. Tilson's colleague, Jethro Batt, was also suffering and his symptoms left him unable to sleep at all. His doctor prescribed a mild sedative and arranged for him to be seen as an outpatient at Harlow hospital.

'The situation is still very undecided,' Graham wrote in his diary on 4 November 1971.

The latest report on D is that he is progressing and once again able to walk. The authorities are still uncertain of the cause of his illness. Apparently, they are not sure that it is poisoning, still half-inclined towards the virus theory. I imagine they will have sent specimens to the path lab for analysis, so all depends upon the results of those tests. A negative finding will re-confirm them in their viral diagnosis. A positive finding would prove disastrous to me. On that front the situation remains dangerous and uncertain.

On the other fronts the situation is more satisfactory. J is unchanged. He is confined to bed and his doctor has come to the conclusion that the illness is due to an unusual virus — in the absence of any positive results from the X-rays, blood tests, etc.

F was ill all over the weekend suffering from vomiting, abdominal pains, diarrhoea, etc. The initial phase has now passed and pains in the legs, etc., have developed. He apparently feels very unwell and his condition is said to be 'not responding as well as hoped. The doctor has said that the illness is due to a virus and that there is quite a lot going around! Is somebody setting up in competition to me?!!!

★ ★ ★

David Tilson was deemed sufficiently recovered to be discharged from hospital on Bonfire Night 1971. On the same day, his workmate Jethro Batt was admitted to Princess Alexandra hospital in Harlow, suffering from crippling pains in his stomach, chest and legs, numbness in the toes, loss of concentration, hallucinations and alopecia. He was examined by Dr Ahmed Abdulla, who recalled that the only abnormality they could find, other than problems with the patient's spine caused by childhood tuberculosis, was the loss of hair 'at a very fast rate'. Dr Abdulla stated that a formal diagnosis could not be made at that stage, but given Batt's symptoms, he and his colleagues discussed three possibilities: Guillain-Barré syndrome, porphyria and lead poisoning. They carried out a number of investigations including bloods, urine tests, electrocardiograms and X-rays. 'Following these tests, we were still puzzled by the diagnosis,' Dr Abdulla recalled, 'and requested the consultant neurologist on her opinion of the patient. She found no neurological abnormalities. In conclusion, when we had completed all our tests and investigations we could not put our finger on the diagnosis.'

In Bovingdon, an atmosphere of fear and suspicion hung over Hadlands like a fog. 'People were taking time off — one or two days, and then things started to get more serious,' Anthony Oldham confirmed. 'There was a particular occasion I remember when I was in one of the buildings looking out and somebody came rushing out of the doors and was violently ill on the grass outside which, looking back on it at the time, we thought, there's something very extraordinary going on there ...' The entire mood of the place had changed, twisting in on itself until everyone dreaded having to go to work. Oldham explains: 'We were a closed group, very trusting and understanding of each other, and suddenly you had this situation where somebody has been very, very malicious. Within a group like that it has a pretty profound effect on everybody. Horror, really, is the only way you can explain it.'

Hadlands' management were deeply concerned about the high rate of sickness among their employees and had to consider whether some form of industrial disease might be the cause. On the day Tilson left hospital and Batt was admitted, Geoffrey Foster telephoned Hertfordshire County Council, where he spoke to their health and divisional medical officer,

Dr Robert Stewart Hynd. Foster wanted to arrange a meeting in person to discuss what was happening at Hadlands but Dr Hynd was not available to visit until the following Friday. He informed Dr Dennis Trott, district medical officer for the HM Factory Inspectorate, about the situation. Trott arranged to look round the factory on Thursday, 11 November 1971.

Graham was making enquiries of his own. Mary Berrow, Hadlands' secretary remembered:

When Mr Biggs was taken ill again, members of the staff came in asking about him, Graham included, but he did not press for more information, but was just given the bare facts that Mr Biggs was in hospital and very ill. I can recall that one evening just as I was preparing to go home about 5:30pm. Graham came into my office and in his hand he had a copy of The Lancet. He handed this copy to me at the same time saying that he had been reading at the library the evening before about an illness in Japan and he thought it very interesting and similar to the illness which had taken place at the firm. I scanned the article very briefly, realised it was far too technical for me to understand and handed it back to him.

Unable to glean much from Mrs Berrow, Graham pressed Peter Buck for information and when he, too, divulged only the barest of facts, he decided to take the extraordinary step of telephoning Annie Biggs, who recalled:

On Friday, 5 November 1971 at about 9:30pm, I was at home with my youngest son and

279

daughter-in-law. I answered the telephone and a voice which I did not recognise said, 'This is Graham from John Hadland.' I realised then that he was the man in stores department who had been working with my husband.

Graham said, 'I have just heard this afternoon that your husband is in hospital. As I live near St Paul's, could I go and see him tomorrow?'

I said, 'I am afraid you can't, Graham, as he only wishes to see the family at the moment.' I did not tell him my husband was seriously ill.

Then he said, 'Well, could I go sometime next week?'

I said, 'Oh I don't know, I'll see you at work sometime.'

He said, 'All right, goodbye,' and that was the end of the conversation.

She was mildly surprised to hear from Graham and a little upset, especially because he sounded as though he had been drinking. To her relief, Graham made no further phone calls.

Graham visited his cousin Sandra and her two young boys the following afternoon. 'Just about as soon as he arrived, he said to me, 'We've got a funny virus at work.' I said, 'What is it?' He said, 'They don't know, but this chap had pains in his arms and legs. He went to the doctor. He told him he thought it was flu started. One or two days later he woke up and he had lost the use of his legs. He was taken into hospital for a fortnight and he was all right while he was in there. When he came out it started again. Then all his hair fell out. This seems to happen at fortnightly intervals. The chap had very long hair before it all fell

280

out.' I said, 'Do they know what is causing it?' He said, 'They think it is a virus of some sort.'' He seemed to be quite calm about the matter and spent the rest of his afternoon playing with the children.

On Monday, hospital patient Fred Biggs began vomiting and complaining of problems with his eyesight. Further tests were conducted and their results awaited. His vision became rapidly worse and, on 10 November, he was transferred to the neurological department of Whittington hospital in Highgate where he was placed under the care of Dr Michael Ashby, consultant neurologist and head of the department. 'Mr Biggs was very seriously ill with general weakness and difficulty in breathing and swallowing,' Dr Ashby recalled. 'No obvious cause was found. We suspected toxic effects from some infection or poisonous substance. We telephoned the Poisons Reference Dept at Guy's Hospital in an effort to relate his symptoms to any known poison but no satisfactory guidance could be given.'

Graham once more turned to his diary as a sounding board for his thoughts:

Nov 10th. Fresh developments, some good, some not so good. D has been discharged from hospital. Analysis apparently proved negative and the authorities returned to their virus diagnosis. They are awaiting the results of the last cultures started just prior to his discharge and after negative results will presumably lose interest, recovery having taken place.

To counter-balance this, both J and F are now in hospital. J has developed severe alopecia, and has lost weight. The hospital is re-checking all the tests previously made. As yet they do not suspect an unnatural cause.

F must have a phenomenal tolerance to the compound for he is still obstinately alive. I can gain little information of his condition although I gather he is not at all well. There does not seem, at present, to be a direct threat to life: the next week will be critical in this respect. If he survives the third week he will live. This would be inconvenient. The hospital authorities do not seem to suspect poisoning. The fact that they are taking lumbar punctures, etc., would indicate that they are looking for a viral cause. There is, therefore, little development on this front at the moment.

On Thursday, 11 November 1971, Dr Dennis Trott of the HM Factories Inspectorate visited Hadlands and launched a full investigation of the premises. Medical officer Dr Robert Stewart Hynd met with Geoffrey Foster the following day at Hadlands. They discussed the history of illness among the staff before Dr Hynd inspected the kitchen and dining facilities. It appears that Dr Trott had grown suspicious of Graham during his visit the day before; Dr Hynd later told detectives that it was 'at Dr Trott's suggestion' that he visited the stores with Foster and spoke to storeman Graham Young. Diana Smart was present; she sat with her back to the three men but listened to every word.

Graham stood by nonchalantly, while Dr Hynd asked him a number of questions, including about his living arrangements. Graham told the medical officer that he lived in digs at 29 Maynard Road, but couldn't remember the name of his landlord.

'Surely, after living there for four months you know

the name of your landlord?' Dr Hynd said.

'I don't know because I have all my meals out. I only sleep there.'

Dr Hynd remarked, 'You must find this rather inconvenient.'

Graham shrugged, 'I've got used to it and it doesn't worry me.'

'Are there any children in the household?'

'There are two young children.'

'Has anyone been ill in that house?'

'No.'

Dr Hynd paused, then said, 'I hope you don't mind me asking these questions, but I am just as concerned for your health and household contacts as I am for the other people in the firm and their contacts.'

Graham inclined his head slightly and murmured his understanding, after which Hynd and Foster moved away. Dr Hynd recalled: 'I informed Mr Foster that in view of my uncertainty of the true nature of the illnesses that I thought it would be wise to call an early conference of all the medical people involved. I felt that the diagnosis and the source of illnesses would be better established by a collective decision rather than by individual decisions. Arrangements were made for such a conference.'

That Friday saw a sharp decline in Fred Biggs' condition. When his wife visited the hospital she felt a stab of fear: 'His eyes were closed and he could hardly speak.' Shortly afterwards, Fred was taken to the respiratory unit where an endotracheal tube was inserted to aid his swallowing. Difficulties with his breathing continued and he was then transferred to the respiratory unit at the National hospital, Queen Square, London. He was semi-conscious when he arrived and scarcely able to respond to the simplest of requests. Annie remained with her husband, but he was unable to utter a single word and almost certainly had no idea that she was there. Within 24 hours he had developed a high temperature and signs of pneumonia, for which he was given intravenous antibiotics. Dr John Meadows, resident medical officer at the National hospital, recalled: 'The diagnosis at the time of his admission was polyneuritis (peripheral neuritis or polyneuropathy) and brain stem involvement. Normally there is no specific treatment for most forms of peripheral neuritis except for anti-inflammatory drugs . . . and the use of assisted respiration if the paralysis becomes severe. Both these were used in Mr Biggs' case. The question of a toxic cause (chemical) was raised but no such cause could be verified.'

While doctors battled to find out the cause of illness, Graham once more visited his cousin Sandra for the afternoon. He raised the subject of the virus again, adding, 'Another chap's got it now. I asked the secretary at work how this chap was. She said he had been taken into the Whittington hospital in London. Do you know it? It's a hospital for neurological diseases.' Barely giving her a moment to reply, Graham went on, 'I rang up the hospital to see how he was and they said they had no one of the name of Biggs there.'

'They probably didn't want to tell you because you're not family,' Sandra said.

Graham shook his head, 'No, they would have said that. They said they had no one of that name. It's strange, isn't it? The only thing I can think of is that he has gone on to an intensive care unit. That doesn't sound too good.'

Sandra told him she was sure his colleague would

make a good recovery, but her words were interrupted by Graham, who said with some excitement, 'I've had the doubtful pleasure of being introduced to the Medical Officer of Health of Hertfordshire at the factory. He's making enquiries about the virus.'

Sandra changed the subject and the rest of the afternoon passed much as it had the week before. But the conversation stuck in her mind, occurring as it had 'the Sunday before he was arrested'.

18

HOW DO YOU KNOW THAT YOU ARE NOT POISONED?

Graham told Diana Smart on Monday, 15 November that he had tried finding out how Fred Biggs was getting on at the Whittington hospital only to be informed that there was no patient of that name on the wards. Later that morning, Graham mentioned it again. 'He had been across to the offices,' Diana remembered, 'and said, 'That would account for it then, Di.' I said, 'What the bloody hell are you on about now?' He said, 'Fred has been moved to the Nervous Disease Hospital. I wonder why they've moved him there.'

'The conversation continued regarding Fred. He further said that he'd heard Fred couldn't speak but he could hear and it was at this stage he mentioned the similarity between the symptoms of Fred Biggs and Bob Egle. During all of that week the conversation was the same regarding Fred. Graham seemed to put himself out to find out [Fred's] condition.'

Diana found Graham something of an irritation that week. At one point he made up a bottle of smelling salts. 'I don't know what he put into it apart from cotton wool and ammonia,' she recalled. 'He was walking around the factory holding the plastic container, inviting people in the laboratory to have a sniff of the contents. I had a cautious sniff and thought it was quite strong.' No one else was interested in Graham's urging to see if they thought he had made the compound well; there were far too many troubling thoughts to occupy the minds of all Hadlands workers during that period.

On 16 November, Graham wrote in his diary:

I now have further information on F's condition, but first news from the other fronts. D is now well and bewigged. The latter may now be considered closed.

J is recovering although totally bald. They are still treating the case as one of natural disease, it would appear. This front is potentially dangerous, although quiet at present.

F is now seriously ill. He is now unconscious and has developed bulbar paralysis, necessitating a tracheotomy. He also has a direct inflammation of the optic nerve or, more likely, a netro-bulbar [optic] neuritis which has produced blindness. It is likely that he will die within a few days. It will be a merciful release for him as, if he should survive, he would be permanently impaired. Even if the blindness was reversible, organic brain disease would render him a husk. It is better that he should die. From my point of view his death would be a relief. It would remove one casualty from what is becoming a crowded field of battle. In the event of F's death, the last remaining problem will be J's, and providing that hurdle is passed, the battle will be over. Too many health authorities are becoming involved for me to press the matter further.

Graham's instincts were correct. The senior public health inspector for Hemel Hempstead Urban

District Council had visited Hadlands on Monday for the specific purpose of inspecting the kitchen and dining room together with the general sanitation of the factory. He found everything was in excellent order. On Wednesday, 17 November, a conference was held in Dr Hynd's office, at his instigation, to discuss possible causes of the illnesses and to determine whether there was any causal of association between the illnesses, and between the illnesses and the premises. Depending on the outcome of the meeting, preventative measures could then be put in place. Present at the conference were Dr Hynd himself; Dr Anne Solomon, who had treated Bob Egle and Fred Biggs; Dr Roger Gulin, who had looked after Bob Egle and David Tilson; Dr Trott, the district medical officer for HM Factory Inspectorate; Dr Malcolm Harrington, lecturer in occupational health at the London School of Hygiene & Tropical Medicine; and Dr Arthur Anderson, GP for Kings Langley and Bovingdon. The medicial registrar at the Whittington hospital was unable to attend. The group discussed at length the medical histories of Bob Egle, Jethro Batt, David Tilson and Fred Biggs while Dr Hynd made notes. Ultimately, they concluded that the problem was probably a virus of some description, and the matter was left open.

That evening, Graham visited his sister. He was garrulous, keen to talk about the public health inspector's visit and the various ailments afflicting his colleagues. He told Winifred that Fred Biggs was seriously ill with a virus, but that it was 'nothing to do' with the infection that had led to Bob Egle's death. Winifred asked if there were any chemicals at Hadlands that might be to blame.

'No, it's all electronic stuff up there,' Graham replied. 'All the health inspector did was to look at the drains and in the kitchen.'

Their conversation turned to other things but eventually Graham brought it back to the health inspector's visit. He tapped his fingertips on his lap, announcing, 'This chap in hospital is very ill — they think he is going blind.'

'That's awful,' said Winifred. 'Will he get his sight back?'

Graham shook his head slowly, 'No, I don't think so.' He paused, then said, 'I'm going down to Sheerness at the weekend. I'm worried about Uncle Jack. He's not been well either.'

'That's a good idea,' replied his sister. Shortly afterwards, Graham got to his feet and said goodbye.

It was the last time she saw him at liberty. Before going to sleep that night, Graham sat on his bed and penned what was to be the final entry in his diary:

Nov 17th. I am most annoyed. The latest news from the hospital is that they 'think F is beginning to respond to treatment'. Of course, they are not yet certain and a relapse is quite on the cards but is [it] is extremely annoying. He is surviving far too long for my peace of mind. It is imperative that he passes on before total alopecia sets in. There is little of interest other than this. I hope that my next entry records the fulfilment of my wishes or, at the very least, a sharp decline in F's condition.

His diary ended there, as abruptly as it had begun.

Graham's iniquitous wish was granted; Fred Biggs failed to recover from his illness. Doctors examining him in the intensive care unit found he was very slowly able to respond to a command while on a ventilator, but in all other aspects he remained locked inside his suffering, with the extensive scaling of his skin one of the most disturbing visible symptoms. To a non-professional it appeared that his entire system was gradually closing down.

Fred's family were with him on Thursday, 18 November. At 7am the following morning, the senior anaesthetist at the hospital, Alice Robinson, was called urgently to the Batten unit; Fred had suffered a cardiac arrest. 'We attempted to resuscitate him by external massage and by inflating his lungs with oxygen as well as injecting heart stimulants,' Ms Robinson recalled, 'but the electrical trace of his heart's action showed no activity and we were unable to produce any.' An hour later, the telephone rang in the Biggs' home. Annie picked up the receiver and was given the news she had been dreading: 'I was telephoned from the hospital and informed that my husband had died at 7am'

Before midday, a leaflet was put into circulation at Hadlands. Diana Smart was working at the far end of the store when she felt a hand on her shoulder. It was Graham. He passed her the leaflet, 'You'd better read this, Diana.' The leaflet informed all staff that their indispensable colleague Fred Biggs had passed away. She recalled:

It hit me like a ton of logs. I said, 'Christ, Graham, what are we going to do? It can't go on for ever, something will have to be done. Poor old Fred.'

He said, 'Well, I don't know about that, Di.' He went quiet for a while, then paced up and down with his hands in his pockets. He then rolled a cigarette and stood there saying, 'I wonder what went wrong. Poor old Fred shouldn't have died. He was taken off the respirator. I thought he was managing to hold his own. That's upset me, that has, I rather liked poor old Fred.'

He then walked off through to inspection. He then spoke to Eric Baxter. After this news Graham could not settle to do any work and did not do any work.

She later insisted to detectives: 'He seemed absolutely shocked at the news — and to a certain extent I think he was genuinely upset.'

The effect at Hadlands was immediate: already unsettled and suspicious about the spate of illnesses at the factory, staff now began handing in their notice and talking about an evil influence at work. Despite the health inspector having found no issues, the main topic of conversation other than their colleague's death was of the curse that was said to have attached itself to the place after the war. The management asked staff to assemble in the canteen that afternoon for an announcement. 'We were informed that Dr Anderson was coming to give us a talk about the illnesses, or as we thought, about the virus,' Diana remembered. 'Graham asked me what the doctor was like and if he would answer some questions. I told him Dr Anderson would answer any questions and that he was very nice because he was my personal doctor. He told me he had four or five questions he had to ask him.'

John Hadland, who had recently returned from a lengthy overseas business trip to find his company in chaos, called in Dr Arthur Anderson. At 2pm, the GP arrived on the premises and made his way to the canteen where the entire workforce had gathered. Looking out at a sea of worried faces, he began by saying that he wanted to reassure them that every safety precaution regarding health was being met. He then expressed the opinion that the illnesses could be due to a local virus with which they were all no doubt familiar: the so-called 'Bovingdon Bug'. This had been around for some time and certain people were more prone to it than others. He assured them that, with the full cooperation of the company management, extensive investigations were being made to formally identify the cause. Certain staff members — those who had contact with all areas, but particularly the kitchen and stores — would be asked to provide blood and stool samples to ascertain whether a particularly virulent strain of the bug had developed at the firm.

Dr Anderson spoke for almost a quarter of an hour. Geoffrey Foster then invited questions from the workforce. The first to pipe up was Graham Young.

'What are the similarities in symptoms of the two people who died and the two people who are ill?'

Dr Anderson replied that there were strong similarities between the two men who were ill but there was no definite link between those who had died and those who were ill.

Graham had another question: 'What is the significance of the alopecia suffered by Mr Batt and Mr Tilson?'

'In the case of Jethro Batt,' said Dr Anderson, 'this

may be due to a nervous condition or stress.'

Graham nodded, 'So complete alopecia due to psychosomatic stimulus then?'

Dr Anderson looked surprised. 'Well, yes. This could have been the cause as Mr Batt showed signs of extreme nervous strain.'

'And would you say,' Graham continued, to the consternation of his colleagues, 'that Mr Batt and Mr Tilson's symptoms are consistent with thallium poisoning?'

The GP drew in his breath. He later recalled:

I was completely taken aback. I had always considered the possibility that the illness and death were being caused by some form of heavy metal industrial poisoning but I was deliberately playing this possibility down in front of the staff because I didn't want to alarm them. But here was Graham Young shouting his mouth off about the subject. He completely lost me in what he was saying. I knew a little about the effects of thallium poisoning but, at that stage, I knew nothing of the neurological damage thallium could do. Young was talking about that type of damage. I tried to shut him up because I was trying to play down that sort of danger and he was going on and on. Eventually, I managed to get him silenced for a while. I didn't suspect him of causing the trouble when he mentioned thallium but I suspected it could be thallium poisoning if the factory used it in the manufacture of camera lenses. A quick check with the factory management dismissed any likelihood of industrial poisoning by thallium because none was ever stocked there.

John Hadland exchanged a perplexed glance with Geoffrey Foster. They brought the meeting to a close and everyone returned to their duties. Anderson spoke to Hadland and Foster about Graham. They explained that he had come to them after spending some time in psychiatric care. Foster added that he wasn't happy about Graham and described him as 'a creep'. The three men then headed for the store, where Dr Anderson sought out Graham, who showed him around the place. 'I was very curious to know a lot more about Mr Young,' Dr Anderson recalled. 'I prodded him on the subject and found he had a very extensive knowledge of one type of poisoning but in other medical subjects he knew very little. I began to think more and more about Young and I found his observations made on that day were rather peculiar. Considering the fact that he had been in a mental hospital it would have been all too easy for this man to be blamed. But as there was no positive evidence to tie him in, we decided to give him the benefit of the doubt.'

When the three men had gone, Graham approached Diana to ask whether she was going to have the tests Dr Anderson had mentioned. She said she would; she trusted Dr Anderson and wanted the authorities to find out what was going on. Graham spoke to other colleagues in the store too, telling them that one of the tests would involve a fairly painful procedure called a lumbar puncture. He kept referring to the meeting that afternoon. 'I got fed up with him and told him to get on with his work,' Diana recalled. 'He said to me, 'You'll have to come and help me.' He begged me, so I had to go and give him a hand. In the end I did all the work. He just paced up and down and talked incessantly.' Among his topics of conversation was a visit he intended to make to see his family in Sheerness over the approaching weekend. Diana prompted him to mention his plans to the management in case he was needed for testing.

He took her advice, calling on Geoffrey Foster in the office at about 4:15pm. He looked a little anxious as he asked, 'Can you tell me when I may be required to give samples as I am going away for the weekend?' Foster reassured him: 'That will be quite all right, Graham. I expect Dr Anderson will send his nurse up here first thing next week.' Graham then returned to the store where, despite having fussed about not getting all the packages out that afternoon, he continued to pace about aimlessly and gaze off into the distance. Diana was exasperated with him and went across to the offices herself, complaining to Foster that Graham was 'prancing up and down and lighting fags and chattering all the while'. She said she couldn't get anything productive out of him and he was getting on her nerves. Foster calmed her down; feelings were running high at the factory that day.

After leaving Hadlands, Dr Anderson had made his way to Dr Hynd's office, arriving there around 3pm. Dr Hynd had learned that morning of Fred Biggs' death and listened to Dr Anderson with a rising sense of alarm as he outlined the medically technical conversation that took place between himself and Graham Young. He decided to call Hadlands and speak to Graham himself. After briefly exchanging polite pleasantries, Dr Hynd asked, 'Mr Young, I understand that you were treated for your mental trouble by a Dr Udwin. Would you mind telling me who he is and where you saw him?'

There was a pause on the other end of the line. Then Graham replied, 'It is a long time since I have seen him.'

'But where did you see him?' asked Dr Hynd. 'Which mental hospital?'

There was a second pause, longer than the first. 'You must know,' Graham said eventually.

'It's very important that I speak to him,' Dr Hynd said. 'It's very important that I know from him the nature of your mental illness.'

'Wait until I close the door then,' Graham said. 'There are people outside.'

Dr Hynd listened. There was the faint sound of footsteps, a door being firmly shut and footsteps again. Then Graham returned to the phone and spoke quietly into the receiver.

'Broadmoor,' he said. 'I was in Broadmoor.'

19

THE ORIGINAL POISON BOY

For a moment there was silence at both ends of the telephone line. Then Graham said, 'I have given you this information because you say it is necessary.'

Dr Hynd recovered from his astonishment and reassured him, 'It will be treated in strict confidence between patient and doctor.' But in that instant, Graham must have known that he had just detonated a bomb in terms of his life and many others. Nonetheless, Diana Smart recalled that when he departed that afternoon at 5pm 'he seemed just his normal self and thanked me for doing his work. That was the last I saw of him.'

Unusually, Graham said nothing about the day's events to his sister when he visited that evening. He made no mention of Fred Biggs' death, Dr Anderson's visit to the factory or Dr Hynd's telephone queries. Instead, he chatted 'merrily' about his plans to enrol in Sussex University the following year, as though a normal future remained an option to him. But at the factory, John Hadland and Geoffrey Foster had discussed everything and concluded that the terrible deaths and illnesses of their staff all appeared to be linked to the young storeman with his strange manner and brilliant understanding of one area of medicine: toxicology.

At 6pm, John Hadland telephoned the police. Two hours later, he and Geoffrey Foster arrived at Hemel

Hempstead police station, where they were shown into a private room by Detective Chief Inspector John Kirkpatrick and Detective Sergeant Robert Livingstone. After listening to the two men's extraordinary story, DCI Kirkpatrick accompanied them back to Hadlands, where he examined the employment register. There was no doubt that the spate of illnesses had begun soon after Graham Young arrived to work at Hadlands. Kirkpatrick wired several employees' names, including that of Graham, to Scotland Yard for scrutiny.

The following morning, DCI Kirkpatrick tried to contact his superior, Detective Chief Superintendent Ronald Harvey, and was told that he was attending a luncheon with forensic science officers in London. Kirkpatrick managed to get a call put through to him and explained the situation at Hadlands. Harvey returned to his seat. On one side of him sat Keith Mant, a forensic pathologist who had worked with the celebrated Sir Keith Simpson, pioneer of forensic dentistry whose cases included the Acid Bath Murderer, Neville Heath, John Christie and the Kray twins. On the other side was Ian Holden, former director of the Aldermaston forensic laboratory who investigated the 1967 murders of two schoolgirls in the Berkshire village of Beenham. Harvey explained the conversation he had just had with DCI Kirkpatrick, telling them about the symptoms suffered by the two men who had died and others at the factory. Either Mant or Holden — Harvey was unable to remember which — remarked, 'Well, it looks as if you've got a case of thallium poisoning on your hands.' Harvey had never heard of such a thing and was keen to learn more before interviewing the suspect. Both forensic scientists recommended J J G Prick's *Thallium Poisoning*, the only book available on the subject at that time. They told him there would be a copy of it in the Royal Society of Medicine's library. Harvey left the luncheon early and telephoned the RSM but it was Saturday and they were closed; however, he did find out that their library books were never loaned to anyone outside of the society, including the police. Harvey then called the police forensic science laboratory in the hope that they might help. They informed him that there was one other copy of the book in the country — it was actually kept in their department in Cheshire. Harvey arranged to have their copy dispatched as a matter of urgency; it was conveyed by squad car down the motorway, blue lights blazing. Later, Harvey discovered there was a third copy of the book in existence and that was only 20 miles away, in the private Barbican home of Professor Francis Camps.

That same afternoon, Detective Constable Michael Grinsted, the divisional scenes-of-crime officer based at Hemel Hempstead, was dispatched to Hadlands, where he removed a number of items from the stores. These included packing material, sweets, an empty tobacco tin and a sample of water from the mains supply. DCI Kirkpatrick, meanwhile, was annoyed with Scotland Yard's response to the list of names he had given them from Hadlands employee list; told they had drawn a blank on everyone, including Graham Young, he insisted they ran another check on the storeman. Together with Detective Chief Superintendent Harvey, he then spoke to John Hadland and Geoffrey Foster at county police headquarters. Shortly after their meeting,

Kirkpatrick took a call from Scotland Yard, who had very different news to impart: namely, that the suspect had been released from Broadmoor six months earlier after spending nine years there for poisoning his father, sister and a schoolfriend. Kirkpatrick telexed Kent police and told them to arrest Graham on suspicion of murder.

A uniformed officer knocked on the purple door of 29 Maynard Road in late afternoon of Saturday 20 November. Mrs Saddiq was surprised to see him there and could only tell him that Graham had gone away for the weekend, but she didn't have an address for him. A short distance away, Detective Sergeant Kenneth Rees and his colleague Detective Sergeant Marsh, both of Kent constabulary, asked the same question of Winifred, who had been writing her Christmas cards when she heard a knock at the door. Her heart raced at the sight of the two officers and she was in such a state that she unintentionally gave them the wrong address in Sheerness, where she said her brother was staying for the weekend. In response to her question, the two men said obliquely that they needed to ask Graham a few questions about 'a disturbance' at Hadlands. Winifred closed the door and stood with her back to it, mind reeling as she grasped the implications of the detectives' search for her brother.

★ ★ ★

'Graham arrived at my home at 5pm,' Win Jouvenat recalled. 'We had had our tea, I cooked him his tea. While I was cooking, he was speaking to me. He said, 'We have had another tragedy at work. Another

300

fellow has died,' and I said, 'What did this one die with?' He said, 'Another obscure virus.' I said, 'That's strange, that's exactly what you told me about the other one.' He said, 'Yes, something similar.' That's all he said about it.' After their meal, Graham left for the Mechanics Arms pub on the High Street and Win herself went out at 6:45pm for a few hours. Unbeknown to them, detectives called at the neighbouring house looking for Graham and left without establishing that he was in fact staying next door.

In Hemel Hempstead, Detective Sergeant Robert Livingstone followed Mrs Saddiq upstairs to Graham's room at 29 Maynard Road, where he would spend the evening in case its usual occupant made an unexpected return. Over the course of two hours, he examined every inch of the small, fairly squalid bedroom and had plenty to impart when Detective Inspector John Ratcliff and Detective Constable Grinsted squeezed themselves into the room just before 11pm. While Livingstone headed back to the station, DI Ratcliff took three photographs of the room, which was as Livingstone had found it, and then sketched out a rough plan of its dimensions and furnishings: the single bed with its striped coverlet under the window, the narrow wardrobe, small table and chair, overflowing ashtray stand and two suitcases. He then started a systematic search, cataloguing every item while DC Grinsted packaged it all securely.

DI Ratcliff's inventory was incorporated into his witness statement and later presented in evidence. It reveals how Graham lived during the six months of what should have been a return to normality after Broadmoor, but which had warped into an unhappy, solitary and ultimately murderous existence with poison at its vortex:

Immediately behind the door was a table upon which was found an:

Avon perfume talc tin
Tincture of Aconite (Flemings) bottle
A poison bottle containing blue liquid, full
A poison bottle containing blue liquid 2/3 full
A poison bottle containing blue liquid almost empty
A bottle containing white crystals labelled poison 'oxalic acid'
A Woolworth's bottle top
A blue stained pipette
A corkscrew
A John Hadland biro
Ashtray with cigarette ends and hair, etc.

Underneath the table we found two empty pie cases.

In the pockets of a jacket hanging behind the door were found:
Young's driving licence
A piece of paper with I.R.A. Levin, etc., thereon
Letter from Sheerness.

In carrier bag no 1 I found:
1 empty bottle of ether, 500ml
1 empty bottle of ether, small size
Address St Albans and times on piece of paper
2 pay slips
2 empty chemist paper bags.

In carrier bag no 2 also near chair I found:
1 pair of cord jeans
1 empty ether bottle
Match box containing bottle cap and dead wasp
1 chemist bag.

A wastepaper bin was found behind the chair near the door in which was a part-written formula and fish and chip papers. A pair of grey trousers were on the chair, in the pockets of which were found a door and locker key and two paper tissues. A brown cord jacket was hanging over the back of the chair, in the top pocket was found a yellow phial containing a white powder, in the same pocket was found a rolled cigarette and a workman's club visitor's ticket. In the left side pocket was an ignition key, goods inward receipt, key ring, Yale key and small mortice, telephone number of F. Biggs on piece of paper. In the right pocket was a metal nail pusher. Also on the chair was a pair of black trousers. On the chair we also found a number of American and English newspapers among which was a drawing of a graveyard and poison, etc. There were three empty wine bottles on the floor in front of the wardrobe. Carrier bag no 3 also in front of the wardrobe contained only dirty washing. Another empty bottle of ether was found under the wardrobe. In a box under the wardrobe was found 6 biros, 2 keys, 1 fir cone, correspondence, chemist bag with script on, a plastic spoon stained with white powder and a skull signet ring also stained. A fly spray on the floor was not taken. A tube of TCP ointment was found under the wardrobe together with an empty bottle stained red, some more drawings on newspaper and an empty chemist bag.

In the bottom drawer of the wardrobe was found a large number of bottles and containers as follows:

Tin of nicotine dust
Bottle half full of formaldehyde solution
Plastic container, potassium ferrocyanide
Acetic acid in bottle
Carbon TC in bottle
Bottle of concentrated hydrochloric acid
Plastic container with lead acetate
Bottle of strong ammonia solution
Unmarked bottle containing liquid
Bottle of concentrate of sulphuric acid
Bottle of strong concentrate of sulphuric acid
Bottle with stopper with liquid
Plastic container with dark crystals
Plastic container with lead acetate
Empty phial with white top
Empty phial with A.H on top
Plastic lid containing white crystals
Book (*Malleus Maleficarum*)
Bottle with white powder with poison antimony.
Together with a quantity of dirty washing which was not taken. We then examined case 1 which was beside the table behind the door in which was found three books together with correspondence and clothing. In case 2 which was beside the head of the bed we found:
a Memorial Book in the name of Gwendoline

Molly Young, Golders Green crematorium
a formula on blue note paper
empty talc tin
pair of hooked tweezers
miscellaneous paper and correspondence
paper Jiffy bag full of white powder
envelope containing pink tablets
Collis Brown compound wrapper.

On the ashtray stand beside the bed we found:
A bottle 2/3 full of eucalyptus oil
A bottle of vitamin C tablets
Empty phial with white powder on sides
Plastic phial containing soaked cotton wool
Small battery.

In a cardboard box beside the bed we found an
empty bottle, hair cream and toiletry waste matter.

There was a battery and a piece of wire in a
paper bag beside the bed, miscellaneous papers
and an empty ether bottle colour blue.

Under the head of the bed was found another
ether bottle together with seven books among
which were:
Aid to Forensic Medicine
1914
When Evil Awakes
The Black Baroness.

Under the foot of the bed was found a loose-leaf
pad, *A Student and Officer's Case Book*, which
contained writing relative to this case.

From a jacket pocket hanging inside the wardrobe we found a letter, an empty container marked potassium bromide, and in the wardrobe with two empty ether bottles, and six empty wine bottle, one collected which had a corroded cap.

On the windowsill of the room was found the following:
A glass which had blue liquid and a spoon in
A small bottle containing blue liquid
A small bottle containing green liquid and a piece of plastic
A bottle half full with nitric acid
A small bottle with glycerine BP
A poison bottle with no label containing yellowish liquid
A small bottle labelled ether containing small amount of liquid with sediment
A small plastic phial with white powder
A goblet type of glass
7 batteries, 3 razor blades
2 polysterene [sic] containers
Wasp with pins in (placed in match box)
Empty aspirin tube
Colourless liquid from pewter pot.

All exhibits listed were removed to Hemel Hempstead police station. Detective Constable Grinsted collected the clothing later.

A separate inventory listed all the books found in Graham's room with brief descriptions of each title. It makes for interesting reading in itself and again reveals where Graham's obsessions lay:

The Accursed by Claude Seignolle — two 'diabolical' takes of French folk involving she-wolves, etc.

The Black Baroness by Dennis Wheatley — story of fictional secret agent in Second World War set in the time of Hitler's invasion of Norway.

1914 by James Cameron — story of a year in the life of Britain and Europe — considered the end of an era.

When Evil Wakes by August Derleth — an anthology of the Macabre.

The Leader by Gillian Freeman — horrifying reconstruction of how a new Hitler might arise.

The Last Leap and Other Stories of the Super-Mind by Daniel F Galouye — science fiction stories of going beyond the barriers of conscious thought.

The German Language Today by W E Collinson — patterns and historical background of the German language.

A Dictionary of Treatment by Sir William Whitla — treatments in medical and surgical practice.

Malleus Maleficarum with an Introduction by Dennis Wheatley — a book written by Dominican monks in 1486 dealing with the powers and practices of witches, the use of torture and methods of Pu.

Funny Ho Ho and Funny Fantastic by Denys Parsons — a book of his prints, oddities and absurdities from newspapers.

Funny Amusing and Funny Amazing by Denys Parsons — as above.

Only with a Bargepole by Joyce Porter — hilarious adventures of the world's most bungling spy.

Aids to Forensic Science

Here We Go Round the Mulberry Bush by Hunter Davies — a picture of the agonies and joys of the struggle of a provincial youth from boyhood to manhood.

I Am Legend by Richard Matheson — a story of vampires.

Lukan War by Michael Collins — fictional story of war on planets.

The Quiller Memorandum by Adam Hall — record of man's mission against a resurgence of Nazi organisation.

The Trojan Horse by Hammond Innes — story of an Austrian refugee from a Nazi concentration camp who brings with him the secret of a new diesel engine.

The Narrow Margin by Derek Wood — a definitive story of the Battle of Britain.

The Troubadour by Louis Vaczek — story of a French scoundrel.

Paths of Glory by Humphrey Cobb — a shocking story of an incident in World War One.

Both officers were laden with bags when they left Maynard's Road. Each item would be thoroughly forensically examined, but it was obvious to Ratcliff and Grinsted that in addition to the multiple toxic substances found, the notepad recovered from underneath the bed would be indispensable in establishing Graham's character, motivations — and guilt.

His personality was present in virtually everything that they collected, from the 'voodoo' wasp stuck through with pins to the subject matter of the books, and there were elements among it all that stood out to anyone with knowledge of his past, including the letters from Broadmoor, his macabre doodles, the memorial book for his stepmother Molly — his first victim — and the scribbled telephone number of Fred Biggs, his last.

★ ★ ★

Detectives Rees and Marsh returned to Winifred's home late that evening to inform her that Graham was not at the address she had provided. Winifred panicked, realising that she had told them her father lived at number 92 Alma Road when in fact it was 93. The two officers sent a message to that effect to Harvey, who instructed Kent police to try the correct property. The house was in darkness, however.

Eventually, the family returned home, with Graham the last to arrive from the pub, at 11:15pm. Fifteen minutes later, Rees and Marsh turned up. Win was in the kitchen, talking to her nephew: 'He said, 'I've been chatting up two old ladies at the Mechanics Arms.' The bell rang. My brother went to the door. I heard a voice say, 'Is Graham Young here? We are police officers.' Two men came in.'

The family's world was about to collapse — again.

Fred Young recalled: 'When Graham got the job at Hadlands, and we heard later that some of the people there were being struck down by a 'mystery bug' it didn't click at first with me. Even when Mr Egle the storeman died and Graham took over his job,

309

and then when Mr Biggs died, I tried not to face the ugly thought growing in my mind ...' But as soon as he opened the door that evening and saw two police officers standing there, reality hit. 'I stood aside,' Fred remembered, 'and pointed to the kitchen where Graham was making egg sandwiches for himself. I would not touch anything he had prepared. One of the policemen immediately strode through and clapped a pair of handcuffs on Graham, while the other officer began to read out some kind of charge. I couldn't take it all in. I felt numb, crushed.'

Detective Sergeant Kenneth Rees introduced himself and his colleague to Graham. They gazed curiously at the young man who calmly placed the butter knife next to the sandwiches he had just made. His clothing was smart: shirt and tie worn with dark trousers, while his hair was neatly swept back too, from the narrow face with its watchful, darting eyes.

Standing in the brightly lit kitchen, while Graham's frightened aunt, uncle and father looked on, Rees asked, 'Are you Graham Young, at present living at Hemel Hempstead?'

Graham returned the detective's steady gaze: 'Yes.'

'Do you work for a photography firm there?'

'Yes.'

Rees declared, 'I'm arresting you on suspicion of murder. I'll be taking you to Sheerness police station where you will be detained until the arrival of police officers from Hemel Hempstead.' Rees then recited the caution and waited for Graham's response. He gave an almost imperceptible shrug, 'All right.'

Marsh stepped forward with handcuffs. Graham held out his wrists. His aunt Win, shaking with distress, shouted, 'What have you done this time?'

'I don't know what they're on about,' Graham said calmly.

Win burst into tears and turned to her husband. Fred Young followed his son and the two officers out into the cold, dimly lit street where Detective Constable John Bibby of Sittingbourne police waited by the police car. Bibby opened the rear door. Graham ducked inside and slid along the back seat, where he was joined by Bibby.

Rees and Marsh returned to the house. Graham waited for his father to follow them, then turned to DC Bibby: 'What's this all about?'

'I'm sorry, I can't tell you.'

Graham nodded towards the house, 'The detective sergeant said I'm being arrested on suspicion of murder.'

'Did he tell you that you weren't obliged to say anything and that whatever you say may be given in evidence?'

'Yes.'

'Well, that still applies, you know.'

'All right,' said Graham, 'but I don't understand *why* I've been arrested.'

DC Bibby replied patiently, 'It's quite simple. You know what 'you've been arrested' means, you know what 'suspicious' means, and you know what 'murder' means. So what is there to understand?'

Graham's next question placed him firmly in the frame: 'Yes, but which one is it for?'

'You probably know more about it than I do,' said Bibby. 'I can tell you no more than you've already been told.'

Sounding slightly peeved, Graham insisted, 'I only want to know what I've been arrested for.'

The police officer said firmly, 'I don't know which one.'

Rees and Marsh reappeared in the doorway, followed by Fred Young. They had searched the room where Graham slept but found nothing of interest. Fred stood on the doorstep, watching as the two men climbed into the car. His sister and brother-in-law remained in the kitchen, too distraught to join him as the car set off quietly down the long terraced street towards the junction at the end. The right-hand indicator winked in the darkness, and a moment later the car disappeared. Fred recalled what he did next: 'I walked slowly upstairs to my bedroom, took out every photograph, tiny snapshot, letter and piece of paper that could remind me of him — even his birth certificate — and tore them in small pieces.'

20

IN THE PORCHES OF MY EARS

Graham was divested of his clothing soon after arrival at Sheerness police station. He removed his raincoat and jacket, shoes and socks, tie, shirt, vest, trousers and underpants reluctantly, handing them to DS Rees, who placed them all inside brown paper sacks for safekeeping. He was given a thick woollen blanket to wrap around himself before being led into a cell, where he would remain for approximately three hours.

DCI Kirkpatrick arrived from Hemel Hempstead shortly after 3am. Standing squarely in front of Graham, Kirkpatrick introduced himself and the two men at his side, 'I am Detective Chief Inspector Kirkpatrick and this is Sergeant Livingstone and Constable Lynch.' He cautioned Graham, adding, 'I am arresting you on suspicion of murder and you will be taken to Hemel Hempstead where further inquiries will be made.'

Still clad only in the blanket given to him by DS Rees, Graham was placed in the police car. Detective Sergeant Livingstone sat next to him, while Kirkpatrick sat in the front passenger seat with Lynch at the wheel. They had scarcely left the station before Graham leaned forward to speak to Kirkpatrick: 'Is it permitted to ask you one or two questions, Inspector?'

Kirkpatrick turned his head slightly to the right,

'Yes, if you wish.'

'What are the precise details of the charge against me?'

'It hasn't yet been decided that you will be charged,' Kirkpatrick replied. 'A great deal of work has still to be done.'

'Agreed,' Graham said, chirpily. 'I appreciate that in a case such as this there is a tremendous amount to do, but surely you must supply us details of the possible charge.'

'A case such as this? What do you mean by that?'

'We won't go into that now,' Graham admonished. 'Surely you are bound to tell me the name of the person I'm supposed to have murdered.'

Kirkpatrick told him, 'We're making inquiries concerning the death of your workmate, Frederick Biggs, who you know died on Friday morning.'

'Yes indeed, Inspector, but as far as I know he died of some kind of virus which appears to have affected a number of other people at Hadlands.'

'That was the doctor's opinion.'

'I presume it's only one man I'm accused of killing.'

'As I said, at the moment I am concerned only with Mr Biggs, but it is more than likely that you can also give me some details of the illness suffered by David Tilson and Mr Batt, and there is also the case of Mr Egle, but at the moment we are only concerned with Mr Biggs.'

Piously, Graham responded, 'I shall want more than that, Inspector. What am I supposed to have done?'

'You tell me what I think you have done.'

'Certainly not, Inspector,' Graham rebuked him. 'As you've told me, it's my entitlement to say nothing and I would much prefer to wait and see what

314

develops. Presuming for the moment I'm guilty of a crime, I remain innocent until you have proven otherwise.' He sat back in his seat and declared: 'No, I shall wait.'

The remainder of the long journey passed in silence. It was 5:50am on Sunday morning when the vehicle pulled into the car park of the modern, elongated police station on Combe Street, half a mile from Graham's digs. Livingstone took him through the building and left him in a detention cell for no more than half an hour. He then collected Graham again and led him into Kirkpatrick's office, where the chief inspector was waiting. Beside him sat Detective Chief Superintendent Harvey, who was reading Graham's diary.

As Livingstone left the room, DCI Kirkpatrick formally cautioned Graham again without introducing Harvey, who did not look up from the blue-backed book. Graham stared at the chief superintendent until Kirkpatrick said, 'As I told you on the journey back from Sheerness, we are making inquiries into the death of Mr Biggs.'

Graham removed his gaze from Harvey and looked at Kirkpatrick. 'You referred to *deaths* before — plural.'

'There's no doubt you'll be questioned concerning other matters,' the detective replied, 'but at the moment I want you to concentrate on Fred Biggs.'

Graham raised his chin slightly: 'I realised in the car that you were trying to avoid the subjects of Bob Egle, Dave and Jeff, but it was you who mentioned their names —'

'For the moment you're under arrest on suspicion of the murder of Fred Biggs,' Kirkpatrick cut in, but

315

then Graham interrupted, 'I maintain that the detective sergeant at Sheerness said murders plural. My uncle will be a witness.'

'He could not have said murders. I spoke to him on the telephone. In fact, I have a copy of the message here and I plainly told him that you were to be detained on suspicion of murder.'

Graham looked steadily at the detective, 'We will agree to differ.'

At this point, Harvey closed the foolscap pad and raised his head. 'I'm Detective Chief Superintendent Ronald Harvey. Mr Kirkpatrick has cautioned you and now I'll do the same.'

Graham replied, 'Yes, the inspector has shown that he's conversant with the judge's rules and I trust you are too.'

Harvey ignored his heavy sarcasm and recited the caution. Having flicked through the enormously technical Thallium Poisoning and then Graham's diary, he had plenty of questions. Not least about possible victims; Harvey had worked out six of those identified by initials in the diary, but was unable to decipher two others. Above all, he was keen to ensure that neither Batt nor Tilson, nor anyone else who was still suffering as a result of Graham's love of poison, paid the ultimate price.

Harvey gestured towards the notepad: 'This diary was taken from your room last night by my officers. Is it yours?'

Graham nodded, 'Yes.'

'I want you to look at every page and tell me if all of the writing is yours.'

Graham thumbed through the diary. 'Yes, I wrote it,' he said.

316

'The diary refers to people by an initial. Who are they?'

Graham shrugged, 'Figments of my imagination. I was preparing to write a fiction story and those are my notes.'

Harvey frowned, 'The initials seem to refer to actual people. They're not people with whom you worked?'

Graham sighed, 'Do I have to repeat myself? They're all imaginary.'

Harvey picked up the diary and thumbed through it himself. 'I think 'B' is probably Robert Egle and 'F' is Fred Biggs.' He glanced up at Graham. 'Both those men are dead. The others are people who've been ill, at least two of them seriously. Did you give these people poison?'

'Absolutely not.'

Harvey said, 'We've also taken various substances from your room. Some of them are marked 'poison'. Do they belong to you?'

'I expect so. I had poisons there but that doesn't mean I poisoned anybody.' Graham paused, then said impatiently, 'Look, Inspector — I'm sorry, Superintendent — you first have to identify the poisons with which you allege I poisoned these people, then you have to show the opportunity. If you say I did it, then how did I do it? Lastly comes motive. I would suggest you need all three, shall we say — means, opportunity, motive?'

A knock came at the door. It was Sergeant Livingstone; he asked Kirkpatrick if he could have a word. The two men left the room and Chief Superintendent Harvey continued questioning Graham.

'For the moment we will forget about the two dead men,' he said, 'and concern ourselves with the living.

317

Two of them are really very ill. I appeal to you to tell me if you've poisoned these people and what you've used. I need to tell the doctors how to treat them.'

Graham sat silently, gazing down at his hands where they clutched the blanket to his chest.

'Look,' said Harvey, 'Some of these people offered you friendship. They tried to help you, now you have the chance to help them.'

Graham looked up, 'As you say, these people are my friends, so where is the motive?' He shook his head vigorously, 'No, you are trying to trick me.'

'I'm not trying to trick you at all. It will take time to analyse the substances taken from your room. In the meantime, people will get worse and others might die.'

Graham glared at him, 'You're suggesting that I'm a monster, some sort of mass poisoner who just poisons people regardless. That is not so.' He sat determinedly upright. 'I've got nothing further to say.'

Harvey persisted, 'If you've done wrong, you can put some of it right by helping people who are sick. Now think of that.'

But Graham said nothing.

★ ★ ★

Later described by Harvey as 'icily polite', Graham subsequently told his barrister that his police interviews had been unduly affected by his having been stripped of his clothing and made to walk about in nothing but a blanket 'like a Sioux Indian'. He had felt 'oppressed' by the nature of his arrest and the fact that 'I hadn't had the opportunity to wash, shave, or comb my hair. My feet were filthy from tramping about the police station. Due to oversight or omission, I hadn't been fed. All these had a depressing influence upon me.'

Together with Graham's emotional state, which he described as 'shocked anxiety', this allegedly coloured what he told detectives, a matter raised by Sir Arthur Irvine QC at trial. 'He never complained to me,' was Harvey's response. 'The office was quite warm and we did get other clothing for him later in the day.' Sergeant Robert Livingstone went home to retrieve some of his son's clothing for Graham. The incident set up the classic good cop/bad cop routine, creating an environment in which Graham was predisposed to view Livingstone (and to some degree, Kirkpatrick) as approachable, while Harvey appeared tough and unrelenting.

Chief Inspector Kirkpatrick took over questioning Graham at 7:20am in his office, while Harvey was required elsewhere. Kirkpatrick began where Harvey had ended.

'As you know, Graham, two of your workmates have been seriously ill in hospital and one of them has not yet been discharged. We are very concerned about him and we need your help.'

Graham looked at him. 'You mean Jeff Batt. I know he's been very ill, Inspector.' He fell silent again and was still but for his fingertips, which tapped lightly on his lap. He met Kirkpatrick's steady gaze, 'I can't possibly tell you everything, but some things I will.' After a pause, his words tumbled out: 'I seemed to be a misfit when I was younger. Not like other children. I used to draw within myself. A loner. I read a lot and became obsessed with the macabre. Toxicology always fascinated me. My father had married again and I began to experiment.'

Kirkpatrick, however, was only concerned at that stage with the recent spate of poisonings. 'Tell me about Bob Egle, Dave Tilson, Jeff Batt and Fred Biggs.'

But Graham refused. 'I'm sorry, Inspector, that's as much as I'm prepared to say. You'll have to give me time, I'm not thinking clearly.' And with that, he would say no more.

* * *

While Graham was being interviewed, Detective Inspector John Ratcliff collected all the toxic substances, chemicals and containers found at 29 Maynard Road and conveyed them to an address in Pinner. This was the home of forensic scientist Nigel Fuller, who examined everything and read Graham's diary. The two men then discussed the case at length. Detective Constable Michael Grinsted conducted another search of Graham's room and took possession of several items of clothing. He then prised open the loft door in the ceiling above the bed and climbed into the attic, where he found one small bottle of tablets. He returned to Hemel Hempstead police station to seal and label everything.

Several witness statements were taken that day, including the testimonies of John Bell & Croyden chemist Albert Kearne and the ailing Jethro Batt. Graham's sister called at the police station. Clearly upset but very concerned about her brother, she asked to speak to whomever was in charge of Graham's arrest. DCS Harvey emerged from his office. He sent for a cup of tea, then sat Winifred down and told her, 'I'm so sorry, but it's about as bad as it can be. I can't pretend there's anything I can say to soften it. We think your brother has poisoned two people. Mr Biggs died in hospital on Friday and two other young men are seriously ill.' Winifred spent the rest of the day 'in a very bad way'.

At 3:45 on Sunday afternoon, Graham was brought back to Kirkpatrick's office. The Chief Inspector waited for him to take a seat, then after cautioning him said, 'I've heard that Batt's condition is deteriorating. He's had hallucinations and appears to be suffering mentally.'

Graham's response was swift, 'Well, that concerns me, Inspector, because it's obvious that the doctors aren't treating him properly. I'm anxious that Jeff *should* be properly treated and I'll tell you what to tell the hospital, although I won't tell you the agent I used.'

'Even that is going to be of considerable assistance. Please tell me.'

'They must treat him with dimercaprol potassium chloride.'

Kirkpatrick reached for a pen, 'Please spell that.'

Graham spelled it out.

Kirkpatrick lay down his pen and looked at him. 'You've told me the treatment. But do you honestly expect the doctors to take notice of this coming from a layman? They'll want to know the cause of the sickness.'

Graham shook his head slowly, 'I'm sorry, Inspector, I can't tell you any more.'

Kirkpatrick got up and left the room to convey Graham's information to the hospital where Batt lay seriously ill. He returned to his office, where Graham was still sitting stiffly as he had before.

'You've told me something about the treatment necessary for Mr Batt,' he said, leaning against his desk. 'I'd like to know something about the death of Mr Egle and Mr Biggs and Dave Tilson's sickness.'

Graham turned his head slightly, 'Is there someone listening at the door?'

'No, one of my officers is sitting out there purely for security purposes.'

'How do I know you aren't recording this conversation?'

'I can only assure you that I am not, and you are at liberty to have a look around the office if you wish.'

Graham bowed his head then and remained silent for some time, apparently deep in thought. He raised his head and gave the chief inspector a direct look. 'I'll tell you about the two deaths and about the sickness of the other two. I cannot tell you the agent I used.' He paused. 'The whole story is too terrible. You'll be disgusted and amazed.'

DCI Kirkpatrick replied, 'Nothing you tell me will amaze me, but carry on. It's important I know the details from you.'

Graham announced: 'Bob Egle: wrongly diagnosed. Not acute infected polyneuritis. Certainly a neurosis, but you and obviously the doctors think the deaths are connected but for the wrong reasons. The agent I used I made up myself.'

'What was it?'

'I can't tell you at this stage.'

'How did you introduce it?'

'By pouring it in the tea.'

'When?'

'At the breaks, sometimes in the morning and sometimes afternoon.'

322

'Was the agent the same in all four cases?'

'Yes. Well, at least for all practical purposes.'

'What do you mean by that?'

'I don't know whether I should say, Inspector.'

'Is it really going to make any difference now?'

At that, Graham got up from his chair and began to pace the room, talking to himself intently, repeating, 'Yes, it's over, the charade is over. It's over, the charade is over.'

Suddenly he sat down and continued as calmly as before: 'It was the same, but in the case of the deaths, I used the powder and the others liquid.'

'You dissolved the powder first, you mean?'

Graham nodded.

'How?'

'Just by dissolving it in water.'

'Was the amount the same in all cases?'

Graham raised his eyebrows, 'No, it certainly wasn't. I gave Bob one very large dose of the powder.'

'How?'

'Always the same, at tea break. I simply poured it in the tea.'

'And the others?'

'Dave Tilson and Jeff Batt: two smaller doses of the liquid. Fred Biggs: three fair amounts of the powder.'

Kirkpatrick said, 'I obviously want you to explain everything in greater detail. Do you wish to make a written statement?'

Graham considered, 'No, I don't think so at this stage. I'm not prepared to commit anything to paper. I may retract all I've said.'

Kirkpatrick warned him, 'Well, that's a matter for you, but as you're aware, a full record of this conversation will be made.' He gave that a moment to sink in, then asked, 'Another employee at the firm with whom you came into contact, Di Smart, has been ill. Have you administered anything to her?'

But Graham drew his thin lips into an even thinner line. 'I'm not prepared to say anything more, Inspector. I must have time to think.'

Kirkpatrick was not prepared to leave matters there, however. Aware that Graham could indeed retract everything he had already said — as he did, sometime later — he consulted Chief Superintendent Harvey. Together with Detective Inspector Alan Newton, Harvey then returned to Kirkpatrick's office to speak to Graham himself. In his hand he clutched the blue-backed notepad. He then began, 'I cautioned you this morning and that still stands. I've been doing some work on your diary and I believe I have identified the persons you refer to —'

Graham interrupted, 'May I say something, Inspector, I'm sorry, Superintendent, I do assure you that was a genuine mistake.' He went on boldly, 'I like you. You have a forthright manner, no sugaring up. We understand each other. What have you learned from your work?'

Harvey replied, 'I think the initial is that of the first Christian name and the symptoms described are those suffered by these people. The dates also correspond to their illnesses.'

'Very well. I'll tell you if you are right.'

Harvey gave a nod, 'So … is 'B' Bob Egle?'

'Yes.'

'And is 'D' David Tilson?'

'Correct.'

'You gave him something different to Bob Egle.'

'Yes, I did.'

'Is 'J' Batt?'

'It is.'

"Di' is Mrs Smart?'

Graham nodded, 'Yes, what I gave her was something quite different to the others, relatively harmless in fact.'

Harvey went on, 'Is 'F' Fred Biggs?'

'Yes.'

Harvey paused, 'I haven't been able to work out 'R'. Is it Ronald Hewitt?'

Graham shook his head, 'No, he did have something, but R did not.'

Harvey thought a moment, 'In the diary you say 'R' should visit in the week 12th October.'

'Yes, he is one of Ryman's drivers. I don't know his name but he didn't come.'

'You also mention getting information from 'P' and 'M' and of 'M' having spoken to 'D's' mother. Who are they?'

He replied, 'M is Margaret [Mary] Berrow and P Peter Buck.'

'Are you now admitting that you poisoned these people?'

Graham stared back at him, 'Yes.'

'Are there any others?'

He responded, 'I've told you of Ronald Hewitt. There's also Peter Buck and Trevor Sparkes. I met him at the Slough government training centre. I believe he comes from Welwyn Garden City.'

'I have not previously heard of Sparkes. Is he dead?'

'No, he had several doses but none were lethal.'

'What about your father and Uncle Jack at Sheerness? Have you done anything to them?'

Graham looked genuinely shocked, 'Good Lord,

no, I think the world of Uncle Jack.'

Harvey frowned, 'Didn't you also like Fred Biggs?'

'Yes, it was a pity about Fred,' Graham said without a trace of irony.

Harvey pointed to the diary, 'In here, on page five, about October 14th, you write of having time to leisurely study the effect on 'D' having had only previous experience of lethal dose. You say both died. Here, read it.'

Harvey passed the diary to Graham, who read the relevant passage.

'This entry seems to have been on 13 October,' Harvey said. 'Only Bob Egle was dead then. Who had the other lethal dose?'

With breathtaking candour, Graham stated calmly, 'I'm referring to my stepmother. I killed her, but that was in 1962.'

Harvey stared at him, then warned he could be charged with Molly Young's murder; all of his previous offences could be brought up if he pleaded not guilty to his recent crimes. Graham made no reply.

Harvey asked, 'You've told Detective Chief Inspector Kirkpatrick the antidote to the poison used on Batt and Tilson. What was the poison?'

'Antimony.'

'Did Egle and Biggs have a different poison?'

'Yes, I gave them thallium.'

'Was it just thallium? In your diary you write of a special compound.'

Graham corrected himself, 'Well, to be precise, thallium chloride.'

'You've admitted giving poison to Bob Egle and Fred Biggs. Their symptoms before they died indicate they died of poison. That is murder. You've also given poison to several other people, six that we know of. That may be attempted murder.'

'That's an academic point,' Graham said dismissively. 'I could have killed them if I had wished, as I did with Biggs and Egle, but I allowed them to live.'

Harvey paused, then went on, 'In our earlier conversation you told me that I had to find the means, opportunity and motive. You've told Mr Kirkpatrick the opportunity, by putting poison into drinks. You've told me the means, thallium and antimony, but what is or was the motive? None of these people were your enemies. In fact, Batt and Biggs were your friends. Why did you want to hurt them?'

Graham hesitated, then spoke slowly, as if weighing each word. 'I suppose I'd ceased to see them as people, or more correctly, a part of me had. They became guinea pigs.'

Harvey was silent for a moment. Then he ran a hand over his forehead and said, 'Look, this has been a lengthy conversation. I've made notes as I was able, but at present I've only got a fraction of what we've talked about. Would you like to make a written statement?'

'What would be the purpose of that, now that I've told you everything?'

'It would ensure that what you have said is accurately recorded and perhaps resolve any disagreement.'

Graham gave a sharp laugh and said scornfully, 'A statement is not conclusive. I could claim that it was made under duress.'

'It's up to you,' said Harvey. 'Any statement I take will be entirely voluntary.'

Graham nodded, 'Yes, you seem a fair man.' He leaned back in his chair, glancing up at the ceiling. 'I'll sleep on it and let you know tomorrow.'

327

21

THE LEPEROUS DISTILMENT

Graham spent a long and dull Monday morning in his cell at Hemel Hempstead police station. At lunchtime he was escorted to the medical room, where Chief Superintendent Harvey waited to question him again. They were joined at 1:30pm by Chief Inspector Kirkpatrick, who enquired of Harvey, 'Is everything alright, sir?'

Harvey nodded towards Graham, 'I think he's feeling some remorse.'

Graham looked up. 'No, Mr Harvey, that would be hypocritical. What I feel is the emptiness of my soul.'

The two detectives exchanged a glance. Kirkpatrick sat down and asked Graham, 'What intrigues me is your knowledge of chemistry and poisons. You must have done a lot of studying?'

'Very little since I was 14, actually,' Graham responded. 'I haven't had the opportunity. But I am fortunate in having a retentive memory. I can give you a complete rundown of the effects of thallium on the human body. Would you like to hear it?'

'Go ahead,' said Harvey.

For over 20 minutes, Graham talked. He spoke in much the same way that a lecturer might address a class, explaining that after taking a fatal dose of thallium, death was inevitable, unless a strong emetic were taken within half an hour of ingestion. After several hours, the person might vomit, but it would be too

328

late: thallium was already in their system. Vomiting was often followed by diarrhoea, although sometimes constipation could occur. Other symptoms included a loss of sensation in the extremities, in the fingers and toes, which would quickly extend to all limbs, caused by the poison breaking down tissue and nerves. He then outlined the effect on the respiratory system, the eyes and the brain, until the afflicted person died. Finally, he told them that in the case of a large dose, death usually occurred before the hair fell out, while fingernails and toenails would display white lines.

Graham paused. 'You must feel repulsion for me.'

Harvey asked, 'Do you know what you have described means in human terms?'

'Not completely,' Graham said. 'I have never seen death.'

Graham's defence counsel later claimed their client had been asked to explain the effects of thallium, rather than volunteering to do so. Harvey told the court: 'He quite spontaneously suggested it. In fact, he seemed eager and proud to tell us of his knowledge of this particular subject.' He added that over the course of questioning, Graham had become more cooperative. Graham stated otherwise, declaring that he had initially maintained his innocence but as time wore on it became apparent that 'we were in a state of impasse'. He claimed to have told Harvey in confidence that he would give him a set of plausible answers to his questions 'in order that and providing that I was then given clothing, food, sleep and access to a solicitor'. Under those circumstances, his statement was a 'mere convenience' and he had expected scientific analysis to demonstrate his innocence 'and therefore my statement was a false one'. He told the court that his intention had been to withdraw his statement at the earliest possible opportunity. When it was put to Harvey in court that Graham had cooperated with detectives in return for the 'amelioration of his conditions of confinement and clothing and so forth', Harvey replied, 'Absolutely not. There was no question of any form of deal with him in any respect.'

To gain more insight into how to handle Graham, and for greater knowledge about his background, Detective Inspector Newton was dispatched to Broadmoor on a fact-finding mission. His visit proved futile: the medical superintendent, Dr Patrick McGrath, refused to divulge anything. Despite being told why such information was necessary, he sent Newton away, citing the unwritten confidentiality clause between patient and doctor.

★ ★ ★

The police inquiry into Graham's crimes continued apace, including the taking of witness statements from his former colleagues and acquaintances. Detective Inspector Ratcliff had also called at Hadlands that morning, Monday, 22 November, to collect Graham's silvercoloured snuff box, while Constable Frank Fuller measured Graham's room at 29 Maynard Road for a scale plan.

In central London, a 30-year-old man from Watford entered the public mortuary on Canley Street in St Pancras, where he was met by Detective Inspector Newton. John Biggs was the eldest son of Fred and Annie Biggs; he viewed his father's poison-ravaged body in Newton's presence. The grieving family had been told that funeral arrangements would have to be

330

delayed while further investigations were conducted.

A larger group of people gathered at the mortuary at 2:30pm. Professor Hugh Molesworth-Johnson was responsible for carrying out the post-mortem on Fred Biggs. Senior lecturer in forensic medicine at St Thomas' hospital medical school, the pathologist had spent his previous weekend reading everything he could about thallium after Chief Superintendent Harvey had explained the case to him. Molesworth-Johnson had already read the Agatha Christie mystery *The Pale Horse*, which led him to strongly suspect that thallium had killed Fred Biggs. He later told the court: 'I was the first to suggest thallium poisoning. I had studied it closely before carrying out my investigation and had heard about its effects before I began. I had also read the thriller and knew something of its effects on people from that book.' Although Molesworth-Johnson was not, in fact, the first to suggest thallium poisoning, he had both an interest and knowledge of the subject, sparked after hearing a professor of forensic medicine at Ghent University read a paper on it. The Belgian expert had dealt with an outbreak of thallium poisoning in the Low Countries during the 1950s; Molesworth-Johnson consulted this same professor, declaring, 'I happened to be interested in poisoning cases and the very bizarre nature of this poison had stuck in my mind.'

Also present at the post-mortem were Professor John Cavanagh, neuropathologist at the University College London Institute of Neurology, Chief Superintendent Harvey, another chief superintendent named Hughes, Chief Inspector Kirkpatrick, Detective Inspector Alan Newton, Detective Constable

Michael Grinsted, police photographer John Mackintosh, coroner's officer Police Constable Bell, Mr Nigel Fuller of the Metropolitan Police Forensic Science Laboratory and Dr Rudge of the National Hospital for Neurology and Neurosurgery (NHNN).

Molesworth-Johnson got to work. Describing Biggs as 'a well-built man, 5'10" in height, in a shroud', he pointed out the discoloration and thickening of the face, particularly the red, scaly skin flaking around the nose and mouth. The same effect was visible on the scrotum and there were other noticeable changes in pigmentation, where the skin had turned purple-brown. The hair on his head came away like that of a moulting animal, even when very lightly touched. These were all signs consistent with thallium poisoning, although there were no tell-tale white Mees' lines on either fingernails or toenails, which led the pathologist to assume that this was due to the relative brevity of the victim's illness and the fact that he had been a healthy man beforehand.

Professor Cavanagh examined sections of the brain, spinal cord and nerves. He found evidence of degeneration of nerve fibres and reactive changes in nerve cells in the spinal cord, together with changes in cranial nerves. His subsequent report examined a number of possible causes, culminating in a superlative description of thallium neuropathy:

This intoxication is characterised by widespread involvement of cranial and peripheral nerves, commonly accompanied by optic neuritis with defects in vision and often associated with bizarre mental disturbances. The onset of the neuropathy is associated with severe and often intense

332

sensory disturbances of the hands and feet, weakness of the limbs following this and progressively affecting the limbs. Most post-mortem examinations have been done within a few weeks of poisoning and have shown peripheral nerve degeneration of varying degrees of severity with chromatolysis of associated nerve cells. Other changes have been described in various regions of the brain but these have been non-specific in nature. Scharer's (1933) case examined many months after poisoning showed distinct loss of fibres in the dorsal columns. There is in fact no specific feature to the neuropathological changes in acute thallium poisoning. The changes in this case are, however, not inconsistent with thallium intoxication, and are consistent with the clinical features noted in this case.

But neither he nor Molesworth-Johnson could find traces of the poison itself. Thus, the pathologist recorded that the cause of death could not be established. He prepared the organs to be handed over to Nigel Fuller of the Metropolitan Police Forensic Science Laboratory for further scientific examination, including toxicology tests which, it was hoped, might confirm the presence of thallium in the body.

But Chief Superintendent Harvey had heard enough. He headed back to Hemel Hempstead.

★ ★ ★

Graham was brought from his cell to Detective Chief Inspector Kirkpatrick's office for questioning again that evening. Lined up neatly on the desk were a number of bottles collected from Graham's room on Maynard Road.

Although Kirkpatrick himself was present, along with Detective Inspector Ratcliff, Chief Superintendent Harvey led the interview. 'I wish to put some questions to you about the offences with which you will be charged,' he began. 'You're not obliged to answer any of these questions, but if you do, the questions and answers will be taken down in writing and may be given in evidence.'

Graham then signed the caution on the first page of the questions Harvey had prepared earlier. Before dealing with those, Harvey wanted to know about the bottles on the desk. Kirkpatrick took notes as the two men parried back and forth.

'When we searched your room, we took possession of certain items over here.' Harvey pointed towards the desk: 'These three tins were found in your drawer. What are they?'

'It's the stores drawer.'

'Is that your drawer?'

'Yes, but I don't know where it comes from. I disclaim ownership.'

'Right.' Harvey then pointed to another item. 'This box. You know its contents. What is this?'

'Potassium ferrocyanide and concentrated sulphuric acid. Just for an experiment.'

'The experiment in question?'

There was no hesitation in Graham's response: 'I wanted to see if the heat on ferrocyanide and sulphuric acid would produce any effect. I was expecting none.'

'Okay.' Harvey pointed again, 'This bottle?'

'Tincture of aconite, purchased relatively recently.'

334

'What purchased for?'

'Merely as a stock item for experiments. It's a tincture for toothache remedy.'

'How did you sign for it?'

'I used the name M E Evans.'

'What reason did you give?'

'I said I required it for alkaline extraction of aconite.'

Harvey pointed to another bottle. 'This?'

'Oxalic acid. It can be used for many things. I kept it merely as stock. It isn't a Schedule 1 item. It's used in the manufacture of straw hats.'

'This dropper?'

'Merely to obtain a specific amount.'

'Will there be traces of thallium?'

Graham shook his head, 'No, certainly not. Merely traces of various harmless chemicals, possible traces of ferrocyanide.'

Harvey ran his finger down a row of containers. 'These nine bottles of ether. What used for?'

'They were all empty. I used them purely for inhalation.'

'Why?'

Graham hesitated, 'I'm not addicted, but its effects are similar to alcohol — the subjective effect is a kind of intoxication.'

Harvey pointed again: 'This?'

'An empty bottle which contained potassium.'

'This?'

'Iodine.'

'This?'

'Lead acetate solution. Merely as a stock item.'

'This?'

'Acetic acid — it looks as if it's leaked. It can be

used in the production of acetates.'

'This?'

'A mixture of ammonia, ether and iodine and a very small quantity of formaldehyde.'

'What used for?'

Graham shook his head slightly, 'No particular use, merely stock.'

'This?'

'Concentrated sulphuric acid from St Albans.'

'What used for?'

'Not used at all,' Graham replied. 'It's a very powerful reducing agent and just a stock item.'

'This?'

'I don't recollect the contents. Probably hydrobromic acid.'

'This?'

'Nitro-hydrochloric acid. I didn't purchase that, actually. I can't remember where it came from.'

'This?'

'Sulphuric acid — stock again.'

'This one?'

'Ammonia solution.'

'This bottle?'

'Lead acetate originally but I may have put something else in it. It's merely an acetate and can be used as an agent. Its toxic effect is very small and its acute toxicity is relatively low.'

'Did you use this on any of your victims?'

'No, I didn't use it.'

'This?'

'Hydrochloric acid — another stock item.'

'Why do you have this carbon tetrachloride?'

'Merely for dry cleaning.'

'This?'

'Potassium ferrocyanide. I didn't use them all for converting to Prussian blue. I only used small quantities.'

Harvey frowned, then continued, 'This?'

'Sodium tartrate mixed with antimony salt.'

'Was this supplied to any of your victims?'

'Yes, Di Smart.' Now Graham frowned, 'I thought you were going to leave that part of the questioning till later?'

'Yes, as you wish,' said Harvey. 'We'll go on. This?'

'Formaldehyde solution — stock.'

'This?'

'I'm not certain whether it's chloride of lime or potassium oxalate used in lavatory cleaner.'

Harvey pointed to a discoloured jar: 'What does this contain?'

'Probably green peas or onions.'

Harvey raised his eyebrows, then continued, 'This?'

'Prussian blue.'

'This?'

'Again, green peas or onions.'

'This tumbler?'

'Probably traces of Hirondelle and white wine.'

'This?'

'A solution of nicotine — very weak.'

Harvey pointed at a smaller bottle, 'Is this ether?'

'It's not ether. It contains a quantity of hydrochloric acid and iodine. Hydrochloric acid is very noxious but there's not much left.'

Harvey indicated another bottle: 'This?'

'Nitric acid.'

'And this?'

'Pure clean water,' Graham replied. 'Completely uncontaminated.'

'This?'

'Aspirin.'

'This?'

'Nitro-hydrochloric acid.'

Harvey picked up a small bottle of tablets, 'We found these in the roof space.'

'They're not mine,' Graham said. 'I've never been up in the loft.'

'What about this spoon?' Harvey pointed to a utensil coated with white residue.

'I don't really know what that is. I used it for grinding up so many things.'

'These tablets?'

'Bismuth of nitrate tablets — antacid.'

'What use?'

'To allay stomach irritation.'

'This?'

'Prussian blue.'

'This box?'

'That's detergent powder, Superintendent.'

'This snuff — is it snuff?'

'Yes, it's mentholated snuff, nothing else.'

Harvey then picked up a bottle. 'What does this contain?'

Graham admitted, 'That contains a residue of thallium.'

'And these smelling salts — did you give them to anyone?'

'It's just ammonia solution in cotton wool. I did say to a couple of people, 'have a smell'. I was using it myself because I had a cold. Nothing toxic.'

Harvey pointed to another bottle, 'This?'

'It originally had ether in it. It's probably ammoniate iodine.' He corrected himself, 'No, it can't be that — I don't know.'

'Can we revert to the antimony?' Harvey asked.

Graham replied, 'Before we continue, do you think I could have a glass of water?'

'What's this formula first?'

'I imagine it's some metallic compound.' Graham squinted, 'I can see salts . . . Oh, I can't tell you — it's so long ago.'

Graham was given a glass of water and a very short break. Chief Superintendent Harvey sat down and began questioning him from the prepared sheet, referring back to the bottles and containers on the desk.

'When your room was searched on Saturday evening, these items were found. Regarding the antimony sodium tartrate, does that bottle contain anything else?'

'Yes, it also contains antimony potassium tartrate.'

'Did you administer it to anybody?'

'Yes, Peter Buck, Diana Smart, Ron Hewitt, Trevor Sparkes.'

'Why did you give those people this poison?'

Graham pursed his lips, 'At present I prefer not to answer the question.'

Harvey nodded. 'The phial which you said contained thallium — where did you obtain it?'

'I obtained the thallium from John Bell & Croyden.'

'Did you sign the poison register?'

'Yes, using the alias M E Evans.'

'Did you give a reason for requiring thallium?'

'Yes, for qualitive and quantitive analysis.'

'To whom did you administer thallium?'

Graham gave a small smile, 'Well, of course you know the answer to that.'

'Why did you give it to them?'

339

'I prefer not to answer that question.'

Harvey let it pass. 'We also found a phial in the top pocket of a jacket on a chair in your room. The substance in the phial has been analysed and found to be thallium and aspirin.'

'Yes — the thallium had been in the phial previously and the aspirin is a method of gauging grainage.'

'Did you administer this substance to anybody?'

'No.'

'Why did you have it?'

'It's just an old phial which contained a residue of thallium.'

'There was another phial on the windowsill that was almost empty but contained particles of thallium.'

Graham shook his head slowly, 'I think we've misunderstood each other. The phial on the windowsill contained a *residue* of thallium; the brown phial in my jacket pocket contained in excess of a *fatal dose* of thallium.'

Harvey nodded, 'All right. Where did you obtain the thallium?'

'It was my original purchase from John Bell & Croyden.'

Harvey returned to Graham's previous reply, 'Why did you have a fatal dose of thallium in your jacket pocket?'

Graham lifted his hands and wiggled his index fingers, 'It was my 'exit' dose, but I didn't have a chance to use it. I hadn't anticipated being arrested in Sheerness.'

Harvey then reached for Graham's sketches. One showed a man with a full head of hair, then thinning hair, followed by a bald head and, finally, a grave. There was also a drawing of an evil-looking genie escaping from a bottle of poison. Another sketch depicted a graveyard where two left hands poured poison into a couple. Harvey asked him about each drawing. Graham replied that the sketch of the genie was 'a symbolic depiction' of the fictional tale he was writing about death by thallium (in other words, his diary). The sketches of the man losing his hair before death was, Graham insisted, 'Just a rather macabre drawing I did under the influence of ether.'

Harvey set aside the drawings and pointed towards two jars containing dead wasps. 'I understand you caught these wasps at the factory. It's been said that you were extremely interested in watching them die. Is this some experiment you were carrying out?'

Graham shook his head, 'No, it was merely a method of keeping down wasps — trapping them or, rather, causing them to be trapped in a solution of sugar.'

Harvey then switched subject: 'In your diary you seem concerned about Fred Biggs not dying as quickly as you anticipated. You seemed particularly concerned that, if he continued to survive, symptoms would become apparent that could connect Biggs' illness with those of Tilson and Batt.' Harvey paused. 'You say that you administered thallium to Biggs and antimony to Tilson and Batt, if this is so why were you worried about the symptoms being connected?'

'I'm sorry, it was a slip of the tongue,' Graham replied. 'I gave Tilson and Batt thallium, not antimony.'

'Why did you give thallium to some and antimony to others?'

'Antimony is a less toxic material, more rapidly eliminated from the system, and unlikely in sub-lethal dosage to cause any lasting ill effect.'

341

'How did you select who should have which poison?'

Graham was silent a moment, then said, 'I prefer at present not to answer the question.'

'Fine. Reverting to what you said last night, when you claimed you had only administered thallium to three persons, is it now correct that you administered thallium to five people?'

'Yes, five and only five.'

'Was it administered in the same form?'

'No, in four instances it was given in a crystalline form and one instance in a liquid form.'

'Would you care to enumerate who had what?'

Without hesitation, Graham responded, 'In chronological order: the four crystalline ones were my stepmother, Bob Egle, Jeff Batt and Fred Biggs; the solution was given to David Tilson. The quantities were approximately in the first instance 20 grains, in the second approximately eight in two doses. In the third approximately four grains. In the fourth instance, probably between five and six. In the fifth, approximately 18 in three doses.'

'Did you measure the thallium against the aspirin we have mentioned?'

'Yes, in an inexact measure.'

Harvey then said, 'You told me yesterday that you had killed your stepmother by poisoning her with thallium. At that time you were a boy of only 15 or 14 and thallium was a relatively unknown poison here. Where did you first hear of it?'

Graham was circumspect: 'It's still relatively unused in this country. It is used in the manufacture of certain types of highly refractive optical glassware, but it's no longer used as a rodenticide. It was at one time used to check night sweats in cases of tuberculosis.'

Harvey looked at him, clearly perplexed, 'Where on earth did you learn of this as a schoolboy?'

'Through my researches into toxicology.'

Harvey gave a bemused shake of the head, then went on, 'In your diary you say that there are few doctors here capable of identifying the substance you had administered. Were you then referring to thallium, which you also call your 'special compound'?'

'Yes, I was referring to thallium, but not to a doctor's ability to identify it by forensic analysis. I meant that few doctors in this country have had experience of thallium poisoning — as a consequence, they'd find it difficult to identify its characteristic symptoms.'

Harvey then revealed, 'We've spoken to Trevor Sparkes. He told us that you used to give him wine. Was the poison in that?'

Graham nodded, 'Yes.'

'Sparkes also says that you gave wine to others, including a man named Ted James and a man nicknamed 'Yorky'. Did you give them poison?'

Graham frowned, 'No. I did not.'

With that, Harvey had completed his list of questions. It was 9:30pm Graham read each page of the interview transcript very carefully, but when asked if he wanted to add his signature, he politely declined. Half an hour later, Detective Chief Superintendent Harvey stood before Graham and charged him with the following offence: 'That you did, on or about 19th November 1971, at Bovingdon in the County of Hertfordshire, murder Frederick Ernest William Biggs, against the Peace.' Asked for his response, Graham shook his head, 'I have no wish to say anything.'

The following morning, news of the case broke in the national press.

22

SWIFT AS QUICKSILVER

Local newspaper the *Evening Echo* had been first on the scene at Hadlands. As a former councillor, Fred Biggs was well known in the area, and the suspicious nature of his death, coupled with the revelation that Bob Egle, another Hadlands store worker, had died only four months earlier, caused considerable interest. The reporter spoke to members of staff at the firm and linked the story to one about possible radioactive contamination from the nearby airfield, unaware that it was actually a murder inquiry.

The *Daily Mirror* knew more but made no mention of Graham by name in their front-page story on Tuesday, 23 November. Under the headline 'Poison Probe CID Halt Funeral', the *Mirror* revealed: 'Detectives halted arrangements for the funeral of a laboratory worker yesterday — and launched a murder inquiry into his death. The man, 56-year-old Fred Biggs, was killed by a mystery illness . . .' The funeral had been delayed because of the post-mortem. Chief Superintendent Harvey spoke to a *Daily Mirror* reporter but divulged little: 'Inquiries are being made into two recent deaths, and we are awaiting the results of forensic tests. A man is helping with our inquiries.'

The man in question appeared before Hemel Hempstead Magistrates' Court early that morning, charged with the murder of Fred Biggs. Graham was represented by a local solicitor, John Pickworth, who had been engaged at the suggestion of Hertfordshire Constabulary. Remanded in custody for one week, Graham would remain in his cell at Hemel Hempstead police station until further charges could be brought.

As Graham was driven back to Combe Road, Detective Constable Michael Grinsted received a number of items from the son of his last victim, Fred Biggs. These, together with blood, urine and semen samples from surviving victims, were conveyed to Nigel Fuller at the Metropolitan Police Forensic Science Laboratory. At the same time, police photographer John Mackintosh returned to 29 Maynard Road to shoot exterior images before driving on to Bovingdon, where he made four negatives of the Hadlands factory.

Chief Superintendent Harvey sent for Graham after lunch. Handing him a cigarette, he enquired, 'Have you slept well?' Graham replied politely, 'I have, thank you.' They sat down together and Harvey recited the now familiar words: 'I wish to put some further questions to you about the offences with which you will be charged. You are not obliged to answer any of the questions, but if you do, the questions and answers will be taken down in writing and may be given in evidence.' That done, he began in earnest, 'Right, I've now got information about several employees at Hadlands, all of whom were sick during the time you worked there. I'm not suggesting that you're responsible for all these people becoming ill, but some of them are married women and four are pregnant. If they've had thallium or antimony during their pregnancy, then there's a considerable risk. Are you prepared to tell me if you've given poison to anybody other than those we have so far discussed?'

Graham gave a nod, 'I'm prepared to tell you.' After listening to the roll call of names, he replied, 'I did not give poison to any of those ladies.'

'Good,' said Harvey. 'Now, in your diary you write of 'R'. That's John Durrant of Ryman's. He says that he had tea in the stores when you were present and afterwards he became ill.'

'I wasn't responsible for his illness.'

Harvey made a note. 'These are also people who've been ill, and some of their symptoms were similar to those who have been poisoned: Alexander Charlmaros, Roland Edwards, John Parker, Norman Smart, Phillip Doggett, Reginald Sharp, Michael Hadland, Duncan Poulton, John Rendell.' He paused. 'There are others.'

'To the best of my knowledge and belief their illnesses were due to natural causes.'

'I understand that you admire Hitler and sometimes argued about him with workmates? The arguments are said to have become quite heated. Did you, as some form of revenge, ever administer poison en masse by way of the tea or coffee, or the drinking water, or any other medium?'

'No. These arguments were conducted without rancour on my part and I did nothing to harm anybody as you suggest.'

Satisfied with Graham's replies, Harvey asked him if he would sign the transcript of their conversation. As before, he declined.

But Graham's name now entered the public domain for the second time as a potential mass poisoner. On Wednesday, 24 November 1971, the *Daily Express* ran a front-page story headlined 'Murder Charge', report-

346

ing: 'Storeman Graham Young, aged 24, of Maynard Road, Hemel Hempstead, Herts., was remanded in custody yesterday accused of murdering local councillor Frederick Biggs. Young, accused of killing 56-year-old Mr Biggs, a storeman with John Hadland Photographic Instrumentation of Bovington 'on or about' last Friday, appears in court at Hemel Hempstead again next Wednesday.'

Despite the story, as yet no one had publicly linked Graham's second spate of poisonings with those of ten years before. But the Home Office were now aware of the matter and the relevant department, C3, scrambled to make sense of the incomprehensible. Division C3 were responsible for helping ministers to enforce the Home Secretary's powers and implement his duties under mental health legislation — especially in relation to offenders detained in psychiatric hospitals whose leave, transfer or discharge was subject to Home Office consent. The archived papers suggest that the department only learned of Graham's repeated offences after reading the national press. An internal memo warns of 'a very serious development in the case of a patient conditionally discharged from Broadmoor earlier this year'. Following a precis of events, the memo states that Dr McGrath had been contacted to explain the circumstances of Graham's discharge from Broadmoor, concluding: 'The newspaper reports make no reference of course to Young's previous history. In the event of his conviction, however, there may well be adverse publicity critical of the decision to discharge.'

It was this, especially, that caused such consternation at C3, whose representative, Mr Law, spoke to Detective Chief Superintendent Harvey the follow-

347

ing day. Discovering that Graham was suspected of two further murders and that an exhumation order had been sought in respect of Bob Egle to analyse his ashes for poison, Law drew attention to police interviews with the two probation officers responsible for supervising Graham after his release from Broadmoor (the underlining is his): 'Both are emphatic that they were not given Young's background or told the nature of his original offence (I find this a little difficult to believe, but the matter can be pursued through Dr McGrath).' Law's report ended: 'Latest inquiries tend to show that Young embarked upon his infamous conduct almost as soon as he arrived at the Training Centre at Slough, one man [Trevor Sparkes] there having become seriously ill with symptoms of poisoning in March this year (Young went there in February).'

With the matter now brought to his attention, the Home Secretary asked for complete disclosure regarding Graham's discharge from Broadmoor and the supervision afforded to him since then. As internal memos flew back and forth and letters were fired off, with various progress reports demanded from the hospital and probation services, one person was most sought after for clarity regarding Graham's early release from Broadmoor: Dr Edgar Udwin. He remained in sunny Barbados, blissfully unaware of the unstoppable storm waiting for him when he returned to work on 29 November. The outlook was grim, with the Home Secretary writing to his assistant private secretary that the case of Graham Young 'will present major problems for our whole present system.'

★ ★ ★

Graham's defence team had already begun work, instructing a pathologist to obtain samples from the body of Fred Biggs. Detective Constable Grinsted and Detective Inspector Ratcliff dealt with the matter before liaising again with Nigel Fuller of the Metropolitan Police Forensic Science Laboratory on other samples. Jethro Batt was discharged from hospital, recovered but far from well; his blood and urine samples were sent to the same laboratory for analysis. Nigel Fuller had visited the Bovingdon factory, where he was shown round by an ashen-faced John Hadland. He paid special attention to the canteen and stores while Grinsted and Ratcliff headed an 'exhaustive' search of the entire plant. More witness statements were taken, including one from a distraught Win, who told detectives, 'When Graham first went to Broadmoor, I saw a young Australian doctor there who advised me to go home and forget about Graham, to treat him as dead. I wish I had taken his advice. As far as I am concerned it was a grave mistake to ever let him out.'

On the afternoon of Sunday, 27 November, police officers from Hertfordshire and Norfolk met at the grave of a young man in Gillingham. It was bitterly cold. A retired farm worker turned church verger began cutting into the earth at the foot of Donald Goldsmith's grave in St Mary's churchyard. After several minutes, an oak casket emerged. Inside were the ashes of Bob Egle, laid to rest in his nephew's grave.

At 2:45pm, District Coroner Frederick Robinson Bell presided over a brief inquest at Norfolk's Loddon police station. Bell released the ashes for analysis, adjourning the inquest until 7 January 1972. The ashes, along with control samples including ashes

349

from another cremated body, were conveyed to Nigel Fuller.

Dr Udwin returned to his desk the following morning, appalled to discover that his first task since returning from holiday concerned murders committed by a recently released patient. He began a letter to the Home Office, robustly defending himself and the system within which he worked, insisting that the first probation officer had ample contact with Graham and background information on him, although admittedly, 'I did not emphasise that Young was a poisoner, nor did I direct him to keep watch and ward lest Young poison anyone.' Udwin was shocked to learn Graham had purchased poison so soon after his release ('I had no inkling that his condition had changed or deteriorated') and based his professional view that 'he was better' on years of treatment and training. He conceded that 'in the event my belief was wrong' but 'this is a clinical error and which of us are to be proof against this?' Reiterating that 'if there had been any thought in my mind that there was a remote likelihood of a relapse on a poisoner's part I would not have sent him out at all', he had regarded supervision as necessary simply to help the patient adjust to life outside after years in the institution.

'The matter of what has to be told to a prospective employer is a difficult one,' Udwin wrote. 'In all cases we consultants pursue a fairly common policy in this matter. We explain clearly that the patient comes from Broadmoor and we explain in vague terms that he was there for 'an act of violence' or some such. We give our assurance that we believe the man to be well.' Here the psychiatrist was mistaken: Hadlands were not informed that Graham's treatment had been at

Broadmoor; Udwin had told his former patient that it was up to him whether or not he wished to mention that fact.

Udwin was of the opinion that the probation officers had carried out their functions 'perfectly well'. He reminded the Home Office that in the last decade 468 patients, all homicides, had been discharged or transferred from Broadmoor:

> in each and every case anxious thought and care is exercised before a decision is made. As far as is humanly possible all factors are weighed and no chances are taken. To date, one homicide has repeated the offence, the initial charge in Young's case being, as I recall, inflicting grievous bodily harm by poisoning. If all error is to be eliminated, we should discharge no cases and we would require a new Broadmoor every three or four years considering our turnover is something in the order of 150 cases a year.

Together with this spirited defence of his position, Dr Udwin compiled a report for the Home Office as requested, explaining Graham's background, treatment and discharge, emphasising that Graham had seemed in no danger of relapse.

But detectives were gathering compelling evidence to show that Graham had not merely relapsed; in layman's terms, he had never been 'cured'. One of the items listed as an exhibit in his case was particularly telling: the poison register seized from John Bell & Croyden, whose staff spoke at length to Sergeant Livingstone and Inspector Ratcliff about the young man who gave the same false name that he had used prior to his years in Broadmoor in order to purchase the poison with which he would kill and torture.

Graham was charged with the murder of Robert Egle in a watershed event in British forensic and criminal history. For the first time, a murder charge was brought against a subject after their victim's ashes were exhumed and successfully scientifically analysed. Tests had also been carried out on one of Bob Egle's kidneys; due to the unusual nature of his illness and death, St Albans city hospital had preserved and mounted the organ. Nigel Fuller examined it and discovered the equivalent of 2.5 micrograms per gram of thallium present and this would have been higher but for the reduction in quantity caused by the mounting process.

Fuller had also tested hair samples from David Tilson and Jethro Batt; hair from the latter had turned coal black at the root. Analysing blood and urine samples from Trevor Sparkes, Peter Buck and Diana Smart revealed no traces of thallium and nor was anything detectable in the soil samples and garden tools taken as a precautionary measure from the home of Fred Biggs. But when Fuller examined Biggs' internal organs, he concluded that the former Hadlands worker must have absorbed or consumed hundreds of grams of thallium.

Finally, Fuller analysed the contents of the bottles and powders found in Graham's room. He made a number of interesting discoveries, not least that the poisoner's 'exit dose' phial contained twice the fatal dose of thallium acetate, while a single bottle bearing a John Bell & Croyden label contained the equivalent of over 200 times the fatal dose. Graham had used that particular bottle to dose some of his victims, though not Bob Egle.

After charging Graham with Egle's murder, Chief Superintendent Harvey asked if there was anything he wished to say. 'No,' Graham replied flatly, 'I have nothing to say.'

Harvey handed him a cigarette. Graham took it and accepted a light, then blew out a pall of smoke. 'Do you know 'The Ballad of Reading Gaol', Superintendent?'

'I've read it,' said Harvey.

Graham took a breath, then recited: 'Yet each man kills the thing he loves/By each let this be heard/Some do it with a bitter look/Some with a flattering word/The coward does it with a kiss/The brave man with a sword.'

He took another drag on his cigarette. 'I suppose I could be said to kiss.'

Harvey merely looked at him. Graham then gave him a nod of acknowledgement, admitting, 'You've treated me very well, far better than I deserve.' The door opened and he went out, following a constable who led him back to his cell where he would remain until a date was set for his committal hearing.

★ ★ ★

Dr Udwin received a somewhat critical response from another member of C3, a Mr Prior, who was sceptical of the psychiatrist's claim that neither he nor Graham's probation officer had felt it necessary to make home visits, given that 'in Young's room at his lodgings were a number of bottles and containers which, had they been seen by an informed eye, might have conveyed a good idea of his activities.' Prior further asserted

353

that Graham's nefarious activities 'might have been detected earlier' had the management of Hadlands known that their new storeman came to them directly from Broadmoor. He added that some sort of review would be necessary to revise general procedures following conditionally discharged psychiatric patients.

Writing within the department, Prior confided that the possibility of a review was something that troubled Dr Patrick McGrath, with whom he had spoken about the matter. McGrath was 'especially anxious at the possibility that, as a result of this most unfortunate case, a more restrictive approach might be adopted in future consideration of the discharge of patients from the hospital [Broadmoor]. This clearly would have serious effects both on hospital administration and for the patients themselves.' Both men agreed that establishing the full facts of the case was a priority and that a meeting in due course would be beneficial.

Prior then had a telephone conversation with Dr Udwin, who reiterated that the probation service had been fully informed about Graham's history, that their supervision was 'entirely satisfactory' and that he had seen no reason to 'keep watch and ward' against the risk of Graham Young 'reverting to playing with poisons'. As far as home visits were concerned, Dr Udwin insisted that these were not part of general practice if — as in Graham's case — the patient was reporting regularly at the probation officer's office. Nor were prospective employers given full details of a former patient's offence, except in the broadest terms.

Mr Prior recorded one last, telling remark: 'Dr Udwin then volunteered quite spontaneously the observation that what has occurred in this case was due to one thing and one thing only, and that was a clinical error. Before Young's discharge was recommended, he had been the subject of a good deal of clinical discussion within Broadmoor, but it was now evident that all those concerned with his care in the hospital had been deceived by his behaviour.'

23
THIS COLD, DELIBERATE, VINDICTIVE POISONING

Two days before Christmas Eve 1971, Chief Inspector Kirkpatrick and Chief Superintendent Harvey completed their report for the Director of Public Prosecutions to show there was sufficient evidence to bring Graham, then aged 24, to trial for 'two cases of murder, two attempted murders and numerous offences of administering poison'. These were the murders by deliberate poisoning of Robert Edward Egle, 60, and Frederick Ernest William Biggs, 56; the attempted murders by the same means of Jethro Walter Batt, 39, David John Price Tilson, 25, and the administering of poison to Ronald Hewitt, 41, Peter Buck, 26, Mrs Diana Smart, 38, and Trevor John Sparkes, aged 35.

At that stage, the final results of the forensic examinations were not known, but initial tests had shown traces of thallium in the pathological samples of Biggs, Batt and Tilson, and in Bob Egle's cremated remains. Inquiries were being conducted to find an expert with knowledge of thallium and antimony, but that was proving far from easy, 'and it would seem that there is nobody in this country qualified by experience to speak authoritatively on thallium and antimony poisoning.' The report included a succinct description of the effects of such poisons on the human body.

The greater part of the report outlined the circumstances in which Graham had committed his crimes, 'a coldly calculated series of deliberate acts by the accused, designed to lead to the death and injury of those named. In carrying out his plans, Young seems to have acted without any understandable motive, and with an utter disregard for human life and a complete indifference to the pain and suffering of others.' The conclusions make for enlightening reading, providing a vivid picture of the culprit:

The murders of Egle and Biggs were apparently without motive. Both were reasonably healthy men with settled and happy lives, it can be said of each that they had been helpful to Young and given no cause for animosity. Much the same can be said in respect of all the victims and the answer undoubtedly lies in Young himself. He is of unimposing appearance, 5'7" in height with a slight frame, pale face and dark hair. He speaks with a cultured voice and at no time since his arrest has he shown any sign of emotion. His callous attitude towards the suffering of others is depicted in many ways, particularly by the seeking of information on those he had poisoned, as exhibited by his telephone enquiry to Mrs Biggs when her husband was so very seriously ill. There can be no doubt of his intelligence; the writing in his diary is grammatically almost without fault and at one stage he treated the reporting officers to a long and accurate exposition on the economic growth of Nazi Germany. When speaking he is precise and dogmatic, but as witnessed by his answers to questions, he becomes carried away by his knowledge and arrogance. There is every likelihood that he will plead not guilty at his trial, enjoying the opportunity of displaying in public his cleverness and conceit.

The report ended:

> The full extent of Young's activities may never become known. The laboratory tests are complex and time-consuming but early results show traces of thallium in the blood of some of those whom he emphatically denies having administered poison to. Many results are waited, of inquiries being made concerning (in excess of 150) persons with whom he came into contact at the Government Training Centre, but some results received show that previously healthy men became sick at this time with symptoms all now too familiar. However, as the excretion rate of the poison is such that it is thought unlikely that traces can be found more than three months after ingestion, there is little chance of proving these forensically.

The report was soon updated to include the results of the inquiries in respect of those people who had attended the government training centre at the same time as Graham. Five men and a woman were sick during that period, with symptoms that might suggest poisoning. Although it could not be proven whether Graham had been responsible for these other illnesses, the witness statements were included to demonstrate further that, within a very short time of his release from Broadmoor, Graham had been 'active in poisoning people'.

Nigel Fuller was, however, able to provide conclusive evidence of thallium poisoning from analysing the remains of Fred Biggs and Bob Egle. Regarding the former, Fuller discovered 120 micrograms of thallium in the gut, 20 micrograms per gram in the left kidney, 10 micrograms in brain matter, 6 micrograms in his urine, and 5 micrograms in muscle samples and also in bone matter. The roots of the victim's hair and his pubic hair had turned black. Fuller was confident that the amounts would have been far greater when first consumed and certainly sufficient to cause death. In analysing Bob Egle's ashes, Fuller discovered 9 milligrams of thallium, which would have been equivalent to approximately 5 micrograms per gram before cremation destroyed most of the poison. Because a person might ingest harmless amounts of thallium from the atmosphere over the course of their lifetime, Fuller then analysed the ashes of a man who had nothing to do with the case to see if any traces of thallium could be found. There were none.

The Home Office continued to be vexed by the prospective criticism that would follow Graham's trial. In a letter dated February 1972, C3 optimistically suggested that when the time came 'we shall be able to make something — but not too much — of the special hospitals' generally good record in assessing fitness for release. But I fear that we may not be able to avoid awkward comparisons between the elaborate safeguards in life-sentence cases and hospital cases in Mental Health Act cases. When the 'line' between hospital and prison cases is as blurred as it is, it is not a wholly convincing answer to such criticism to say that Broadmoor releases are basically a matter for medical judgement.' C3 had decided boldly that there should be no need for any inquiry to establish the facts of the case or where the decisions taken had gone so catastrophically wrong, since that could be attributed to a clinical judgement which, 'though now known to have been wrong, was reasonable when made. Everything followed from that. Its results could not have been foreseen.' Nor did the department feel there were any lessons to be learned from the case, since procedures were already being examined to pinpoint where improvements could be made. A note of caution was sounded: 'We must obviously be prepared for the possibility — indeed the likelihood — that public opinion will not be satisfied by departmental assurances and that there will be strong pressure upon Ministers to have some form of independent — and public — inquiry.' It was still a matter of conjecture what form such an inquiry might take.

Buckinghamshire Probation and After-Care Service had contacted C3 to support Robert Mynett, who had been Graham's probation officer immediately after his release from Broadmoor. The principal probation officer confirmed that Mynett was of the opinion that Dr Udwin had failed to discuss Graham's background, offences and needs fully with him and that the further information he had requested from Broadmoor was insufficient and provided only with 'reluctance'. Mynett had several suggestions for going forward, chief of which was that 'the maximum written information to which referral can be made during supervision is essential. Mr Mynett feels strongly that a person who has been in a mental institution for a very serious and dangerous offence and separated from the outside world for many years presents very real potential difficulties when he is released with very limited preparation and under the supervision of an officer who has not had the benefit of the considerable knowledge gained about him in a treatment situation.' The principal probation officer was nonetheless keen to confirm that they had 'valued the services of Dr Udwin in other matters and found him extremely helpful and cooperative'.

In due course, Graham's second probation officer, Susan Vidal, contacted the principal probation officer herself, expressing the muted view that more information in Graham's case would indeed have been helpful prior to working with him and making suggestions for improvement in the future. 'Broadmoor seemed to occupy a rather remote position in the total picture,' she wrote. 'Having said that, I must say that I would not have hesitated to contact Dr Udwin at Broadmoor if Mr Young's behaviour had given me cause for concern.'

* * *

At the Hemel Hempstead Magistrates' Court on 22 March 1972, Graham was committed for trial. He had been held on Brixton prison's sick wing for several weeks, where Dr Peter Scott kept him under observation. John Pickworth of Lloyd & Steel solicitors visited him regularly, imparting the news that Hertfordshire constabulary had constructed a formidable case against him. Graham seemed unperturbed, as he did when he stood in the dock at the Magistrates' Court while the charges were read out followed by a list of 75 witnesses for the prosecution. Of this, 35 witnesses were ordered to attend the trial, and the remaining 40 bound over. The fact that John Walker, representing the Director of Public Prosecutions, had tried to prevent their names being read out in court was a measure of the nervousness with which the Home Office viewed the case. Mr Lewis Dean, the magistrate, overruled the request.

Graham's sister and cousin attended the committal, sitting side by side for support. The two young women were both mothers now: Winifred had two daughters and Sandra two sons. Much to the surprise of the police officer accompanying him, Graham broke down completely when he saw them; the officer remarked that it was the first time he had shown any sort of emotion. Winifred took home some of Graham's shirts to wash, returning them a fortnight later when they met again in Brixton prison. He told her that many of the prison rules were nonsensical; he was not permitted a tie, gloves or belt because he was deemed a suicide risk, and could understand the logic in that with regards to the tie and belt, but what was he supposed to do with the gloves — strangle himself?

Graham's most frequent visitor at Brixton remained his solicitor, John Pickworth. As Hertfordshire police had suspected, Graham was determined to seek maximum publicity by pleading not guilty to each charge at trial. This would be his big moment, particularly when he appeared as the only witness for the defence. The eyes of court and country — and to some extent the rest of the world — would alight on him as he took his place in history as an eminent poisoner. Aware that his background would give the press a field day, he knew and welcomed the headlines that were to come. His attitude drove his solicitor to distraction; John Pickworth pleaded with Graham to let him handle matters differently, but without success. Finding a suitable QC to defend Graham under those circumstances was no easy task and, as a result, the trial was postponed twice. Finally, a date was set: 19 June 1972. Just a few days beforehand, Pickworth secured the services of Sir Arthur Irvine, QC, who had acted as Solicitor General for England and Wales for the last three years of Harold Wilson's government. Mr Freddie Beazley would assist as his junior.

Graham remained convinced that he would walk free from court and chafed against the tedium of life in prison, writing to his sister: 'I attempt to circumvent it by reading or playing chess against myself. The latter is a somewhat schizophrenic exercise, calling for almost superhuman detachment, but at least I have the consolation that I invariably win! At present I exist in a sort of limbo, my remands having finished and my trial yet to come. I can imagine how anxious you are to see the whole thing finished with. I, too, wish to see the end of this unfortunate episode. I trust that it will end in victory — the alternative would be the finish of me.'

Further evidence of Graham's troubled mental state was presented by Dr Peter Scott, who examined him on 18 April to ascertain whether he was fit to stand trial. Much of Scott's report is familiar territory, but there are some fresh insights. Noting Graham was 'always neatly dressed' and physically 'normal', albeit with bad teeth and red marks on his upper arms ('said to be sulphuric acid burns'), Scott documented Graham's regret at never having married, continuing:

He has exceptional ability to hide or deny sympathy and affection so that he tends to be described as 'devoid of feelings'; he gives the impression of having to force himself to be callous and hard. He says that he is 'sombre' in all his tastes and that gaiety embarrasses him. He shows a very strong tenacity of purpose and rigidity of character, but is not obsessional. He recognises a 'streak of arrogance' in himself. He tends to drink fairly heavily and to inhale ether for its interesting effects. He has a fantasy of having sufficient money to own a fast car and to live in a large, secluded Gothic house, where he could pursue his studies and thus gain power over people.

Scott went on to describe him as:

cooperative, never challenging authority, nor trying to manipulate people, though sometimes insistently demanding. He is in excellent touch with reality and shows no disorder of perception, except that very occasionally, at times of particular stress he suddenly feels 'detached', as though looking in on himself (a not uncommon phenomenon occurring widely in psychiatric patients and normal people). He shows a dry sense of humour, and has been observed to show anger, despair, self-criticism and to weep, quite appropriately. He seems reluctant to be friendly and, if he becomes so, seems to make a conscious effort to withdraw again. Similarly, he will sometimes express remorse or affection and show considerable insight into his own personality but next time he is seen it has all been withdrawn. Throughout the great stress of this long remand he has always maintained his innocence in regard to the current charges. He has not shown any disorder of thought; he has not been hallucinating and there are no paranoid or depressive delusions. He has expressed hopelessness and failure and has felt 'I might as well be dead.' He has been a considerable worry lest he should kill himself and will continue to be a risk in this respect.

Scott explained his clinical viewpoint:

If convicted he will need long-term treatment in secure conditions. It is very difficult to know whether this would be most appropriately achieved in one of the special hospitals or in the prison system, bearing in mind that if within the prison system a transfer to a special hospital would be a possibility, whereas transfer in the reverse direction would not. There is the additional point that there may be some hostile reaction towards him from other patients within the special hospitals and that this might be less marked in prison; perhaps anticipating this, the defendant himself has told me that, if convicted, he would much prefer the prison system and does not think he could face a return to the special hospitals. In my opinion there would be a very much higher risk of suicide if he were transferred to a special hospital. If a hospital order were made and (as seems likely) the Health Authority decide that it would be unwise to return him to Broadmoor, then the remaining two special hospitals might be even less suitable for him than Broadmoor. For these reasons I would prefer him to be placed (if convicted) within the prison system. From the medico-legal point of view he would have known what he was doing and that it was wrong. He has

a mental abnormality which substantially diminishes his responsibility but does not fall within
the definition of psychopathic disorder in terms
of the Mental Health Act 1959. He is likely to be
fit to plead and to stand his trial.

* * *

One week after Dr Scott had compiled his report
on Graham's mental health, Chief Superintendent
Harvey wrote to the Director of Public Prosecutions
regarding a troubling exchange involving Graham in
Brixton. A solicitor acting for a felon named Leon
Carlton had written to Harvey, stating that his client
had some information to pass on regarding Graham.
Harvey agreed to meet Carlton, who was married
with children and in his mid-30s. A club owner and
company director, he had been arrested in August
1971 with three other men, two of them brothers, all
accused of running protection rackets and handing
out punishment beatings. Harvey visited Carlton in
his solicitor's presence and listened as the prisoner
described how he had arrived in the HMP Brixton
hospital in February 1972, where he met Graham.
They struck up a conversation and spoke on several
occasions during exercise periods. Graham discussed
his case, specifically referring to thallium, and spoke
about medical matters.

Carlton recalled: 'He asked me about witnesses in
my case and if there were any who were a nuisance
to me. I told him that one or two were lying and he
said he might be able to help me.' Carlton stated that
Graham went on to explain 'how thallium could be
purchased from a chemist and warned me to avoid

the chain chemists such as a Boots and go to an old established chemist who was more likely to have thallium in stock. He specifically warned me not to go to John Bell & Croyden but I had never heard of this firm and so it didn't mean anything to me. He described how thallium came in the form of crystals which could be dissolved in water and then become odourless and tasteless.'

Claiming to be troubled that Graham 'could kill innocent people', Carlton asked him to write down the details of what he had told him regarding thallium. Graham did as he asked, and they continued to chat:

On one occasion [Graham] told me that he went with the managing director of the firm he worked for to the funeral of one of the men he had poisoned. He said the man had been cremated and there was no hope of the police finding sufficient thallium in the body to prove murder. I asked him to explain this and was told that there could be thallium there, but by that time there would not be enough to show that he had given the man a fatal dose. At the same time he told me that the managing director was a capitalist pig and that he was lucky.

Carlton told Harvey that he had asked Graham whether he had meant to kill this man:

Young laughed and said that he had but couldn't get the opportunity. Another time he told me there was a bug going round where he worked and the symptoms were very similar to poisoning by thallium and he had been able to give people poison and it was thought that it was the bug. In connection with this, he made particular mention of poisoning somebody in a garden.

During his first meeting with Harvey, Carlton refused to make a written statement. He said that Detective Chief Superintendent Bert Wickstead of New Scotland Yard's Serious Crime Squad had 'got it in' for him. Wickstead was then well known in London as the 'Gangbuster', having jailed several gangland bosses, but he was frequently accused — though never convicted — of malpractice. Carlton wanted Harvey to get Wickstead off his back, insisting that he was innocent of the charges against him and that he had been threatened by a gang, which made him want to turn Queen's evidence. Harvey told him he would speak to Wickstead, certainly, but had no influence over him. Carlton seemed satisfied by this and asked, 'I'll be exercising with Young this afternoon; are there any particular points you want me to cover?' Harvey told him to keep his ears open.

Harvey spoke to Wickstead that same day, relating the meeting with Carlton. For his part, Wickstead said he had no interest in Carlton as a witness, telling Harvey that he was an East End gangster whose crimes included bribery and impersonation of police officers. Harvey then informed the Director of Public Prosecutions about the entire affair. At the request of Carlton's solicitor, he returned to Brixton for another meeting, accompanied by DCI Kirkpatrick. Carlton said he had decided to make a statement because Graham was 'confident of an acquittal' and the possibility of this disturbed him. Harvey then recorded

Carlton's statement and took possession of the piece of paper on which Graham had scribbled details pertaining to thallium acetate in his neat handwriting:

Thallous Acetate: (pronounced thall-youss asset-ate)

Description: white crystals, odourless, tasteless, colourless when dissolved in water.

Fatal dose: 15gms (¼ level teaspoonful).

Produces symptoms of Landry's Paralysis. Time of action: symptoms appear 24 to 48 hours after administration, death occurs within 7—10 days.

Post-mortem appearances: multiple nervous inflammation consistent with Landry's Paralysis.

To obtain: purchasers should go to large retail chemist, representing himself as either: 1/ chemistry student or 2/ gemmologist. He should request chemist to order 25mgs of thallous acetate for him from Analar Dept of British Drug Houses Ltd. If asked for reason he should say that he requires it for 1/detections and estimation of metallic thallium or 2/ for making up into Leclerc's Solution (used in gemmology). Having placed his order the purchaser should be prepared for a 1 to 2 week delay whilst chemist awaits delivery from BDH. Chemist will then request him to sign the poisons register before sale is effected. This is only a formality, the chemical will then be supplied to purchaser and the transaction is completed.

Purchaser is advised to select old established firm as it is possible that the latter will already have thallium in stock. It is NOT advisable to use chain chemists, Boots, Co-op, etc., and John Bell & Croyden's must NOT be approached.

15gms of thallous acetate will dissolve in 1—2 drachms (teaspoonsful) water, forming a colourless, odourless and tasteless solution. It will not alter the taste or colour of spirits, tea, coffee, foodstuffs, etc.

Harvey contacted the Director of Public Prosecutions immediately to ask them to consider Carlton's statement 'worthy of credence'. Although most of it was already known to the Prosecution 'none of it has been published in any manner which would make it accessible to Carlton'.

When Graham discovered that Carlton had spoken to Harvey and passed on the note, he was disgusted: 'To me, the whole thing stank. I was sure it was a police set-up. I decided to play along with the idea and see if it was used in court.' It was also a means of allowing Carlton himself to be shown in a better light, which had the potential to be useful to him. During Graham's trial, little was made of the incident. It became noteworthy only because Prosecutor John Leonard revealed a streak of sexism in telling the jury that the paper Graham had handed to Carlton 'revealed that a quarter teaspoonful would dissolve in another teaspoonful of water to give a colourless, tasteless, odourless clear liquid. It said that thallium would not affect the taste of tea, coffee, wine or spirits. There, members of the jury, you have the recipe handed to a fellow prisoner in much the same way as your wife might hand over a cooking recipe to her

370

friend.'

Carlton's trial at the Old Bailey for conspiracies to cause grievous bodily harm, to blackmail and for running a long firm fraud concluded on 4 July 1972. Together with his co-accused, Phillip Jacobs and George Dixon, Leon Carlton was sentenced to 12 years in prison.

★ ★ ★

A meeting about Graham's case and its implications had taken place at the Home Office in April. Those present included Sir Philip Allen, acting as chairman, and Sir George Godber, Chief Medical Officer, for the Home Office and Department of Health and Social Security, and Dr Patrick McGrath of Broadmoor. According to the minutes of the meeting, the discussion revolved mainly around damage-limitation measures. Dr Udwin, although not present, was not criticised: 'It was recognised that, although there had been a mistake in clinical judgement, the opinion formed by the doctor was reasonable in relation to the facts then available to him' and that 'prognosis was especially difficult because the clinical history was in many respects unique'. In addition to considering what could be done 'going forward' to prevent a similar case happening, there was also some deliberation on Graham's own future: 'DHSS representatives and Dr McGrath expressed the view that it would be inappropriate for Young to be returned to Broadmoor on re-conviction, since on present information he appeared to be unlikely to benefit from further hospital treatment and he would be in danger from other patients there.' Whatever the outcome in court, the idea of Graham returning to Broadmoor was palatable to no one, including Graham himself.

As the trial loomed, C3 were especially concerned about media interest in the case and the Home Office role. They had been contacted by Bernard Scarlet, chief crime reporter of the Press Association, who was compiling a 'now it can be told' background story on Graham for release to newspapers and broadcasting outlets throughout the UK as soon as the verdict was passed. Scarlet warned that 'the case is likely to raise some awkward questions for some government departments, including ourselves'. He had spoken to the management of Hadlands and informed C3 that 'the firm are not 'gunning' for anyone, although they naturally feel aggrieved at not being told in confidence about the true nature of Young's medical history. Evidently they have a fairly good record of employing ex-prisoners and say that they might well have taken Young on anyway but of course they would have kept him under some kind of supervision.' Scarlet's request was followed by numerous other enquiries, including one from the BBC, whose research assistant Angela Holdsworth was 'preparing a documentary film on the problems of people leaving Broadmoor'. She intended to refer to Graham and hoped to be given access to medical reports from his earlier trial, along with the transcript. The Home Office politely declined to get involved with any media outlets, having enough to deal with in ongoing communications between themselves, Broadmoor, the department of employment and the probation service. Any observations about the case were kept strictly to themselves.

The Department of Employment eventually took responsibility for the information that was given — or rather, not given — to Hadlands about Graham's background. In a letter to C3, one of their senior staff explained:

> We had to view him also against the background of our policy for dealing with those who have been convicted. When the offence is relevant to the job (e.g. a man convicted of fraud being considered for a position of financial trust), the employer (with the applicant's agreement) is informed. In this case the 'offence' of Young was linked to a mental illness which preceded its commission. Again Dr Udwin's report stated in unqualified terms that Young had made a full recovery. There was therefore no reason to believe he would repeat the 'offence'.

He reiterated that the responsibility for Hadlands not being informed of this, or that Graham had been treated and 'recovered' at Broadmoor 'is our responsibility'. Staff at the Slough government training centre knew no more than those who went on to employ Graham. There was consternation at C3 over Graham's reference for Hadlands, which was in the form of Dr Udwin's psychiatric report, from which the normal 'Broadmoor' heading was mysteriously absent, but this was never resolved.

Prior to Graham's trial, a second psychiatric report was commissioned from Dr Connell, physician at the Maudsley hospital, on behalf of the Director of Public Prosecutions. Like Dr Scott, he had found Graham 'cooperative, talkative and clearly intelligent' while continuing to 'maintain his innocence' of the charges brought against him. He deemed him to be 'fully in touch with reality and did not show, at interview, any disorders of perception. Nor did he appear clinically depressed though he shows some anxiety concerning the hearing of his case.' As regards his previous crimes, Graham told Dr Connell 'I was emotionally disturbed' and 'I had acquired a psychopathic disorder.' He said that he had acted up at first but as time went on his disorder remitted so that he was normal on discharge from Broadmoor. There was not a great deal that they could discuss regarding the present charges since Graham denied them, 'but he noted that his diary was merely fantasy and nothing to do with real events.' Dr Connell then made several observations, including that Graham was 'suffering from a psychopathic disorder' and 'a mental abnormality which substantially diminishes his responsibility and which can be regarded as a psychopathic disorder under the definition of the Mental Health Act 1959.' Furthermore, at the time of his crimes, 'he would have known what he was doing and that it was wrong'. Looking to the future, Graham needed 'to be looked after in a situation of maximum security since in my opinion he is likely to commit similar offences in the future if he has the opportunity.' On balance, Dr Connell felt a prison placement would be 'more humane since there is little that direct treatment can offer him in a special psychiatric setting'. He would also require psychiatric supervision; in the event of being found guilty of the offences, he should be closely watched 'since he may well become depressed and even suicidal'. Dr Connell concluded: 'He is fit to plead and to stand trial.'

On 8 June 1972, Dr Christopher Mark Fysh, formerly senior medical officer of Ashford Remand Centre, contacted the Home Office regarding approaches he had received from the press about Graham's case. Fysh had examined Graham on numerous occasions during 1961 and 1962; it was he who had submitted a report to the Central Criminal Court giving evidence that Graham 'was prepared to take the risk of killing to gratify his interest in poisons. The prognosis is frankly bad.' Dr Fysh wanted to know if he could grant certain interviews, having been asked repeatedly about his earlier prognostications, declaring:

The implications are obvious but, believe me, I feel no satisfaction in the possibility of having been correct in my opinion. However, it is not at all surprising that I have been approached by the BBC and the press who of course like myself realise that the matter is sub-judice, but have asked whether I would be prepared, if Young is found guilty, to be interviewed and comment on the report I made to the Central Criminal Court and the evidence I gave in public to that court.

I pointed out that as an ex-civil servant I regarded myself as bound in certain respects by the Official Secrets Act, but did not know how far this extended, for instance, in expressing my opinion of his then condition and the evidence I gave in court. I may be wrong, but I have gained the impression that a great deal of pressure will be put on me to comment if Young is guilty.

I realise that the treatment of dangerous offenders is a matter of great public interest and controversy, as well as material for the sensational press. If Young is found guilty I feel that I can properly comment on my evidence given in public and defend (if necessary) and explain my recommendation to the court. I would also like to express, if asked, my confidence in the integrity of Broadmoor even if, in common with all humanity, their judgement can be at fault, and that they must have the freedom to exercise that judgement if any progress is to be made in the treatment of dangerous offenders.

Finally, I would like to show that the medical side of the prison service is very much aware of its responsibilities to the public as well as the individual offender. Frankly, I took a very great deal of trouble in this case as well as the advice of outside consultants. I had many interviews with Young, and [am] profoundly concerned to avoid further tragedy.

May I therefore be instructed as to whether I am liable to commit any offence under the Official Secrets Act or contempt of court. Since I am now happily retired I do not wish to spend my remaining years in Brixton.

My direct approach to yourself is dictated by a desire for completely impartial and authoritative advice in connection with my service to the court and its consequences ...

Almost ten years to the day had passed since Graham's first trial and his second. When Dr Fysh was initially told that his former patient was about to face another round of murder charges, he responded calmly: 'I am not surprised. I am no prophet, but I thought he would remain a permanent danger to the public for the remainder of his life.'

24

A DEVILISH THING TO DO

'Make me so famous that I wind up in the Chamber of Horrors at Madame Tussauds. I want to go down in history as a really famous murderer.'

The writing on the note was unmistakable; it came from the man in the dock, who basked in the attention bestowed upon him like an actor at the opening night of a roaringly successful play. The room thronged with people, although Graham's aunt Win, sister Winifred and cousin Sandra only attended sporadically due to commitments with work and childcare, and in the case of Win, looking after her husband Jack who was again unwell. Fred Young did not attend. But representatives from all the national newspapers and other media were present, including the recipient of that note and more: writer Anthony Holden, there to report on the trial for his local newspaper. Throughout proceedings, Graham unabashedly courted the media and would probably have held his own press conference after each session if such a thing were possible.

Despite his anxiety about the trial during his time on remand, when he appeared in court, all nerves fled, and he performed before his audience with enormous confidence. 'His demeanour was very arrogant, detached,' Holden recalled. 'Like one of those dictators who doesn't recognise the court.' Even the presence of stern Mr Justice Edward Eveleigh, a former British army officer of 54, who still carried his black cap to every murder trial, failed to dent Graham's enjoyment of the judicial process. 'He was very proud of being the first person to use thallium in a poisoning case in Britain,' Graham's defence lawyer Peter Goodman recalled. 'I suppose the trial was an experiment in seeing if he could use his knowledge to argue his way out of it.'

Court No.1 of St Albans Crown Court had certainly never hosted a case quite like it. The newly designated court building, granted its superior status following the termination of assizes and quarter sessions, was ill-equipped to deal with the sheer volume of interest in a trial that began with an error: the clerk of court read the wrong oath to the all-male jury, who were sworn in at 10:40am. Peering from behind his large, black-rimmed spectacles, Mr Justice Eveleigh looked distinctly unimpressed. 'I suppose we had better begin again,' he grumbled. The correct oath was then read.

Shortly before 11am, Mr John Leonard QC — 'a small, neat convivial man with wiry hair' — rose to outline the case for the prosecution. Graham beamed as Mr Leonard referred to him as a young man 'with a great knowledge of poisons and a macabre interest in their effects. He studied poisons in the public library as a boy, reading books about mass murderers.' Forbidden by the legal process from referring to Graham's teenage offences, Leonard was at pains to present a picture of the defendant as an almost lifelong enthusiast of poison and its criminal practitioners, particularly William Palmer, whose biography he read compulsively: 'He expressed some admiration for him.' He described how Graham had told detectives that he was a misfit and loner as a youth, 'sniffing bottles of ether or nail polish', and felt very different to his peers: 'He is alleged to have said, 'I became obsessed with the macabre. Toxicology always fascinated me."

Leonard then turned to Graham's diary, 'a chilling document' that was 'almost unbelievably callous'. There was nothing fictional about it, despite the defendant hoping to convince them otherwise, but it was in every other sense 'almost unbelievable, the record of a poisoner with the power to choose the fate of other people. He noted their symptoms, tried to visit them in hospital, made various drawings showing their deterioration and pointed out mistakes being made by the doctors.' The diary entries bore out the prosecution's submission that Graham had wanted to play God, or act as a Nazi commandant at the ramp of a concentration camp, deciding who should live and who should die. Graham had insisted there was thus method to his madness, telling detectives: 'You are suggesting I am some kind of monster, a mass murderer who just poisons people regardless — this is not so. I suppose I ceased to see them as people, but to me they become guinea pigs.'

His diary underlined the point, revealing 'a possible motive' in the defendant's 'scientific experimental approach to the whole problem. It is a very macabre situation if he did — and perhaps he had a tendency to treat human beings as guinea pigs ... It may well be that you may well come to the conclusion eventually that this young man has a desire to establish his power over other people and that is the real motive for what has happened.'

It was this ambition which informed Graham's

comment to police after his arrest. Remarking on his alleged attempted murders, he had declared: 'That is an academic point. I could have killed them if I wanted, but I allowed them to live.' His conceit in his own skill as a poisoner was his undoing, since he 'took great care to let detectives know the extent of his activities, how many victims had been chosen, and his ability to decide between a lethal and sub-lethal dose.'

Leonard then spent 20 minutes reading almost the entire content of Graham's diary. He explained the use of initials to represent individuals such as Bob Egle, about whom the diarist had written: 'In a way it seems a shame to commit such a likeable man to such a horrible end. But I had made my decision and therefore he is doomed to premature disease.' Leonard provided the jury with another example:

'F' [Fred Biggs] is being obstinately difficult. If he survives a third week he will live. That could be inconvenient. I am most annoyed. He is surviving far too long for my peace of mind ... F is now seriously ill, he is now unconscious and has developed paralysis and blindness. It is likely that he will die within a few days. It will be a merciful release for him. He would certainly be permanently impaired. Even if the blindness is reversed, organic brain disease would render him a husk. It is better that he should die. From my point of view his death would be a relief. It would remove one casualty from what is becoming a crowded field of battle.

The prosecutor allowed the sheer inhumanity of that entry to sink in before describing how Fred Biggs was

380

treated in three hospitals for chronic nervous disorders and died from bronchial pneumonia after receiving assistance with breathing. Leonard told the court that the diary also revealed a macabre plan to administer poison to David Tilson while he was already hospitalised. Graham's intention had been to offer him a toxic nip from a miniature bottle of brandy with the aim of bringing about Tilson's death 'within a week'. His diabolical plan was thwarted by the hospital's strict visiting policy. Another entry implied that the killer had come to realise that detection of his crimes was inevitable.

Leonard also referred to the sketches found in Graham's room: 'They showed a man with hair, then little hair, then baldness and finally the grave. There was a drawing of a bottle with a genie rising from it and a skull-and-crossbones on the head.' Finally, he turned to the formula for thallium poisoning, which Graham had passed to Leon Carlton on remand in Brixton prison, 'in much the same way as your wife might hand over a cooking recipe to her friend'.

Leonard had outlined the case for the prosecution with ease, but it was not until the following day that the emotional impact of Graham's obsession with poison shook the court.

★ ★ ★

Mrs Dorothy Egle clutched a handkerchief as she entered the witness box and pulled at it repeatedly while giving evidence of her late husband's suffering. Sitting on the chair offered to her, she told the court that Bob had been a healthy, happy man until the illness that killed him. Their last holiday had been a good one, and he had been perfectly fit upon their return, but then he went to work 'and the next day came home and said his fingertips were numb. He didn't want any tea and lay down on the settee.' Mrs Egle hesitated and began to sob. Mr Justice Eveleigh, recognising a witness who needed time to compose herself, adjourned the hearing for a few minutes.

When the court reconvened, Mrs Egle was able to describe that last day with her husband at home, when they had gone out to stable their daughter's beloved horse:

> He couldn't walk, he was feeling so ill. We went out about nine o'clock. He tried to get down the road with me but I had to bring him back. He was just staggering along like someone who was drunk. I got him back home and straight up to bed. He said he couldn't feel his tie or the buttons on his shirt so I helped him. That night he was groaning with pains in his back. The doctor came twice early next morning and later I went in the ambulance with him to hospital.

After eight days of unimaginable suffering, her husband died from a paralysis which started at the extremities and affected his breathing.

Hadlands' managing director, Geoffrey Foster, then took the stand to tell the court about attending Bob Egle's cremation with his killer. He recalled the young storeman remarking that it was sad Bob should 'come through the terrors of Dunkirk, only to fall victim to some strange virus'. Graham had asked him about the cause of death. 'I had that morning received a copy of the death certificate. I told him it

382

was polyneuritis,' Foster related. 'He remarked that polyneuritis was only a general term and there must have been some further indication on the certificate of the type of polyneuritis.' Graham had then mentioned some syndrome and Foster recalled that 'when he said that I remembered that was on the death certificate.' Graham had then explained to him how polyneuritis generally caused bronchial pneumonia. 'I recalled that that was also on the death certificate,' confirmed Foster. 'I was very, very surprised at the apparent depth of Graham's medical knowledge.' Pathologist Dr John Pugh then gave evidence about the post-mortem he had conducted on Bob Egle's remains: 'My findings about the cause of death correspond with thallium poisoning — heavy metal poisoning.'

The earliest known survivor of Graham's post-Broadmoor poisonings then stepped into the witness box. 'I used to go out drinking with Young,' Trevor Sparkes told the jury. 'In March last year I got the first pain on the football field. I was aching in the groin and weak in the thigh and leg muscles. I had to leave the field and I have never played again ... I am better now but I still get these aches in the groin.'

On Wednesday, 21 June, one of Graham's most recent surviving victims took the stand: Jethro Batt, still showing clear signs of debilitation and hair loss. He had never dreamed the man he regarded as a friend might try to kill him, but the means by which the defendant was able to dispense poison so readily soon became apparent. Batt told the court that Graham had made him a bitter-tasting cup of coffee: 'I had only one mouthful and put it down again. Young asked me, 'What's the matter, do you think I'm trying to poison you?' Twenty minutes later something came up in my chest and I had to rush to the toilet and vomit.' Excruciating pains then attacked his legs, stomach and chest and within six days he could no longer stand. He was taken to hospital a fortnight later, with his hair 'falling out by the handful. By this time I was having hallucinations and I wanted to commit suicide. That is certainly something that I have never felt before.' Batt then told the jury that Graham had confided that it was quite easy to poison people and make it look afterwards as though they had died from natural causes. He had never named the poison but described it as 'tasteless and odourless and that even the doctors would say the death was from natural causes'.

David Tilson confirmed that he, too, became ill after drinking a few sips from the rancid-tasting cup of tea Graham had handed him. His legs had gone numb the following day and then the pain began: 'I could not breathe very deeply because of the pain.' While in St Albans city hospital, 'I immediately began to feel better and within five days they allowed me to come home. I felt I was well enough to go back to work.' But his illness had returned. Towards the end of November his hair began falling out in handfuls and he was readmitted to hospital. Leonard then produced photographs showing the normally hirsute witness almost completely bald. 'I'm sorry to remind you of it,' said Leonard, 'but these photographs do not show you as you are now.' Tilson admitted: 'I had to wear a wig for a time but my hair has since grown again.' He added that he had recovered without specific treatment during his second stint in hospital, but he had lost 21 pounds in weight. Dr Edward Cowan, consultant physician at St Albans city hospital, confirmed that Tilson had come to them 'looking like a three-quarters-plucked chicken. This was very unusual and significant. It made us think of heavy metals and the possibility of thallium poisoning.'

Diana Smart confirmed that she had suffered sickness, body odour and cramp after drinking coffee in the workplace: 'My legs were so weak, it was agony to walk. For three weeks I was ill. I was sick every afternoon following the coffee break.' She usually recovered over her weekends away from the firm. But on later occasions, when Graham brought her coffee, the symptoms returned with a vengeance. She told the jury, 'When this happened, Young was always very concerned. On one occasion he went and got a chair and made me sit down near an open door and brought me a glass of water.' She recalled speaking to Graham about Fred Biggs shortly after the older man's funeral: 'He said to me, 'Poor old Fred, I wonder what went wrong. I was rather fond of Fred." She added that although she herself had an interest in medicine, it was nothing compared to Graham's understanding of the subject, which he liked to demonstrate regularly, using technical terms. 'He was very morbid,' she remembered. 'He was an unusual character and spoke a lot of medical terms. We used to have conversations. He would always go out of my reach.' Then she said, with evident bemusement, 'I have never done anything to inspire Young to do what he did to me. I always thought I got on very well with him.'

Peter Buck, import-and-export manager at Hadlands, told the court that he too had been sick after drinking tea while working in the stores with Graham one afternoon the previous October. Fifteen minutes later Buck felt nauseous: 'I got a headache and had to sit down and was still being sick when I got home that night. I was quite sure it was something to do with the tea Graham had served me. I was sure of this because I had not eaten any breakfast that morning and the vomit consisted of the tea only.' Buck also told the court how he had once found Graham skipping work to read a book concerned with humanity's 'preoccupation with death'. He added that Graham had frequently asked after Biggs and Tilson, remarking that he understood the latter was losing his hair. 'We were not aware that this was common knowledge at the time,' said Buck.

Dr Arthur Anderson recalled the staff meeting at Hadlands where Graham had displayed an 'extremely extensive knowledge of both medical expressions and the cause of illness and in particular, poisoning'. Anderson admitted: 'To be quite honest, his questions showed that he knew a very great deal about poisoning and I as a GP did not know all that much about it. I had been taken aback by his knowledge, which was far above that which I would have expected to find in a person doing his kind of work.'

Detective Chief Inspector John Kirkpatrick gave evidence, recalling Graham's remark, 'The whole story is too terrible. You would be disgusted and amazed.' Then Detective Chief Superintendent Ronald Harvey, 'in a well-pressed grey suit' according to the *Daily Mail*, took the stand. He was a sturdy presence in the witness box, with all the paraphernalia of police work within his reach. This included a vast brown wooden pegboard on which there hung bottles and phials of poison removed from Graham's lodgings. Harvey described how Graham had told him that a fatal dose of thallium found in his jacket pocket was 'my exit dose — exit in inverted commas — but I didn't have the chance to use it.' He recalled asking the defendant if a bottle of sodium partrate mixed with antimony salt had been supplied to any of his victims. Graham had replied, 'Yes — Di Smart.' The accused had admitted that some antimony sodium tartrate found in his room also contained antimony potassium tartrate. When Harvey enquired if he had administered this to anyone, Graham had nodded, 'Yes. Peter Buck, Di Smart, Ron Hewitt and Trevor Sparkes.' When Harvey had asked him to whom he had administered the thallium, the accused had replied, 'Well, of course you know the answer to that.' He recalled Graham's recital of the verse from 'The Ballad of Reading Gaol', and how, when it was suggested he was feeling some remorse, Graham had interrupted, 'No, Mr Harvey. That would be hypocritical. What I feel is in the emptiness of my soul.'

The second woman to be widowed while her husband worked at Hadlands gave evidence: Fred Biggs had likewise enjoyed an active life, filled with gardening and ballroom dancing, until his sudden illness at the end of last October. Annie Biggs related how Fred had made a brief recovery and then felt unwell after Graham had offered him a cuppa during stock-taking fortnight. Her husband had visited his doctor who gave him medicine, but it had no effect: 'He had great difficulty in walking and complained of pains in the chest.' At night, his feet hurt him so much that he couldn't even bear the bedsheets on them. Fred Biggs' doctor had sent him to the local hospital, but he was transferred a few days later to the Whittington hospital where he was put in intensive care. Graham had then telephoned Annie Biggs. She recalled: 'He said to me, 'Oh, I have just learned today that your husband is in hospital. Could I go and see him?' I said no, as I thought my husband would only want to see the family.' Fred Biggs had died on 17 November, following the doctors' suspicions of toxic effects.

Dr Hugh Johnson, forensic pathologist and senior lecturer in forensic medicine at St Thomas's hospital, London was the main prosecution witness to take the stand on 23 June. He told the court how Agatha Christie's novel *The Pale Horse* had led him to conclude that Fred Biggs had died of thallium poisoning. 'I was the first to suggest thallium poisoning,' Dr Johnson insisted. 'I had studied it closely before carrying out my investigation and had heard about its effects before I began. I had also read the thriller and knew something of its effects on people from that book.' He recalled being telephoned after Biggs' death and being told his case history along with those of Batt and Tilson: 'I happened to be interested in poisoning cases and the very bizarre nature of this poison had stuck in my mind.'

As far as Johnson was aware, there had never been a case of thallium poisoning in England. Asked to define thallium, the doctor said it was a metallic element used in making optical glass. It could also be used for killing rats and had even been used in the medical treatment of scalp disorders. He added, 'This however was discontinued because some children had died as a result of this treatment.' Dr Johnson said a fatal dose of thallium would be between ¾ and 1 gram, the equivalent of 12 to 15 grains. He said he had contemplated taking some of the poison himself as an experiment but decided against it. In the case of antimony, this was also a metallic element and a large dose could cause death from shock and dehydration.

The case for the prosecution ended there. It was 3:30 on Friday afternoon. There had been no intense or controversial cross-examination of any of the witnesses as such, more a straightforward corroboration of facts. Throughout the entire proceedings, Graham had observed and listened intently to his former colleagues, detectives and doctors giving evidence against him. But he remained impassive. 'The Man in the Dark Suit Just Listens' was one headline. The *Daily Mail* reported:

> The man in black seemed in his brooding, intense way to dominate the proceedings, though he took no active part. Fingertips together. Brown suede shoes peeping below the dock rail. Sharp, pale face bent forward to miss not a word they were saying about how he was alleged to have mixed poison potions for his unsuspecting friends and workmates. He listened as a police witness spoke of his highly sophisticated knowledge of poisons and their effect on the human body and gave a sharp shake of his black hair if, as happened once or twice yesterday, a witness stumbled over the unfamiliar language of pharmaceuticals.

The defence was due to begin its evidence the following week, with the jury expected to retire to consider their verdict on Thursday, according to Sir Arthur.

On Monday, Graham would take the stand.

25

HE IS JUSTLY SERVED

Monday, 26 June 1972 was a brighter day, weather-wise, than it had been since the trial began. It was still cooler than was usual for that time of year, but the sun glimmered on the cascading fountains outside the court building and the rosebuds of the public garden were in full bloom.

There was not a single seat free in Court No. 1. The public gallery was packed with attentive spectators and alert reporters who shuffled in anticipation as the legal personages took their places and the defendant was brought up in a state of barely repressed elation. Journalist Arnold Latcham, who had reported on Graham's first trial, was at his second to see him emerge as 'totally wicked. A complete psychopath, a living Jekyll and Hyde. Confident, at ease, left hand always lounging in his trouser pocket.' Anthony Holden noticed the same calculated performance: 'Neat black suit, immaculate grooming, one hand generally in his left trouser pocket, the other resting on the bar rail, the refusal to sit, the occasional sip of water, the requests for adjournments to gather his thoughts — all combined to produce the impressive histrionic performance designed to earn him the publicity he coveted.' Near Latcham and Holden sat Susan Nowak of the *Watford Observer*, who thought the man in the dock 'clearly a very intelligent fellow, but he also came across as incredibly creepy. You

390

didn't want to make eye contact with him because he just had this unnerving aura about him.'

At 10:30am, Graham strolled into the witness box and stood with his hands resting lightly on the wood surround. Defence counsel, Sir Arthur Irvine QC, rose to his feet and began leading his client through the tangle of charges against him. Regarding the veracity of the allegation of administering poison to Trevor Sparkes, Graham responded, 'Certainly not. I emphatically deny it.' He recalled that sometime in March of the previous year Sparkes had mentioned suffering persistent groin pains.

'Did you offer him anything by way of medicinal treatment?'

'On a couple of occasions during the time he was ill he came to my room to talk to me and on these occasions — as was my habit when he came to visit me — I offered him a glass of wine. I believe he complained of tension one day and I suggested that he take some 30 grains of potassium bromide. I myself use it as a sedative to enable me to sleep. I tend to be an insomniac. I find difficulty sleeping.'

Asked about his colleagues at Hadlands, Graham said that he had been on friendly terms with his fellow store workers: Bob Egle, Fred Biggs and Ronald Hewitt. In August last year the stores had been plagued by wasps: 'Fred suggested we use sugar and water placed in a bowl outside the doors,' Graham told the court, 'the theory being they would be attracted to the water rather than the interior of the stores. As a result of this, we struck up a general conversation about market control.' They discussed insecticides and Biggs mentioned that his garden had been invaded by some sort of bug. Graham suggested using nicotine to get rid of the pests; three or four days later he brought in a tin of nicotine dust and offered it to Biggs, who wasn't convinced of its effectiveness. Graham said he had taken the tin home and then recommended a thallium solution: 10 grams (about 150 grains) to a gallon of water. He again offered to provide some, explaining he had bought 25 grams of thallium from a chemist using the pseudonym M E Evans, purely for the purpose of scientific study. Returning to the subject of thallium and its use as a garden pesticide for Fred Biggs to try, Graham told the court, 'Because of my knowledge of chemicals and toxic substances I was able to warn him how dangerous it was.'

Irvine asked him about his arrest. Graham replied that he had felt embarrassed walking about the police station in a blanket 'like a Sioux Indian'. This and other factors, including not being allowed to wash, shave or comb his hair, and the lack of food and drink, influenced him during his interviews with detectives at Hemel Hempstead. In a state of shocked anxiety, he had maintained his innocence until they reached an 'impasse' when he told Detective Chief Superintendent Harvey that he would give him a plausible set of answers to his questions 'in order that and providing that I was then given clothing, food, sleep and access to a solicitor. I emphasised that I would withdraw the statement at the earliest opportunity. It was done purely to enable me to get away from the police station and see my solicitor.' There was no question of him practicing deception; the statement was a 'mere convenience'. He had felt certain that scientific analysis would show his innocence 'and therefore my statement was a false one'.

Irvine then brought him to the subject of his diary.

Graham responded that it was 'not a diary at all. It is set out in diary form, but it is not a number of entries set out over a period of days or weeks. It is a document which was completed on one occasion.' Asked if he could elaborate on that, he said that as far as he could remember, it had been written on 18 November and therefore he would agree to refer to it as a diary only 'under protest — for the sake of convenience'. Asked what led him to write it, he replied, 'The diary, as it were, was the exposition of a theory — not one I seriously held — a somewhat fanciful one which I outlined for my own amusement, although that is not a very apt word.'

He told the court that he had been grimly inspired by what was happening at his workplace:

> The illnesses were unusual in origin and many of us were naturally concerned to know their cause. A number of things sprang to mind, one being virus infection. Something that also sprang to mind — well, to my mind, at any rate — was the similarity of symptoms displayed by people at the firm and the symptoms of heavy metal poisoning. In consequence I decided to elaborate my theory and suggest circumstances under which these things could have come about.

The cause that he ascribed to these illnesses was purely his own invention. The way that the illnesses had come about for the purpose of his theory could not have been the result of a multiple accidental dosage or multiple suicide dosage. So for the purpose of the story, it was necessary to create a homicidal reason. The 'I' in the diary was not him, he said: 'I am writing in the first person but I am not referring to me.' Mr Justice Eveleigh asked, 'You had to postulate someone with homicidal tendencies.' Graham nodded, 'Yes. I intended to elaborate it in the form of a short story or novel, for this was not something I seriously believed. I did at first attempt to set it out in the form of a novel, but my style of writing is somewhat stilted. In consequence, I tore out the first one or two leaves.' He said that other authors had used the same literary device, including two writers he admired deeply: Dennis Wheatley and Bram Stoker.

He said writing was 'something I have always dabbled in' and he had in the past submitted stories about both world wars to an English teacher 'for critical analysis' and a short story to Reader's Digest: 'I never heard any more about it but at least I submitted it.' He said that on a number of occasions in the document he gave way to temptations and wrote to conjure up an atmosphere of horror. He agreed with his defence counsel that part of the document was 'an exercise in the macabre'. If it had been intended to be serious, he would 'certainly not' have left it lying around at the foot of his bed. He had no reason to suppose anyone would take it seriously and there was no reason for him to hide it. The document did not strictly refer to previous illnesses at the firm but one of the fatalities he had in mind was that of Mr Robert Egle. The second he had mentioned was a non-existent fatality which was put in for 'padding'. He agreed that there were parts in which he had deviated from accuracy. The court adjourned for ten minutes for him to sort out the parts in the diary where this had occurred.

Graham's first day in the witness box ended at 4:15pm. The press scrambled to send in their copy;

the following morning, every newspaper in the UK led with the story of the 'Poison Diary'. The Sun had a front-page scoop: 'Accused! The First Picture of the Man in Poison Trial'. Taken in a photo booth, the image showed Graham with his head slightly bowed, eyes raised to the camera in a psychopathic glare. Although it came to personify the murderous turmoil of a man who had spent his life in thrall to poisons, Nazism and other British serial killers, in reality Graham's ferocious expression was the result of being short-changed by the photo booth. Aware that it was just the sort of thing the tabloids would relish to illustrate their accounts of the trial, Graham asked Chief Superintendent Harvey to release the image to the media. There was an embargo on its publication, but *The Sun* released it on Tuesday, 27 June, ahead of Graham's cross-examination by Mr John Leonard QC.

Graham stepped into the witness box quite prepared to do battle with the QC. This, more than the previous day, would determine how he was remembered as a killer: he could either slip up and give away more than he intended, making himself appear cuckolded by a legal brain, or he could remain cool and sinister, the intellectual equal — or even superior — of the man who had spent years training to expose people such as him. Graham was ready.

As the exchange began, Leonard pointedly told the defendant that he was not prepared to regard him as an expert on poisons for the purposes of the case. 'I don't profess to be so,' Graham answered. However, when he referred to a question that he said he had been asked about David Tilson's urine sample, he was quick to make the point that the quantity seemed far less than that found in recorded cases of non-fatal thallium poisoning. With affected modesty he said as an aside to the court, 'Nonetheless, my opinion is that of a layman and must be treated as such.'

Regarding his police interviews, Graham told the court that 'at my own request' he had seen a senior police officer to impart his theory on the illness of Jethro Batt, explaining that he understood Batt's condition to have been caused by a form of heavy metal poisoning. If that were the case, then he would have expected doctors to use dimercaprol and potassium chloride.

'Do you honestly believe, Mr Young,' asked Leonard, 'that the doctors needed your advice? You do, by your own admission, have an extensive knowledge of toxicology, but did you really know more about these things than the hospital doctors?'

'No,' Graham conceded. 'I assumed they would have already commenced this treatment. It would have been highly presumptuous of me to tell a hospital what treatment should be given.'

Leonard pointed out that dimercaprol was mentioned in a book as an antidote for thallium. Graham corrected him: it was not specifically for thallium, but rather for use against a host of heavy metal poisonings.

'You were quite prepared to give the antidote but not prepared to say what the poison itself was?'

'No, that is not the case.'

Leonard then raised the idea of 'the deal' that Graham had talked about the previous day, in which he claimed to have made his confession in exchange for clothing, access to a solicitor and food, etc. 'That is a complete nonsense, is it not?' asked Leonard.

'I'm afraid it isn't. This is exactly what happened.'

He repeated that he spoke freely to the police in a 'spurious' confession, which 'I had no doubt could never be substantiated.'

Leonard said if that was so, then why did he continue 'the process of confession' after achieving his alleged aims of being given clothing, etc.

'Because that was still my part of the bargain.'

Leonard frowned at him, 'Are you seriously saying that an experienced chief superintendent was prepared to enter a deal with a man charged with murder, the effect of which was that the man was going to make a plausible confession, which he would withdraw subsequently?'

'I did not say I was going to give plausible answers,' Graham replied circumspectly. 'I said I would give answers which would satisfy him to the extent of enabling him to press his charges but I said I would later withdraw them.'

Leonard tried to pin Graham down: 'You are an intelligent person. Are you really saying you were prepared to confess in those circumstances merely to get your material comforts?'

Graham was not deterred: 'Yes, because I was convinced that subsequent analysis of the deaths and illnesses of the people concerned would prove they had not suffered from metallic poisoning.'

'Was it not curious then, that the two poisons named in your diary — thallium and antimony — were the very two that your victims were later found to have suffered from?'

Graham made no reply.

'And why did you go on to tell Chief Superintendent Harvey about other victims not even named within the pages of your erstwhile diary?'

Graham answered blithely, 'From my point of view if I was making a spurious confession, the more the merrier.'

Leonard gave a small snort of derision, 'You were certainly giving value for your part of the bargain.'

Graham replied, 'Yes, because I had no reason to think any of the charges preferred against me could be substantiated.'

'Well, you were certainly taking a chance mentioning two poisons which you had previously purchased and of which you knew there were still residues left in your room which the police would find.'

Sounding a trifle bored, Graham answered, 'My confession had to have a semblance of credibility as far as the police were concerned.' He paused, 'Though this revelation may take you aback, Mr Leonard, if I give my word, I tend to keep it.'

There was a ripple around the court. Mr Justice Eveleigh leaned forward to ask a question of his own: 'What sort of odds did you think there were of your suggestions to the police about these people turning out to be true?'

Giving a slight shrug, Graham responded, 'I didn't think there was any chance of my suggestions turning out to be right.'

Leonard then questioned him about remarks he had made to police about his past. Graham denied having told Harvey that he was not like other children, that he was a loner who had read a lot of macabre books, but he admitted to being fascinated by pharmacology from the age of ten. When they discussed his purchasing poisons under a false name, Graham declared smoothly: 'To obtain a Schedule 1 poison the prospective purchaser has to complete a form under Section II of the Dangerous Poisons Act. This has to be countersigned by a householder to the effect that the purchaser is of good character and it has also to be signed by the local police. As you can imagine, this is a time-consuming and somewhat tiresome procedure so I decided to take a short cut.'

'But you used a false name?'

Graham replied, 'I simply used the pseudonym of Evans so as not to be involved in an embarrassing dispute if I were found out.' He smiled at his interrogator, 'You may think this irresponsible, Mr Leonard, and I may agree, but it was hardly felonious.'

The prosecutor was plainly rattled, 'I suggest you knew perfectly well you were buying those poisons for use on human beings.'

Graham shook his head. 'That is not so. I performed various tests on the thallium I bought to establish its solubility and its compatibility or incompatibility with other chemicals.'

Leonard almost caught him out by declaring that he did not have the necessary equipment for full tests.

Graham hesitated, 'No, but I did as much as I could. I also tested thallium's power as an insecticide on wayside weeds.'

'For clarity then,' Leonard said, 'you administered thallium to no one?'

Graham shook his head again, 'No, I performed the tests to satisfy my own curiosity about certain chemical problems. To some extent, one might say that my interest in these substances was that of a collector.'

Leonard then asked him why, if his experiments were so innocent, he carried an 'exit dose' of thallium on his person.

Graham responded that there was no 'great significance' to that fact. 'Had I genuinely wished to commit suicide, Mr Leonard, I had other agents available which would have killed me in a far shorter space of time.' Realising his mistake, he said quickly, 'I have a tendency to stockpile, but I don't believe the fact that a person stockpiles dangerous poisons means he is going to use them against people.'

There was not much to be gained from Leonard's viewpoint in their discussions about the victims. Graham referred archly to 'our old friend, the 'Bovingdon Bug',' causing Leonard to remark, 'If I may say so, Mr Young, you display during the course of your evidence a remarkable calmness.' Graham merely inclined his head, as if to acknowledge a compliment. On the subject of Fred Biggs' death, Leonard asked him, 'Were you so concerned about what had happened that you were unable to do any work that day? You knew you had just killed a second man.'

'That is not so,' Graham said tartly. 'From the picture you paint of me you would have thought that I would have been gleefully rejoicing.'

'Your expression of regret at Mr Biggs' death was pure hypocrisy,' Leonard retorted. 'His death satisfied you.'

Graham slowly shook his head. 'No, I can see very little satisfaction to be derived from the death of a man in circumstances like that.'

Leonard said dryly, 'Neither can I, Mr Young.'

When it came to the matter of the drawings found in Graham's room, Leonard was at a slight advantage, passing them to the jury for inspection before holding them aloft for the entire court to see. 'They have the classic look of shock for a horror comic,' he declared.

400

'The figures written on them correspond exactly to the fatal doses of thallium involved in this case.'

Graham denied the accusation: 'They are a symbolic representation of scenes from my novel. The baldness is not significant. They are clearly gross distortions. The faces could be expressing aggression as much as shock.' Asked about his sketch of an evil genie rising from a bottle of poison, Graham repeated that this, too, was a 'symbolic depiction' of his fictional tale, along with every other sketch.

Leonard then turned to Graham's diary and the tension between the two sparring men spilled over. 'As a work of fiction it jumps into the middle of the story pretty quickly, doesn't it?' Leonard asked.

'Yes, but diaries often do.'

'Did you intend the diary for publication?'

Graham was able to answer honestly: 'No, I had no intention of pushing it for publication. As I have said, I was writing it for my own amusement.'

Leonard gave him a long, searching look. 'You have great confidence, Mr Young, in your ability to escape detection in the first place, and in the second place to escape conviction.'

Graham replied tartly, 'That is your opinion, Mr Leonard. You can hardly expect me to agree with it.'

Leonard frowned. He then turned to the diary passage concerned with the escalating illnesses at Hadlands, after which Graham had written: 'Is someone setting up in competition to me?!!!'

'Three exclamation marks. Isn't that a rather flippant remark in what is purported to be the serious journal of a fictitious poisoner?'

Graham clearly felt he had the upper hand, responding, 'I was introducing a bit of macabre humour.

Since when have poisoners been known for their lack of humour?'

The prosecutor played straight into his hands: 'I don't know, Mr Young. I've never met any.'

Graham gave a deep bow, 'Why, thank you, Mr Leonard.'

His interrogator gaped at him, then recovered, 'You appreciate, Mr Young, that this trial is not yet concluded.' But as far as Graham was concerned, in a very public battle of wits, he had won hands down.

* * *

'He was not unimpressive, was he?' remarked Graham's counsel, Sir Arthur Irvine, softly to his team at the end of his client's ten-hour questioning in the witness box. Reporter Arthur Latcham agreed: 'Eloquent, precise, impressed by himself and his medical know-how. Ready with well-phrased and plausible answers. And with cunning counter questions for the prosecuting QC.' But Graham failed to realise that 'the more he got going on his pet subject, the more he seemed to show himself as incapable of accepting his obsession as evil'. Latcham recalled that a woman next to him in the packed public gallery summed him up well. 'A good brain gone wrong,' she said.

Neither defence nor prosecution felt that a lengthy summing-up was necessary. Both spoke for less than an hour. Sir Arthur presented Graham's defence and tried to do a little damage limitation to counter his client's unabashed confidence. He told the jury that Graham might have 'a morbid and unsavoury' interest in poisons but that must be kept in perspective on a number of points. He referred them first of all to the meeting at Hadlands when Graham had questioned Dr Anderson in such a way that it finally brought suspicions about him to a head: 'He chose to flaunt his knowledge,' Sir Arthur admitted. 'Now, while it was perhaps extraordinary to find a man at the meeting with such knowledge, but it would have been even more extraordinary if he *was* guilty, that he should display the extent of his knowledge.' He then invited the jury to consider a hypothetical case of a valuable postage stamp stolen from a collection in a country house: 'Let us say that several people are present in the house and let us suppose that one of the guests is a philatelist, and suspicion will centre on the philatelist in that context. But I suggest that it would be the same duty in that instance not to permit such a thing to play a disproportionate part.'

Nor should the 'Bovingdon Bug' be overlooked, Sir Arthur entreated. After all, there appeared to have been a sufficient spread of upsets to attract notice and warrant a name. 'It is quite extraordinary that the concept of the 'Bovingdon Bug' should ever have taken life and yet it did. More than one witness spoke of it,' he reminded them. 'It was the sort of illness one might unfortunately encounter at family seaside holidays.' As for the damning diary: Graham claimed it was a novel. Sir Arthur, on less firm ground, told the jury that for all his faults, there was not much sign of his client being a liar. The diary had been left lying about Graham's room. No effort had been made to conceal it.

Mr Leonard had recovered from his clash with Graham to offer the simplest of condemnations. He reminded the jury of Graham's allegations of a deal with the police. That, he insisted, told them all they needed to know. 'In my submission,' he said, 'if you can swallow that, you can perhaps swallow anything.'

It was almost 4pm. The room was hot with the June sun outside and with the press of bodies in a space where most of them had spent the entire day, concentrating on every word. Mr Justice Eveleigh wanted to make a start on his summing-up, nonetheless. He told the jury that it was said Graham had administered poison to eight people, aiming to observe its reactions and workings. It was not necessary that there should be any motive. But consideration of a motive might play a part, because without being able to see one the jury might find it difficult to bring themselves to believe that the alleged offences could have taken place. He warned them to be wary of accepting a confession Graham was said to have made to police 'for it is known that people will confess to things they haven't done.'

The judge paused and glanced at the clock, then at the sea of hot, tired faces before him. He decided to adjourn the court for the day; his summing-up would conclude tomorrow, and he asked the jury to refrain from reaching any conclusion until then.

In Whitehall, C3 were jittery. The public relations branch of the Home Office sent round a memo on the subject of the considerable press interest surrounding the case and put forward the names of those reporters it might be worth consulting regarding the material gathered. The main area of concern remained the decisions that had been taken by the psychiatrists and Home Secretary. A final draft of the ministerial statement was feverishly completed that evening, noting that the verdict was expected the following day. It pointed out: 'Poisoning is a unique crime. If violent offenders on release return to violent ways, this is apparent at once. But the use of poison can escape detection for a long time — and in this case the nature and effects of the poisons used made it especially difficult to recognise that the resulting symptoms were not due to innocent cause ...'

Suggesting which steps should be taken, the attached memo admitted:

The present case is one giving rise to great anxiety and it was important for the responsible Ministers to make immediate improvements in the procedures and to take independent advice on them. Whether further fundamental changes should be made raises issues which are complex and difficult and need full investigation by an authoritative body such as is now to be appointed.

Another memo discussed what should be done if Graham was acquitted. The overriding view of C3 was that he should then be returned to Broadmoor immediately.

As a final word of gloomy caution, the memo warned: 'There is every indication, assuming he is convicted, that we must expect a first-class press and Parliamentary row ...'

On that at least, they were correct.

26
THE TREACHEROUS
INSTRUMENT

It took the jury scarcely an hour to reach their verdict. The bravura Graham had displayed throughout John Leonard's often aggressive questioning deserted him. Increasingly overwrought, in the cool cells below the court, Graham told his warders that if he were found guilty, he would kill himself there and then by smashing his head and neck against the dock rail. It was not a risk the authorities were prepared to take; two extra guards were called and as he was led back up the steps into court, four burly officers kept a tight hold on him.

In the public gallery, Graham's Aunt Win clutched her daughter's hand as the foreman of the jury stood to announce the verdict: guilty of the murder of Robert Egle; guilty of the murder of Frederick Biggs; guilty of the attempted murder of David Tilson; guilty of the attempted murder of Jethro Batt; and guilty of poisoning both Ronald Hewitt and Diana Smart. There were just two acquittals: he was found not guilty of poisoning Peter Buck and Trevor Sparkes because the evidence was deemed insufficient to reach a definitive answer. The alternative charges with regard to Jethro Batt and David Tilson were likewise dropped. But it was enough.

Graham's narrow face showed no emotion throughout the reading of the verdicts. Nor did he betray any inkling of thought when his defence counsel, Sir Arthur Irvine, then rose and braced himself to reveal that Graham had been convicted of a series of near-fatal poisonings as a young teen, hence the hitherto obscure years in Broadmoor. It was the proverbial 'pin drop' in court, met by an audible, collective gasp from the jury and the curious onlookers in the public gallery. Reporter Susan Nowak recalled: 'The blood drained from their faces when they heard about his previous convictions. The verdict had not been a foregone conclusion and they were probably thinking, what if we'd let this maniac out on to the street?'

But advances in forensic science since he had first put into practice his passion for poison, coupled with the seething obsession that coloured every page of his murderer's diary, had left little serious room for doubt. Before taking his seat again, Sir Arthur addressed Mr Justice Eveleigh:

> In considering sentence, I submit that your Lordship should bear in mind one matter which I mention with the greatest reluctance. I refer to it in my duty, as I conceive it to be, to my client Graham Young. It is that it was possible for Graham Young to commit these offences only because he had been released on licence from Broadmoor. This release may appear to have been a serious error of judgement, but the authorities had a duty to protect Young from himself as well as a duty to protect the public. If your Lordship is balancing the desirability of a custodial sentence with that of a hospital order, I think it is right that I should say to your Lordship that Young himself thinks that the prison sentence

would be better for his condition than a return to Broadmoor.

He paused,

> The Broadmoor experience thus far has had the tragic consequences of which we have learned in this trial. Your Lordship may think a prison sentence is preferable.

A thin smile crossed Graham's face. He had got what he wanted; to be seen as evil rather than mad. And to serve out his days somewhere new, rather than return to loathsome Broadmoor and its 'goons' — staff and patients alike. He was quite calm as the judge handed out four life sentences: one each for the two counts of murder and two attempted murders, and ten years in total for administering poison to Hewitt and Smart.

As Mr Justice Eveleigh ended his short speech, the foreman of the jury rose again to ask if he might make a statement on the jury's behalf. The judge frowned behind his thick black spectacles: 'In the circumstances, that would be highly undesirable.' The foreman explained that they simply wanted to say something about the sale of poisons. Mr Justice Eveleigh then indicated for him to go ahead and the foreman read from a prepared statement: 'The members of the jury in this case consider it to be our duty to draw the attention of the authorities concerned to the failings of the present system by which poisons are sold to the public. We urge that the system be reviewed in order that in future the public may be more consistently safeguarded.'

'Thank you,' said Mr Justice Eveleigh, with a nod. 'And thank you, too, for your close attention in this nasty case.'

★ ★ ★

Win and Sandra had already spoken to Chief Inspector Kirkpatrick to ask if they could see Graham before he was taken away by prison van; as they left the public gallery, Graham's solicitor, John Pickworth, appeared and led them downstairs.

Pickworth showed the two women through a corridor and into a small room divided by a window with a grille. Sergeant Livingstone stood to greet them, drawing up chairs. Win began to cry when Graham entered on the other side of the glass. He was particularly pale-faced and subdued, asking how they both were, before stating quietly, 'You'd do better if you followed the advice given you ten years ago and forget all about me.'

Win wept, insisting that nothing could be further from her mind or that of her daughter. 'Why did you do it, Graham?' she asked with a bewildered shake of her head, 'Why did you do those things?'

Graham looked down and bit his lip. He said nothing.

His aunt leaned forward, 'Don't waste what little time we have — talk to me.'

But having always appeared so eloquent, now he seemed unable to find the right words. Eventually, he looked up. 'I am so sorry for the trouble I've caused you all.'

His aunt and cousin had no doubt that he meant what he said. Sandra recalled afterwards that he

409

seemed 'genuinely upset and what I call 'his look' was entirely missing'. She had brought him a packet of cigarettes but had to pass them on to Sergeant Livingstone, who explained he could not take them into prison and would have to smoke them before he got there. But, he added, there were no restrictions on how many parcels and cigarettes that could be sent to him, unlike Broadmoor.

At this, Win glanced at her nephew: 'Do you think you'll prefer prison, Graham?'

'Well, if this is what Broadmoor did for my condition in ten years, then I think I'll be better off in prison.'

The guards approached Graham's side of the divide. He looked over at Sergeant Livingstone. 'Please send my regards to Superintendent Harvey and tell him there are no hard feelings as far as I'm concerned.' He told his aunt to give his regards to everyone, including Rupert, his sister's dog.

'Write and let me know where you are,' said Sandra. 'You will write, won't you?'

'Yes, I will,' he said. 'But don't tell Dad — let him come round in his own good time. Give my love to Uncle Jack too.'

One of the guards touched his shoulder.

Graham got up, his chair scraping on the floor. He stood at the divide for a moment, then put his fingers to his lips, kissed them and pressed them against the glass. Then he turned and went out.

★ ★ ★

The verdict was of sufficient interest for the BBC to interrupt their afternoon programmes with the announcement, while news of the trial's end and its revelations saturated the tabloids and broadsheets, all of which featured the story on their front pages. Most newspapers ran a whole slew of accompanying stories examining the issues raised and featured interviews with those whose lives had been directly affected by Graham's first and second welter of poisonings.

'Scandal of the 'Cured Killer'' announced the *Daily Mirror*, whose chief crime reporter had tracked down Graham's first victim, John Williams, 'twenty-five now, a successful salesman, happily married — and healthy'. Williams recalled: 'All those years ago, a detective told my mum that I was lucky to be alive. I reckon I am.' His last surviving victim, Jethro Batt, described the slow process of recovering: 'I couldn't eat properly for weeks and I was impotent for two or three months after I was discharged from hospital. The doctors have tried to reassure me, but they can't be certain that I won't have some lasting effect from all this. The terrible part is that whatever I suffered, you can multiply five or six times over for my workmates Fred and Bob, who died.' Diana Smart continued to suffer vomiting, stomach ache, diarrhoea and muscular pains. Equally distressing was the depression that smothered her after the trial, leaving her unable to return to work until shortly before the new year.

Hadlands' managing director, Geoffrey Foster, was deeply regretful:

Had I known of Graham Young's background and subsequently employed him, then as soon as anyone was ill, particularly anyone working closely with him, I could have taken the appropriate action to see that this was investigated. As it was, Robert Egle was ill for four or five weeks before he was finally taken ill at the time which resulted in his death. Not only his life could have been saved but the second death would never have occurred and the people associated with this business who've experienced extreme suffering would have been protected from that.

Unbeknown to Geoffrey Foster and John Hadland, the Department of Employment held discussions about the situation, with one internal memo noting soberly: 'One thing which remains to be done in the Young case is to mend our fences with the unfortunate employer Hadlands …' At the foot of the memo is an update: 'Mr Walker rang. He spoke to the firm at length by phone and is satisfied that fences are now mended. The firm do not blame the Department of Employment. But is nevertheless very scarred by its whole experience.'

Graham's family spoke to the press in some depth. Winifred commented: 'I feel now as I did then, that he should have had more supervision.' Her story of growing up with a poison-obsessed brother was serialised in the *News of the World*, while the *Sunday Mirror* ran an extensive interview with Fred Young, who declared: 'As far as I am concerned, my son Graham doesn't exist any longer. From this moment on, I never want to hear his name mentioned.'

The crooked path Graham had taken from school to Broadmoor, then to Hadlands and back into captivity was the subject of lengthy media attention. Dr Hynd, the Medical Officer of Health who had investigated the 'Bovingdon Bug' at Hadlands, had his say in the press: 'It seems vital that the community physician, as the Medical Officer of Health is to be called in the future, is given all the information necessary for carrying out his duties to protect the community. Surely this includes information about people like Young? The medical association urge that if there is any doubt about someone being a danger to the community, then the Medical Officer of Health should be told. That did not happen here.'

Dr Fysh was approached by reporters at his home in mid-Wales but had been forbidden from speaking about the case by the Home Office. He told them: 'All I can say is that I have not seen this former patient for ten years, but I am likely to be of the same opinion now as I was ten years ago without having any further information to modify that opinion.' He could not resist adding: 'He was put under the care of the Home Office who were responsible for deciding to release him. I am sure those concerned acted in good faith and gave honest advice. Sometimes people are wrong.' A grim-faced Dr Udwin confronted reporters who gathered on his doorstep in Reading, asserting: 'Medical ethics and the Official Secrets Act forbid my saying anything at all.'

★ ★ ★

Home Secretary Reginald Maudling addressed the House of Commons within an hour of the jury delivering their verdict. He declared that there would be two inquiries and pledged a review of every case of a patient on conditional discharge from hospital under Section 66(2) of the Mental Health Act 1959. One inquiry would be chaired by Sir Carl Aarvold, Recorder of London; the second by Conservative

MP and former Home Secretary, Lord Butler of Saffron Walden, who was also president of the National Association for Mental Health (later, MIND) and chairman of the trustees of the Mental Health Trust and Research Fund.

Maudling revealed that a number of changes had already been introduced, specifically to protect the public from conditionally discharged patients. This included permitting social workers and probation officers to fully inform potential employers about such patients' backgrounds, and further safeguarding the process of release. Shadow Home Secretary Shirley Williams wanted an assurance that all findings in respect to mistakes made in the Graham Young case would be made public. Maudling agreed: 'The whole circumstances should be made public and they will be made public. We have nothing to conceal and nothing we want to conceal.' But when the time came, his promise of total transparency was not fulfilled.

The Aarvold Report was the first to appear. Published in January 1973, it examined specific details of Graham's case and led to reforms in how conditionally discharged patients were monitored upon release; it resulted in the newly established Advisory Board on Restricted Patients to screen all admissions and discharges. The Aarvold committee was comprised of medical professionals, lawyers and criminal justice experts. Their focus was to ascertain what had gone wrong in the exchange of information between the Broadmoor authorities, the probation service and the police. Their suggested amendments were accepted by the new Home Secretary, Robert Carr.

Considerable efforts had been made to examine the process of conditional discharge and after-care from Broadmoor. Information was requested on all patients released since the 1960s who were still under active supervision, 'with a view to identifying any cases giving rise to concern and, where possible, rectifying the situation'. A total of 331 Broadmoor patients had been discharged since 1960 into the community on the authority of the Home Secretary. Graham aside, two of those patients had subsequently committed homicide, and in both cases the offence occurred after active supervision of the patient had come to an end. Around 1,200 files were examined during the review. Most of those concerned had gone on to live lawful lives in the community, but the inquiry highlighted several cases where serious offences had been committed following discharge.

One example was that of Alan Gay, sentenced on 5 February 1963 to six years' imprisonment for the attempted murder and rape of his sister. Reported to be suffering from psychopathic disorder, he was transferred to Broadmoor in October 1963. A doctor recommended his return to prison in December 1966 after finding him 'basically unchanged, unwilling to accept help and not requiring or susceptible to hospital treatment'. Gay remained in Broadmoor, however. In spring 1968, another consultant reported an 'improvement' in Gay's attitude and asserted that he 'would not be a danger' to women. Gay was discharged in October 1968 into the supervision of a probation officer. He 'quickly' broke the conditions of his discharge 'but restrictions ran out before he could be recalled'. In October 1969 he raped a 16-year-old girl and threatened to strangle her. He was then sentenced to life imprisonment. Another case was that of a Mrs Giles, who in March 1958 killed her 16-year-old son by putting sleeping pills in his tea and then striking him over the head with an axe. Sentenced to Broadmoor, she was conditionally discharged in October 1961 after Dr McGrath had reported no suggestion of depressive psychosis since autumn 1958 and found that she was unlikely to relapse, and 'even if she did, [was] no danger to anyone except possibly herself'. In October 1968 Mrs Giles repeatedly attacked her husband about the head with a chamber pot. He died a few days later. Mrs Giles was convicted of manslaughter and returned to Broadmoor where she was diagnosed with 'recurrent psychotic depression'.

The findings of the inquiry into the specific circumstances of Graham's release took the form of over 80 questions and answers. Declaring that 'this particular case — of a boy poisoner — is unique in forensic psychiatric experience,' the review noted again that 'Young is probably unique but there are some 600 patients who are subject to conditional discharges from various hospitals.' Many of them were concerned in offences far less serious than Graham Young's, including non-violent offences. It was extremely unusual that Graham should have been admitted to Broadmoor at such a young age, given that in the five years preceding 1971, ten patients aged 14 were admitted to special hospitals, though none of them to Broadmoor. A total of 147 patients aged over 14 and under 18 were admitted, of whom 17, all over 16 years old, entered Broadmoor. The review confirmed that Graham had been released 'on the advice of the experienced consultant psychiatrist (Dr Udwin) at Broadmoor Hospital who was in charge of his treatment there, by authority of a warrant issued on behalf of the Home Secretary after careful review within the Home Office.' The Home Secretary had been able to set aside the restrictions on discharges which the court ordered to last for 15 years because the effect of the restriction order was to make Graham's release within that period subject to the Home Secretary's consent, not to forbid it entirely. Dr Udwin's recommendation of discharge was endorsed by the DHSS before the decision as to discharge was reached; furthermore 'all the consultants at the hospital knew of the intention to discharge Young and none said that they felt it to be undesirable. The other consultant who was directly responsible for Young's treatment in his early years at Broadmoor examined him again in 1969 and found him very much matured, relaxed and controlled. He knew of and concurred with the proposal to discharge Young in 1971.' Dr Udwin had been responsible for the discharge of 13 patients — including Graham Young — since February 1971 and the transfer of another 34 into the care of NHS hospitals.

The much-vaunted media suggestion that doctors were under pressure to release patients from Broadmoor to allow new admissions was specifically answered by the DHSS, who declared: 'The hospital has been overcrowded for many years but there has been no pressure to discharge patients prematurely for this reason; each case is considered with great care.' Positing the question 'Are the doctors at Broadmoor well enough qualified to do the job expected of them?' the review stated emphatically: 'Yes, they have unrivalled experience of the problems involved in the treatment of mentally disordered patients with violent, dangerous or criminal propensities.'

Regarding Dr Fysh's prescient conclusion in 1962 that the outlook for Graham was troubling and that he was likely to repeat his offences if the opportunity were available, the review sidestepped the issue of whether his views were taken into account at the time of Graham's release, but insisted: '. . . in the earlier stages the doctors at Broadmoor were also very dubious about Young's prospects but their views changed after observation of his response to treatment.' The supervision afforded Graham after his release failed to detect his crimes because 'it would have been impossible for the probation officers to maintain surveillance for 24 hours a day. Young showed himself co-operative towards his supervisors, anxious to keep his appointments with them and ready to discuss his own progress. Poisoning is a clandestine activity and Young gave no indication of sinister behaviour.' The review found that arrangements for training and employment of Broadmoor patients generally worked well: in the past four years, 14 patients from Broadmoor, including Graham, had taken courses at government training centres; eight had successfully completed their courses and two were still under training; one returned to Broadmoor voluntarily and three either gave up their courses or had them terminated. The disablement settlement officer at Reading had, in the last two years, successfully placed Broadmoor patients in employment or in training centres. The majority of patients discharged from Broadmoor found work by other methods, with the help of the hospital authorities 'and these arrangements appear to work well'.

Regarding the issue of how Graham was able, as a conditionally discharged Broadmoor patient who had been convicted of poisoning, to obtain poisons, the review stated: 'Before his trial only three purchases of poisons by Young had been traced. These were made at two retail pharmacies and on each occasion an entry was made as required by law in the seller's poisons book, but Young appears to have given false particulars, including a false name and address. Further investigations are being made into this aspect of the affair — they could not be started before the conclusion of the trial — and no further comment can be made until they are completed.'

In terms of what was being done to prevent similar purchases being made in the future, the review found that:

the question is really whether the purchases we know about show that the law is defective, or that it simply was not properly observed, and this cannot be fairly answered until we have the results of the investigation now in progress. However, it is necessary to stress that the law has been framed to deter, but cannot be expected totally to prevent, the purchase of poisons by a person who is intent on poisoning, and almost certainly, therefore, trying to disguise his intentions. In the case of the more dangerous poisons (e.g. arsenic, potassium cyanide, thallium salt) the law provides that the purpose for which the purchaser requires the poison is declared and recorded in the seller's poisons book along with particulars such as the name, address and occupation of the purchaser. Furthermore, the purchaser must be known to the seller as a person to whom the poison may properly be sold, and the purchaser must sign the entry in the poisons book.

As to why this system had failed in Graham's case: 'The clinical history was unique. Poisoning is an uncommon crime and a case of this nature — by a boy of immature and disturbed personality — is unique in forensic psychiatric experience. The opinion formed by the doctor was reasonable in relation to the facts available to him at the time.'

Positing the question 'Can an assurance be given that Young will never again be released?', the review declared: 'Obviously no absolute assurance can be given about the view that might be formed, many years hence, by a future Home Secretary (acting on the advice of the Parole Board). But it is clear that it is out of the question at present to think of Young's possible release.' The review also passed final judicial comment on the question of Molly Young's murder, when it stated that 'this has not been substantiated and no action can be taken'.

Pointed questions were asked about Graham's mental state and whether, if he was still regarded as 'mentally disordered', his condition might be curable. The review answered: 'This is not a question on which a layman can enter into details — it is understood that he appears to have an abnormality of personality which is not susceptible to psychiatric treatment.' There were also several very succinct replies to some questions that had been repeatedly raised in the press, such as whether disciplinary action was being contemplated against any of the individuals involved, to which the response was a flat 'No'. Regarding the issue of 'Who took the actual decision to discharge?', the review refused to say, stating: 'It is not the practice to disclose the identities of individuals acting in the name of the Home Secretary. The decision was taken at a high level.'

Returning to the wider issues raised by the case, question 56 asked: 'The system is being improved: in what ways was it inadequate? There seem to have been big loopholes: is not the stable door being shut after the horse has gone?' The answer given stated that the resettlement of patients from the special hospitals into the community had been 'remarkably successful', but the close examination given to the general procedures had revealed the need for 'a well-understood code of procedures', including the improvements mentioned in the ministerial statement.

To avoid similar cases, the committee suggested that 'the social worker who is likely to supervise [the discharged patient], and the local consultant who will be taking over responsibility for the medical aspect of treatment if the patient is going to an area distant from the treating hospital, should be brought into consultation at an early stage. Not only will this enable the decision about discharge to be taken with the best possible knowledge of the likely circumstance, but it will allow time for the patient and those who will be concerned in the followup process to become acquainted with each other and the problems which they will be facing.' This could best be achieved, it was felt, by an extended use of case conferences, which would involve the relevant professionals:

Assessment of individual patient's personality, the nature of his mental disorder, his response to therapeutic help, the circumstances, both material and emotional, in which the offence took place, the likelihood of those circumstances recurring, the resources available in the social situation the patient would go into on leaving hospital, the likely reactions to that situation, and the chances of his successful reintegration in the community despite any stresses which may develop.

The use of case conferences would also help maintain a vital balance between what was best for conditionally discharged offenders and the right of the public to be protected. At that time, rehabilitation was a major aim — if not the primary aim — of those agencies concerned with managing offenders; it was a common belief that such people should be able to move forward, and indeed perhaps could only move forward without having to disclose their history, since that was regarded as a burden that might prevent their successful reintegration into society. In Graham's case, a perfect storm had been created by the absence of coordination between the various agencies involved, leaving him free to realise his ambition of becoming an infamous poisoner.

The code of procedures suggested was introduced as a direct result of the review and covered a number of changes in the after-care and follow-up of conditionally discharged patients as a result of the review. The key amendments were:

> We now look, at the time of discharge, for more information than in the past about the social setting in which the patient will live after discharge.
>
> We ensure that the supervising officer (and the local consultant psychiatrist who undertakes medical surveillance, if he is not the responsible medical officer) is fully briefed on the medico-social history of the patient and on his responsibilities.

Consideration is now given to whether, and how much, the patient's employer, landlord or others need to be told about his past.

Reports by the supervising officer are now sent to the Home Office direct rather than through the former responsible medical officer, and we look to the local consultant psychiatrist for reports at similar intervals. Copies of the reports by each are sent to the other.

We ensure that the police force for the area in which the patient is to live are aware of his presence.

Other conditions, not made public at the time, were implemented regarding cases requiring a patient's urgent recall to hospital; these in effect gave the Home Secretary complete power over such situations. Ultimately, the Aarvold committee found that 'from our enquiries we are satisfied that the case was dealt with in accordance with the procedures accepted at the time to ensure that proper weight was given to questions of public safety.'

1972—1990
PARKHURST

'Life is always dangerous — never forget that. In the end, perhaps, not only great forces but the work of our own hands may destroy it.'

Agatha Christie, *The Pale Horse*
(Collins, The Crime Club, 1961)

27

A POISON TEMPER'D
BY HIMSELF

Although the recommendations of the inquiry were implemented immediately, there were soon instances where all the safeguards failed.

Six months after the publication of the Aarvold Report, Graham's case and the flaws that had led to it were linked in the press to the breakdown of Genevieve Parslow, granddaughter of a police officer and a 29-year-old Buckinghamshire mother of two, who had suffered severe mental health problems. She had spent several periods in care; during one stay at a mental health facility, she had become pregnant by another patient. Doctors refused to allow her to have an abortion on the NHS and therefore she arranged the procedure privately. Her mental health deteriorated rapidly again as a result and, one weekend in March 1973, she tried to poison her children by feeding them jam contaminated with cleaning fluid. When her husband discovered what she had done, he made her leave the house. After wandering about the streets all night, she made her way to Aylesbury police station and pleaded with an inspector for help. She informed the startled inspector that she was a witch more than 1,000 years old and that it was her destiny to 'kill everyone in the world', especially babies. The inspector asked if she was fond of her own children. 'No,' Genevieve replied, 'They ought to be dead, like me.' Local mental welfare officials were called in, who in turn sent for a GP, 27-year-old Dr Adrian Burch. He talked to two doctors from St John's hospital at Stone, where Genevieve had had two spells of treatment. But all three thought it unnecessary to admit her to hospital again, believing outpatient treatment was a better option.

Genevieve then walked away from Aylesbury police station, where, according to the prosecution at her subsequent trial, it had not been possible legally to detain her. What happened next would forever scar all those involved in her case: Genevieve somehow made her way approximately five miles south-east to the pretty market town of Wendover. In Nash Lee Road, she approached a bungalow and looked through the window, where a ten-week-old baby lay sleeping in his cot. She climbed through the window, snatched the child and carried him to a ditch half a mile away. There she drowned him before stamping on his body.

The baby was Jonathan Snasdell, the younger son of television film editor David Snasdell and his wife Vanessa, both 25 years old. They raised the alarm and their child's body was discovered that afternoon, in the ditch where Genevieve had killed him. Genevieve herself was located in a private garden shortly afterwards. She was tried at Reading Crown Court on 18 July 1973. Pleading not guilty to murder, she admitted manslaughter on the grounds of diminished responsibility, a plea that the prosecution accepted. Mr Justice Thesiger sent her to Broadmoor and ordered that she should not be released from strict security 'whatever doctors or tribunals recommend'. Genevieve Parslow died 40 years later at a care home for those

428

with 'challenging behaviours associated with complex neurological, physical and mental health needs'.

In the wake of the trial, Vanessa Snasdell offered to adopt Genevieve's son and daughter and raise them with her own. She told reporters: 'If the doctors had given Mrs Parslow the help she clearly needed, I would still have my baby. The police officers had done their best and they could see she was not fit to be left wandering around. Refusing as they did, these foolish doctors are guilty of crass stupidity. They should have been made to appear in court to explain their decisions.' Dr Burch moved away after the trial but told those reporters who tracked him down: 'The reason I did not certify her that night was simply because at the time she was not certifiable. As a doctor I will listen to the advice of others when dealing with a case. But in the end I have to make my own decision and that is what I did with Mrs Parslow.' The Snasdells were promised a full inquiry by the medical director of Stone mental hospital (as it was called then), although he admitted: 'Knowing only what the doctors then knew, I would not have recommended that the patient be detained. If we had thought that this woman would harm someone, it would have been a different matter.'

The case gained widespread attention in the media. Referring to the Graham Young case, an editorial in the *Daily Express* declared:

Once again the failure of those charged with securing the mentally disturbed is exposed. A mad woman, Mrs Parslow, killed a baby boy ... The public is becoming increasingly alarmed at the number of unbalanced people who are being freed, or being given diminished sentences, at the say-so of psychiatrists ... Psychiatrists are not omnipotent. Their prime duty must be to the interests of society. But society too has a duty: to provide comprehensive facilities for the care of those who have long periods of lucidity along with recurring bouts of murderous obsessions. Here is a branch of medicine which is being starved of resources — at the public's expense.

Another article titled 'How We <u>Can</u> Cut the Mad Killer Menace' thundered: 'This is the third case recently when people known by psychiatrists to be mad have killed. Poisoner Graham Young murdered shortly after his release from Broadmoor and 38-year-old psychopath Wesley Churchman was recently jailed for life for a killing he committed several years after serving a six-year jail sentence for murder.' The newspaper suggested a three-point plan that was more or less an echo of the recommendations of the Aarvold committee, advocating a full and adequate treatment programme worked out for each mental patient; the strengthening of community services — health visitors and social workers — who should remain in close enough touch with their charges to identify any relapse and a consultant psychiatrist on hand for swift assessments in acute situations. The column ended: 'Psychiatrists must realise their responsibility cannot end once they have discharged a patient from hospital. A closer surveillance must be kept on doubtful patients once released.'

Some of the press was plainly inflammatory, but agreed the responsibility had to lie with those in the relevant branch of medicine, declaring:

The streets of Britain are filled each day with thousands of mentally disturbed people … when does a disturbed person become a dangerous lunatic? It is normally left to the welfare services to alert the community to the hazards that accompany mental disorder. Social workers with close firsthand knowledge of families are trained to spot the potentially dangerous people … But nevertheless at the end of the day the responsibility lies with the medical men. We must put our trust in their training and their judgement.

But the ink was scarcely dry on the newspaper reports of the Snasdell killing before another Broadmoor-related case reached the media. Terrence Iliffe had been sent to Broadmoor in September 1970 for the attempted murder of his second wife. Three years later, aged 53, he was conditionally discharged. The hospital had declared him to be no risk to the general public, but 'If Iliffe were to remarry, there might be a specific risk to his wife.' The Aarvold recommendations were in place, putting him under supposedly strict supervision, but he managed to remarry clandestinely. Three weeks after the wedding, neighbours raised the alarm when he and his new wife suddenly seemed to vanish. Police who broke into his home in Swanage found Iliffe severely injured and his wife's body in the freezer. He had strangled her. In hospital, Iliffe was found to be suffering from acid poisoning.

At Winchester Crown Court, Iliffe made no attempt to deny strangling his wife, who was his third. He was convicted of murder and sentenced to life imprisonment; he died in 2002, aged 81, while still serving his sentence. The case was raised in a House of Commons debate in January 1976, when MP Michael Alison stated that there was 'real, noticeable and widespread public disquiet' over mentally disordered offenders. He referred to Graham Young, Terrence Iliffe and Ian Dunlop.

The latter, who had spent all but three of his 39 years in institutions, was admitted to Broadmoor for sex offences in 1964 with — like Graham — a restriction order for 15 years. In 1973 he was transferred to a prison on medical advice. After four months, he was allowed out to work as a plumber and was given periods of weekend leave. A female acquaintance contacted the prison to warn that Dunlop had been paying 'abnormal interest' to her seven-year-old son. Dunlop was interviewed by a medical officer who accepted his insistence that the claim was untrue. The Home Office likewise accepted the doctor's report on the matter. In May 1975, a family with whom Dunlop was lodging twice called Broadmoor to express concern at the former patient's behaviour towards their children. Nonetheless, the responsible medical officer decided this did not affect his advice to the Home Office that Dunlop was suitable for conditional discharge. But the following month, Dunlop went on leave and failed to return. He was eventually captured, but by then he had committed 13 offences against young boys and was jailed for life after admitting the offences, which included abduction, wounding, assault and acts of gross indecency. His own defence counsel stated that allowing him out of hospital was like letting a mad dog loose and expecting it not to bite.

Five years after the Dunlop case, the British press was filled with the story of 44-year-old labourer Ronald Sailes. He had spent 16 years in Broadmoor on a rape conviction and was released in November 1978. Seven months later in Plymouth, he killed 16-year-old Anita Quayle, leaving her gagged and mutilated body on a sun-lounger. Sailes had been released on the recommendation of Dr Edgar Udwin. When reporters discovered that this was the same doctor who had recommended the conditional discharge of Graham Young, they did a little more research and found that six men who had been released on Udwin's recommendation had gone on to commit major crimes. However, it has to be borne when considering such cases that we rarely if ever hear of the successes, only the failures — but these failures can be deadly.

Dr Udwin was made physician superintendent of Broadmoor in October 1981; he had been running the hospital since McGrath retired earlier in that year after 25 years in charge. Newspaper articles on his appointment noted that he was a controversial figure for his decisions in the past. Udwin held the post for only 18 months; he retired in 1983.

★ ★ ★

The findings of the Butler committee had first appeared in an interim report in 1974 with its final form published in October 1975. Its official remit had been to consider to what extent and on what criteria the law should recognise mental disorder or abnormality in a person accused of a criminal offence as a factor affecting his liability to be tried or convicted, and his disposal; and to consider what, if any, changes were necessary in the powers, procedures and facilities relating to the provision of appropriate treatment in prison, hospital or the community for offenders suffering from mental disorder or abnormality, and to their discharge and after-care. One hundred and forty recommendations were put forward, including several for the psychiatric hospital systems, of forensic psychiatry and in regard to the insanity defence.

The interim report appeared because the members of the committee were so appalled by their findings, particularly with regard to gross overcrowding in the special hospitals. In some Broadmoor wards there was barely a gap of 18 inches between beds. The report declared: 'Patients obviously have no privacy. And as there is no cupboard room, they are living out of suitcases.' The committee urged an immediate overhaul to improve conditions, leading Social Services Secretary Mrs Barbara Castle to promise the House, 'We shall remedy the overcrowding at Broadmoor as soon as possible.'

The report further warned: 'Between the overcrowded but secure special hospital and the National Health Service hospitals providing no security, there is a yawning gap.' Secure units were recommended for all 14 regional health authorities to relieve pressure on special hospitals but would also allow the NHS to concentrate on those patients who would most benefit from an 'open door' regime, relieving prisons of some of the more disturbed inmates. The committee believed there were around 500 patients in special hospitals who had no need to be there. Barbara Castle pledged between £12 and £14 million to begin an early programme of building to provide units for 1,000 patients, which was half the number deemed necessary by the Butler committee. A new unit at Maghull near Liverpool was almost complete; this would become Park Lane hospital, later Ashworth,

434

whose most infamous resident was Moors Murderer Ian Brady. Fifty-eight beds would also be added to Rampton. A new hospital at Broadmoor to replace the present one was expected to be completed by 1979; it finally opened in 2019.

In the strangest of ways, Graham Young was responsible for bringing about the most important and wide-ranging inquiry into the laws regarding the mentally ill during the entire 20th century. Broadmoor 'biographer', Dr Harvey Gordon, recently commented that the effects of Graham's case were 'considerable and still reverberate to an extent today'. As a result, a complex of forensic units providing medium security was established where newly released Broadmoor patients could be transferred to provide a more successful — and safer — transition for rehabilitation within the wider community.

Epilogue

POISON BY DEGREES

From St Albans' Crown Court, Graham was sent to HMP Wormwood Scrubs in West London, where two months earlier there had been a sit-down protest by 350 prisoners. It was part of a wider campaign for better conditions and improvements in legal rights; the Scrubs had long been regarded as having one of the most punishing and brutal regimes in the country. Graham was expected to spend several weeks there on the hospital wing under close observation, partly due to his threat to kill himself. Psychiatric tests would be carried out, after which a decision would be taken on which prison would suit him best.

At first, Graham's main concern was whether Madame Tussauds had been in touch to ask for his measurements in order to create his waxwork for the Chamber of Horrors. He was delighted when he learned that this particular ambition had been achieved and his effigy would stand alongside his heroes William Palmer, Dr Harvey Crippen and John Reginald Christie. But his mood changed when he was shown the serialisation of his father's story in the *Sunday Mirror*. Fred was quoted as saying that if he could have got his hands on his son ('this bloody monster'), he would have 'cheerfully strangled him' and that 'I never want to hear his name mentioned.' Those who knew him thought Graham genuinely distressed. He wrote to his aunt and uncle that the break with his father was 'final', and he was 'terribly sorry for all the trouble he had brought on the family' but he knew they would stick by him.

His sister admitted that her feelings were 'very confused and ambivalent', not least because the courts had thought him sufficiently disturbed to send him to Broadmoor ten years before, but latterly had decided he was sane. Soon after his arrival in Brixton she wrote to him, making it clear that she would always be his sister but felt sickened by his crimes. Graham was again devastated, replying that he wished she had 'more faith' in him. 'I can't believe in you,' she wrote back, but she would stay in touch with him regardless.

The stories that appeared sporadically in the press did little to help. In August 1972, the *Sunday People* announced: 'From his top security prison cell, double killer Graham Young is still managing to spread poison ... verbal poison.' According to unnamed staff, Graham and another prisoner had repeatedly threatened two officers who were subsequently transferred to another part of the prison. Their colleague told the reporter: 'Young is an extremely dangerous man. Unlike many killers, he is very intelligent, and quite capable of influencing other inmates. With a life sentence hanging over his head, Young feels he doesn't have anything to lose.'

That same month Graham put in an application for leave to appeal against his conviction and sentence but was told within a fortnight that it had been turned down. As a result, he was being transferred to the prison known as Britain's Alcatraz where — with one brief exception — he would live out the remainder of his days: HMP Parkhurst on the Isle of Wight.

Part of almost one square mile of penal establishments, which included the prisons of Albany and Camphill, Parkhurst was situated two miles north of the island's capital, Newport. Originally a military hospital, its first prison inmates, in 1838, were 102 boys under the age of 15, who were previously incarcerated on the rotting hulk of the prison ship HMS York, anchored in the Solent. Some of the boys were bound for Australia's correctional facilities. In 1856 the prison received its first short-term adult male prisoners and the population switched from youth to adults in accordance with the laws regarding the punishment of children. Parkhurst received a large number of female convicts from London's Millbank gaol in 1863. One year later, the last juveniles were transferred to Dartmoor prison and five years later, all female inmates were sent to a new women's-only prison at Woking. Parkhurst then became a gaol for men and over the years its buildings were adapted and extended. Capital punishment was never carried out there, but the regime had a reputation for severity. In 1963 work began on the special security block, which was in effect a prison within a prison, completely self-contained, and which provided accommodation for inmates convicted of particularly notorious crimes, including the Great Train Robbers and the Kray twins. Parkhurst was the scene of an infamous riot in 1969, when 28 inmates and 35 officers were injured; one officer had his throat cut but survived, while another suffered a fractured skull and a third had his arm broken.

The first few years of Graham's incarceration were unremarkable. Notorious prisoner Charles Bronson, who was sent to Parkhurst in 1976, has a possible explanation for that. He recalls that although the other inmates 'hated' Graham because they feared his reputation as a poisoner, he pitied him: 'It was obvious to any rational man that Graham Young was mad. All that prison did was keep him drugged out of his head. His life was a constant daze. He was a very dangerous man but he should have been in an asylum, not a prison. I always felt sorry for him as I know the long-term effects of isolation. It's as painful as any form of torture.'

The death of Graham's beloved uncle, Jack Jouvenat, in January 1977 unbalanced his behaviour. After once more threatening prison staff, he was placed under observation by two experienced senior prison medical officers: Dr David Cooper and Dr Jim Dexter at Wormwood Scrubs, where he was also examined by the ex-director of the prison medical service, Dr Ian Pickering, who was then consultant psychiatrist at Rampton. As the re-assessment of Graham's mental health continued, Dr Patrick McGrath was invited to offer his opinion. Dr McGrath's views were unchanged since his previous examination of Graham as a youth; he diagnosed process schizophrenia and found him to have suffered, over a two-year period, persecutory auditory hallucinations and paranoid delusions. Nonetheless, the possibility of returning Graham to Broadmoor was deemed unfeasible due to the hostility towards him from staff and patients.

For the time being, he remained in Parkhurst where IRA prisoners held a rooftop protest in March 1979, complaining about rations and conditions at the prison. Approximately 100 inmates were on hunger strike. Extensive damage was done to the buildings, including C-wing, where those inmates with several psychological problems were treated. The protests lasted for several days until the demonstrators surrendered peacefully but C-wing remained closed as a result for the next 14 years.

Seven months later, in October 1979, Graham was transferred to Park Lane advance unit in Liverpool. In bleak surroundings just outside the town of Maghull, the site originally housed a hospital, then a convalescent home for workhouse children. It was taken over by the Red Cross during the Great War, when shell-shocked soldiers were treated there. In 1933 the building then known as Moss Side became a special hospital. As a result of the severe overcrowding in Broadmoor, construction began on Park Lane, adjacent to Moss Side, in 1974. It opened in stages until its completion ten years later, operating independently from Moss Side. In later years, two inquiries uncovered appalling abuse meted out towards patients from staff in an institution that was described as 'brutalising, stagnant and closed'. *The Guardian* noted: 'Even by the chequered standards of the special hospitals as a whole, [its] profile is profoundly negative and its history a catalogue of controversy, mismanagement and ill treatment of its patients.'

Three experts — Professor Robert Bluglass, Dr James Higgins and Dr Christopher Hunter — were engaged to advise on Graham's mental state. Park Lane's medical director, Dr Malcolm MacCulloch, also spoke with Graham at length and provided an insightful analysis that examined his entire history with perhaps a better understanding than ever before. Dr MacCulloch found:

In discussing his childhood he told me that he was a boy of intellectual pursuits with very few

440

close friends, a very studious child who learned that knowledge is power. His first motivation became the pursuit of knowledge and his parents became alarmed and sought to divert him to boyish pursuits and the relationship then deteriorated. By ten, his interests had settled on medical sciences, chemistry, pharmacy, pharmacology, pharmacodynamics, general medicine, toxicology, pathology, forensic medicine. He thus came to have an intense emotional investment in the subject [and] wanted to qualify in medicine but had bitter opposition from his father. His father blamed the death of his mother on Graham, or at least Graham felt so, and also on the incompetence of the medical profession. The father banned all medicine-type books from the house and accused Graham of having a twisted mind, therefore Graham carried on covertly and came to hate his father and decided to punish him, first by killing the stepmother by poisoning her slowly. As we went along, I learnt that the different kinds of colour of dress are important in Graham's life: black is aggressive, brown is aggressive, blue is tranquil, green is flamboyant. He came to tell me how he came to look at death as an ideal state. Death is neat and orderly, sterile. He said of his victims that he thought of them being better off when they were dead. He himself felt that he had more in common with death than with life and he saw himself as an agent of mortality, an agent of death.

Dr MacCulloch described how, during his many long interviews with Graham, it had become apparent that he was not in fact as 'emotionally cool' as might have been expected but was instead 'highly sensitive'. Nonetheless, he found it extremely difficult to show his emotions. The medical director noted:

He has got a deeply embedded resistance to discussing his inner feelings and a deep revulsion of discussing matters which are sexual or emotional, although he does turn out to be deeply emotional. This is evidenced by extreme anger which he can manifest readily and it is apparent in his previous history in relation to his victims and he had also manifested it here. Sometimes when his wishes are frustrated he has become very angry. He does work over his experiences many times and has come back to a discussion from previously and has sought to put right points which he thought I may have misunderstood . . . He shows chronic uncertainty. There are some asthenic qualities in his personality and elements of ambitiousness 'to be the greatest poisoner ever' and there is quite a bit of moral pride. He is deeply against Pavlov whose experimentation on animals he abhors. I pointed out to him his inconsistency in that he had given 'aconite' to mice as a child but he brushed this off by saying he had become disgusted by what he was doing and stopped it. I think he has a deep affection for animals. He is self-critical in that he tends not to excuse himself and is peculiarly a man of conscience.

On 2 June 1982, all the reports, tests and observations of Graham's mental health were brought together when a multidisciplinary conference was held at Park

442

Lane. Over the course of exactly 20 years, he was found to be suffering from a mental illness that saw him confined to Broadmoor, where doctors believed him to have made a full recovery; then when his crimes brought him before the law again, he was deemed sane and sent to prison, but later returned into a psychiatric environment. Now, finally, the decision was to 'recommend that Graham be returned to whence he came and repay his debt to society and his victims in the normal way'. There would be further, sporadic consultations over the years, but in June 1982, he was transferred once more to Parkhurst.

Also arriving in Parkhurst that year was paedophilic child-killer Ian Brady, then a quarter of a century into his lifelong sentence. Brady later compiled a study of serial killing that was controversially published in 2001. Graham loomed large in the book, which contained several factual errors but nonetheless provided some further insight into his character ten years after his second period of imprisonment. The familiar tropes were there: the intelligence, the obsession with poison and Nazi Germany, smoking, reading, and the persistent habit, revived again, of growing a Hitler-style moustache which he trimmed so often that the skin around it beaded blood. Graham had never been particularly keen on music, other than a love of Wagner, which was another Hitler-led affectation, but Brady recalls him listening repeatedly to Ray Charles' 1950s smash 'Hit the Road, Jack' and Jeff Wayne's debut album, a progressive rock adaptation of H G Wells' *War of the Worlds*.

The two prisoners found a friendship of sorts over their mutual circumstances, admiration of the Nazi ethos and chess. Brady liked to claim that Graham — who always favoured the black pieces — never won a match against him, but the opposite was true. Otherwise, his observations were clinically precise: he described his fellow inmate as asexual, excited only by the power afforded to him by his deadly experiments with poison. Graham's moods were extreme; he would be in the depths of despair or on top of the world. During the former, he would sit in his almost bare cell 'as though it were the Berlin Bunker, listening rapturously to *Götterdämmerung*, a doomed figure with his grandiose dreams in ruins'. Brady writes of him frequently suffering depression or being 'in the throes of a schizophrenic fugue', when he could be seen displaying 'an air of general abandonment, hair prematurely grey, features jaundiced and drawn, his frame physically shaking, wrecked by the daily high dosages of prescribed drugs'. Brady observed that when in deep melancholia Graham 'repressed a great deal and had developed an acute anxiety neurosis. Highly aware that his peers were shrewdly suspicious of him and in constant fear of being poisoned, he nevertheless genuinely yearned for their approval and trust. Failure to achieve this emotional goal compounded his frustration and anxiety.'

There were occasions when Graham flew into 'violent, maniacal rages which further depleted his reserves of nervous energy and kept him thin and gaunt'. Such explosions left him feeling that his own death was imminent; he would draw up another draft of his will and solemnly and ominously tell everyone within hearing, 'I shall return.' When in a more optimistic frame of mind, he was capable of creative thought and methodical planning, relaxing in his cell by reading *The Times* obituaries, remarking, 'Better to be a live dog than a dead lion.' Brady passed on some of his favourite literary quotations to Graham, who was especially taken by the opening soliloquy from Shakespeare's *Richard III*, in which the alleged murderer of the two princes in the tower declares: 'Now is the winter of our discontent/Made glorious summer by this sun of York . . .' He was unfamiliar with *Death's Jest Book*, a play by 19th-century poet and dramatist Thomas Lovell Beddoes, who later committed suicide, but asked Brady to write down the lines that resounded with him. These ran:

The look of the world's a lie, a face made up
O'er graves and fiery depths, and nothing's true
But what is horrible. If man could see
The perils and diseases that he elbows
Each day he walks a mile, which catch at him,
Which fall behind and graze him as he passes;
Then would he know that life's a single pilgrim,
Fighting unarmed amongst a thousand soldiers
It is this infinite invisible
Which we must learn to know, and yet to scorn,
And, from scorn of that, regard the world
As from the edge of a far star.

Graham features in the memoir of another Parkhurst inmate, gangland leader and armed robber Bobby Cummines, who first encountered him in the exercise yard in 1983. Charlie Richardson, an infamous East End criminal with a host of appalling offences to his name, pointed out a 'furtive character, glancing round all the time' with 'a thin, long face, dark hair that came forward in a V, thin, cruel lips and staring eyes. His nose had a bit of a point on it. Those eyes were

445

really scary.' A swirling wind whipped up on that day in October 1983, blowing leaves around the nervous inmate and his guards. 'Be careful if you have a cup of tea with him,' Charlie Richardson warned, as a twinkle appeared in his steely blue eyes. 'That's Graham Young . . .' Handcuffed to two prison warders, Graham was led towards the vulnerable prisoners' unit. Cummines, now a leading penal reformer, referred to Graham in his memoir as 'the most evil man in Parkhurst', an epithet that would have delighted Graham, had he known. Charlie Richardson was fascinated by him, but thought him 'totally bonkers'. According to Cummines, neither the prison chaplain nor the prison warders would go near Graham unless unable to avoid him during the course of their work.

Parkhurst medical officer Dr Stewart was approaching retirement in April 1990. One of his last tasks was to ensure that Graham, who was showing increasing signs of mental disturbance, should be examined by one of the Ashworth hospital (formerly Park Lane) medical experts with a view to transferring him once more into the secure psychiatric system. But Graham was deemed 'untreatable' and made to remain in Parkhurst. And it was there that he died four months later, having outlived his sister, who passed away in 1983, and his father, who died in 1987.

★ ★ ★

Wardens making a routine visit to Graham's cell on the evening of 1 August 1990 found him lying unconscious on the floor. Attempts were made to resuscitate him but to no avail. He was rushed to the prison hospital but was pronounced dead on arrival, having suffered a fatal heart attack. Inevitably, there were rumours that Graham had either poisoned himself or that he had been killed by prison officers or inmates, all of whom were wary, if not terrified, of him. An inquest into his death was held at Newport on the Isle of Wight in October 1990; pathologist Dr Neil Greenwood told the hearing that one of Graham's coronary arteries had closed to the size of a pinhole, which could have been caused by something as simple as excitement or a fattening meal. Thus a jury found that Graham had died of natural causes. His passing was scarcely mentioned in the press, who had all but forgotten him. He was outlived by his beloved aunt Win, who died in 1999, and his cousin Sandra.

Five years after Graham's death, interest in the case was revived with the release of *The Young Poisoner's Handbook*, a black comedy very loosely based on his crimes. Starring Hugh O'Conor as Graham Young, Roger Lloyd-Pack as his father and Charlotte Coleman as Winifred, it is now regarded as something of a lost minor classic. The film provided spurious inspiration however: in November 2005, a 16-year-old Japanese schoolgirl in Shizuoka Prefecture was arrested for poisoning her mother with thallium. The unnamed girl, a promising chemistry student, had bought thallium on the internet and tricked a chemist into selling her a small quantity of the substance, telling him she needed it for a college project. She had become obsessed with the 1995 film and, subsequently, with Graham, after reading Anthony Holden's 1974 biography *The St Albans Poisoner: The Life and Crimes of Graham Young*. In a modern-day version of his diary, she kept an online blog recording the dosages she administered in her mother's cups of tea and the results. On 3 July 2005, she typed on her blog: 'Let me introduce a book: Graham Young's diary on killing with poison — the autobiography of a man I respect.' One month later she wrote, 'It's a bright, sunny day today and I administered a delivery of acetic thallium. The man in the pharmacy didn't realise he had sold me such a powerful drug.' Her mother was admitted to hospital, but the girl continued to find ways of poisoning her.

The girl's crimes came to light when her brother became suspicious. The case was assessed in a family court, where the girl was found to be developmentally disturbed. The girl's mother remained in a coma. A senior investigative official declared, 'She did not hold a grudge against her mother — she just wanted to do an experiment.' The court ruled that a structured education would be most effective; she was sent to a reform school where the emphasis was on mental health care. In 2013, a Japanese movie based on the case was released. It was called *Poisoning Diary of a Thallium Girl*.

★ ★ ★

The case of Graham Young forces us to look at one of the most unsettling aspects of our society, namely, whether someone who has committed appalling crimes can ever be safely released back into the community. Should a person be locked up forever or ought they be given a chance to start afresh, providing certain criteria — which can never be infallible — are met? At Graham's second trial, his defence counsel asserted: 'His release from Broadmoor was a serious error of judgement with tragic consequences. The authorities

448

had a duty to protect Young from himself as well as a duty to protect the public.'

There was undoubtedly a compulsion in Graham's actions, a sense that he was unable to control his impulses where poison was concerned. He described himself as a coward, a term used repeatedly, albeit obliquely, in studies of poisoners. Those studies, coupled with the papers now released to the public on this most contentious of cases, give us greater insight into the character and crimes of Graham Young than was previously possible, and to see where those terrible mistakes were made, and why, on the part of the authorities.

'Chance favours the prepared mind,' declared scientist Louis Pasteur. Graham's story demonstrates the veracity of his words; the poisoner has perhaps more control than any other killer over his crimes, his victims and their detection — or lack of it. Direct contact between killer and victim is not necessary; we know that poison is a stealthy, silent weapon rendering its victim totally vulnerable and oblivious to danger, permitting no defence. Forensic toxicologist John Harris Trestrail clarifies this deadly depersonalisation: 'In the mind of the poisoner, he merely sets the trap, but the victim actually springs it. This attempts to rationalise and to lessen the guilt that the poisoner may feel by being the one who actively pulls the trigger of a gun or plunges a knife.'

Poisoners are less vulnerable themselves: a gunman risks being disarmed and having their weapon turned on them, but poisoners are unlikely to meet a similar fate. Nor is the weapon easily discoverable, for unlike a gun or knife, powder or fluid may be overlooked or concealed in another substance at a crime scene.

449

Returning to the matter of control, poison allows the killer to determine with extreme accuracy the level of a victim's suffering and the span of time between administration and death. The killer may single out a victim in a crowd, committing murder before an unsuspecting audience. Poison may be administered in a variety of ways: hidden in drinks, food or medicine, injected or inhaled, even absorbed through contact with the skin. Those who are subjected to acute poisoning usually die quickly, while those subject to chronic poisoning suffer results for weeks, months or even years, and when death occurs, it is often regarded as expected, the result of a long illness.

Prior to modern forensics, murder by poison was difficult and often impossible to prove. It is still a challenging means of death for police, pathologists and other medical experts to establish. There are rarely any obvious signs of the ordeal that the victim has endured, and sometimes little or nothing to suggest that their demise was due to anything other than natural causes. Trestrail points out: 'Bullets leave holes, knives leave cuts, and clubs leave bruises, but the poisoner covers the murder with a blanket of invisibility. Important clues are usually buried with the victim.' It is also a relatively uncommon form of murder, accounting for only 3-6 per cent of homicides.

Despite the preponderance of factual and fictional stories involving a female poisoner, most real-life cases feature a male protagonist. Nonetheless, poison has often been the weapon of choice for female killers throughout history. A study of the 49 women executed in Britain during 1843-1890 revealed that 29 used poison to kill, with arsenic employed in 23 of those cases. But this may be due to the fact that divorce was difficult for women to obtain during the Victorian era, when traditional gender roles also resulted in women making and serving meals, or supervising the process in middle-class households, leaving them free to add poison to their culinary creations.

Further studies explore whether a 'typical' poisoner can be said to exist. John Rowland, author of *Poisoner in the Dock* (the 1960 book that so enthralled Graham Young), considered 12 historic cases and found a number of 'primary characteristics' common to poisoners. These include a 'streak of complete ruthlessness', which shows itself in an absolute defiance of legal authority, and 'the refusal to accept any moral basis for life'; and a venal and egotistical nature, which convinces the poisoner they are invincible: 'They cannot be found out, they think; they treat it as a cruel whim of fate when the doctors or the police reveal some fact that they thought could not possibly be discovered ... The fact that they have been clumsy, that they have made stupid errors, does not ever, as far as one knows, occur to the unsuccessful poisoner.' Rowland suggests that poisoners are peculiarly vain and partial to media interest. In the case studies he presented, four of the 12 were connected with the medical and pharmaceutical world, but that was significant only insofar as their professions afforded them easy access to poison.

More recent studies include Dr Robert Brittain's work on the sexually sadistic killer. In his research, which as we know was drawn primarily from his contact with Graham Young, Brittain found a number of common elements, albeit not related specifically to poisoners as a 'group'. He identified an individual whose fractured developmental history included

451

problems with the mother and an authoritarian father; an introspective, solitary, prudish and socially inept character who is rarely overtly confrontational but possesses a deep, hidden aggression and enjoys cruelty, usually towards animals in childhood and later seeking out stories of black magic, torture and Nazism. As patient or prisoner, the sadistic killer can often seem rehabilitated but is likely to murder again if given the opportunity.

Other studies and discoveries abound. Dr Malcolm MacCulloch, who worked with Graham, identifies the experience of power and control during sexually sadistic killings as the single most important factor. Alphonse Poklis, Director of Toxicology and Professor at Virginia Commonwealth University School of Medicine in the US, states that poison is the weapon of 'controlling, sneaky people with no conscience, no sorrow, no remorse. They are scary, manipulative.' Author Michael Farrell finds that 'when someone poisons, the distinctive aspect of the crime is the planning and calculation that is associated with it, implying a self-directed shaping of events.'

Poisoning expert John Harris Trestrail describes such killers as 'for the most part cunning, avaricious, cowardly (physically or mentally non-confrontational), child-like in their fantasy, and somewhat artistic (meaning they can design the plan for the murder in as much detail as if they were writing the script for a play). Why does the poison murderer select this weapon as the means of getting to the goal? One of the major reasons is that they stand a very good chance of getting away with the crime. Other reasons include the fact that a poison allows completion of the assault without physical confrontation with the victim. The poisoner is truly an intelligent coward, or we could say has the mind set of an 'enfant-terrible' in the body of an adult. This is a very dangerous combination.' Among the traits he identifies, which includes those already highlighted by other studies, are 'a tendency to turn the victim into an object with no feelings', a belief that they are unlikely to be discovered given their careful calculations, 'a limited mind without sympathy' and something in the poisoner that keeps him or her 'permanently immature; they never seem to grow up. They try to make the world obey their will by cheating it in minor ways, and thereby stealing what it refuses to give them.'

Graham Young emerges forcefully from these findings; indeed, it seems possible to measure his character against the elements of the poisoner's table: the fractured early childhood; the somewhat author-itarian father; the lack of 'normal' relationships as he matured; the interest in supernatural evil — black magic and voodoo — and in the totalitarian murders of the Nazi regime; the detachment of his crimes and the depersonalisation of the victims ('I'd ceased to see them as people,' he admitted, 'they had become guinea pigs'); his prudism whenever sexual matters were mentioned while privately acknowledging that he had gained sexual stimulation from experiment-ing with poison; the cunning, preparation and sadism in administering poison over a long period in order to observe its effects, even to the extent of keeping a diary of his victims' sufferings; the extreme vanity in his knowledge of toxicology and the need to 'show off' about it, which led to the discovery of his crimes; the twisted virtue of his genuine horror at the suggestion that he might have been willing to poison his beloved aunt and uncle; the desire to leave a morally deformed mark upon the world in his urging to reporters to 'make me famous'; having fooled the authorities into believing him 'cured' only to kill again; the obsession with power and control ('I could have killed them if I had wished … but I allowed them to live'); and, above all, his addiction to poison: 'The doses I was giving were not fatal, but I knew I was doing wrong. It grew on me like a drug habit, except that it wasn't me who was taking the drug.'

Perhaps the latter, more than anything else, goes some way to explaining why his family and friends were so remarkably forgiving of him. They felt more than a little pity for the youth who was, as his sister put it, 'obsessed with poisons and their effects and the power it gave him, the way other young men are obsessed with football'. And in many ways, Graham forever remained that thin, pinched-faced youth in the playground, whom his classmate Clive Creager remembered habitually taking a phial of poison from the pocket of his school blazer: 'This is my little friend,' he'd say, and chuckle over it like a gangster over his gun.

His crimes were exceptionally cruel, with many different kinds of torture inflicted upon the victims, some of whom died in lengthy and excruciating agony, while others survived with emotional scars as severe as the physical effects. Yet lawyer Peter Goodman stated with authority that Graham had no 'ill will towards the people he killed. He just had no morals. The reason he poisoned those closest to him was simply that he could closely observe the symptoms. He was a deranged scientist, essentially.' Meanwhile, Graham's first biographer, Anthony Holden, described his subject as possessing a 'deadness to normal human interaction. He had no compunction, no remorse, no guilt.'

And yet there were indications that Graham desperately wanted to be 'normal', even to get married, as he told a social worker, and to divest himself of the 'terrible coldness' he felt inside, which caused him to break down completely on a visit to his sister shortly before his arrest in 1971. Winifred's memoir, filled with love and affection as much as horror and incomprehension, includes a 1972 letter her brother sent to their cousin Sandra, while he was on remand. Aside from Graham's nonsensical comments about his lack of guilt, the genuine warmth he felt for the small band of people he regarded as his closest family shines through almost every line:

Dear Sandy,
Thank you for your last two letters and for the enclosed cigs and tobacco. The tobacco was fine — indeed, if you'd sent me straw it would have been welcome in my present impecunious circumstances.

I was really delighted to hear from you. I have yet to receive any reply to my letters to Win and Auntie Win. Perhaps they were discouraged by my grim attempts at humour. Honestly, though, I see little purpose in writing sepulchral, doom-laden epistles to them. I wish to ease their anxieties, not increase them.

To you, however, I can be honest, Sandy. I stand a good chance of acquittal, for the Prosecution case has a number of inherent weaknesses and a strong point in my favour

455

is that I am not guilty of the charges against me — antecedents notwithstanding. My trial will, I hope, vindicate me. If, by ill chance, it should find me guilty, that will be the end of me, Sandy.

I'm glad the boys are well. I wonder if Andrew misses his 'mountaineering sessions' clambering all over me. At times I gained the impression that I was the Eiger!

Time travels very slowly here, and tends to hang heavily upon me. There is still considerable time before my trial and a number of sessions with Counsel scheduled before then. The first should occur sometime this week.

I am not maltreated here, it is merely a question of finding ways to pass the time. The fact that I have always been a prolific reader on a variety of subjects has stood me in good stead, although I regret that my choice of literature is somewhat limited.

I do hope that the family are all well. When I don't hear from them I worry but I don't want them to feel obligated to write so do not pass this comment on to them.

I am writing this in my cell, late at night and am a little influenced by my Nembutal night sedatives, so excuse the untidiness of my hand-writing.

The few friends which I made upon my admission here have now been consigned to their various fates, so I feel a little solitary. However, there are some advantages to solitude, at least it gives one the opportunity to reflect upon the past and to plan for the future.

456

One of the things I miss in here is my intermittent sessions in the arms of Bacchus! As you
can imagine, the prison is dry and no alcohol
has passed my lips for many a month. I have
been transformed into an abstemious person fit
to grace the board of a Temperance Society!

Well, San, I don't have much more to say
now, so I'll sign off with love to Tony and
Andrew and of course, to yourself.

Keep well and happy, look after yourself and
write to me soon.

With all my love,

Graham XXXXX.

Contemporary articles on the case suggest that if
Graham Young existed today, he would probably
be assessed for evidence of a spectrum disorder,
but such approaches fail to understand his motivation. Dr Christopher Fysh's analysis of the murderer
aged 14 remains the most accurate: 'As far as can be
seen, he chose his relatives for his poisoning experiments because of their propinquity and he admits
as much. There seems to have been no animosity
towards his victims. He describes the administering
of poison to them rather as an adult might describe
a chemical experiment which took place in a laboratory unconnected with human victims. He describes
the symptoms of his victims freely, with interest, but
without emotion.'

Thus Graham was not only 'prepared to take the
risk of killing to gratify his interest in poisons' but
came to regard murder as another form of experimentation. For the unambiguous truth is simple
if incomprehensible: Graham Young was a toxico-

maniac. The epitome of a rare condition, he was a lover of poison, and the euphoric sense of strength that he gained from its mere presence set him almost inevitably on the path to murder, where control and dominion were absolute. 'I miss my antimony,' he told officers who arrested him in 1962. 'I miss the power it gives me.'

All that remains is a single, enduring mystery, as fitting an end to the life of Graham Young as anything dreamed up by the Queen of Crime, Agatha Christie. It is this: when the prison guards entered his cell for the last time in August 1990, was the man lying prone on the floor killed by natural causes or had he chosen one final, deadly poison?

Acknowledgements

It was a strange experience, researching and writing this book during the lockdown imposed by COVID-19. I had been able to visit the National Archives just prior to March 2020, but a second visit was delayed until November of that year because of closures. In that time, my world, like that of everyone else, shrank considerably and during that period and after, as sole carer for my mother, who has several serious health issues, and my sister, who has severe learning difficulties, writing necessarily grew further and further delayed. I mention this because without the support of those closest to me, this book would still be unwritten.

With that in mind, I want to thank the following people for supporting me through a period where my mental health difficulties became almost overwhelming: my partner Lee, my son River and his partner Morgan, my friends Sharon Moore, Tricia Room, Tina Barrott, Ali Dunnell, Sarah Barnes, Kirsty Koch, Angela Handley, Alan Bennett and Keith Skinner. I haven't been in touch as often as I should have been, but not a day goes by when I don't feel grateful to have such amazing people in my life. Additionally, I must thank Mo Lea and Eugene Scardifield, who have endured so much in their own lives but offered such kindness and compassion to me; I am deeply grateful to you both and hope that your books, which I cannot recommend highly enough, reach and touch as many people as they deserve.

I also want to thank the staff of York Hospital and our local doctors' surgery in Pocklington for everything they have done over this past year for my family and others. And equally, if not more so, I would like to thank all the staff at my sister's day care centre, Woldhaven, which must be the best unit of its kind in the country. Although the centre was closed to its usual day visitors, the staff remained a huge source of support throughout the lockdown period and I cannot thank them enough.

My research for this book relied almost entirely then, given our strange global circumstances and the passing of those who knew Graham best, on written sources from the National Archives. The voluminous files on the case were released fairly recently, and this book has benefitted considerably from having access to the thousands of papers contained within the cardboard folders. I must also thank those other authors, documentary makers and journalists who have written about Graham since he first came to public attention in 1962; I would recommend especially Winifred Young's book, *Obsessive Poisoner*, as one of the most compelling true crime memoirs I've ever read.

Finally, I must thank my agent Robert Smith, as always, for being the most terrific literary agent and friend, and also Justine Taylor, Lisa Dyer and all the wonderful team at Bonnier for having such patience, faith and trust in me and my work. I know just how fortunate I am, so from my heart — thank you.

Bibliography

BOOKS

Christie, Agatha, *The Pale Horse* (London: Harper-Collins, 2017).

Cummines, Bobby, *The Parkhurst Years: My Time Locked Up with Britain's Most Notorious Criminals* (London: Ebury Press, 2017).

David, Jenni, *Poison, A History: An Account of the Deadly Art and Its Most Infamous Practitioners* (London: Chartwell Books, 2019).

Emsley, John, *The Elements of Murder: A History of Poison* (USA: Oxford University Press, 2006).

Farrell, Michael, *Criminology of Homicidal Poisoning: Offenders, Victims and Detecting* (Switzerland: Springer International Publishing AG, 2017).

Farrell, Michael, *Criminology of Serial Poisoners* (Switzerland: Springer Nature Switzerland AG, 2018).

Farrell, Michael, *Poison and Poisoners: An Encyclopedia of Homicidal Poisonings* (London: Bantam Books, 1994).

Gordon, Dr Harvey, *Broadmoor* (London: Psychology News Press, 2012).

Grant, Thomas, *Court Number One, The Old Bailey: The Trials and Scandals That Shocked Modern Britain* (London: John Murray, 2020).

Harkup, Kathryn, *A is for Arsenic: The Poisons of Agatha Christie* (London: Bloomsbury Insignia, 2016).

Harris, Robert and Paxman, Jeremy, *A Higher Form of Killing: The Secret History of Chemical and Biological Warfare* (London: Random House, 2002).

Hawksley, Lucinda, *Bitten by Witch Fever: Wallpaper and Arsenic in the Victorian Home* (London: Thames & Hudson, 2016).

Holden, Anthony, *The St Albans Poisoner: The Life and Crimes of Graham Young* (London: Hodder & Stoughton, 1974).

Hubbard, Ben, *Poison: The History of Potions, Powders and Murderous Practitioners* (London: Welbeck Publishing, 2019).

Levi, Jonathan and French, Emma, *Inside Broadmoor: Up Close and Personal with Britain's Most Dangerous Criminals* (London: Blink Publishing, 2019), Kindle edition.

Lowe, Gordon, *Escape from Broadmoor: The Trials and Strangulations of John Straffen* (London: The History Press, 2013).

Macaskill, Hilary, *Agatha Christie at Home* (London: Frances Lincoln, 2009).

Manser, Brian, *Behind the Small Wooden Door: The Inside Story of Parkhurst Prison* (Isle of Wight: Coach House Publications Ltd, 2000).

Marriner, Brian, *Murder with Venom* (London: True Crime Library/Forum Press, 2002).

Private Eye, The Anatomy of Neasden (London: Quartet Books, 1973).

Rowland, John, *Poisoner in the Dock: Twelve Studies in Poisoning* (London: Arco Publications, 1960).

Stevens, Mark, *Broadmoor Revealed: Victorian Crime and the Lunatic Asylum* (Berkshire Record Office, 2011), Kindle edition.

Thompson, Peter, *Bound for Broadmoor* (London:

Hodder & Stoughton, 1972).

Trestrail, John Harris, *Criminal Poisoning: Investiga-
tional Guide for Law Enforcement, Toxicologists,
Forensic Scientists, and Attorneys* (New Jersey:
Humana Press, 2000).

Valentine, K J, *Neasden: A Historical Study* (London:
Charles Skilton Ltd, 1989).

Wilson, David and Day, Jenni, *Broadmoor: A History of the Criminally Insane* (Dreamscape Media
LLC, 2018), Kindle edition.

Young, Winifred, *Obsessive Poisoner: The Strange Story
of Graham Young* (London: Robert Hale, 1973).

BIBLIOGRAPHY: PERIODICALS AND OTHER PUBLICATIONS

Bowden, Paul, 'Graham Young (1947—1990), The
St Albans Poisoner: His Life and Times', *Criminal
Behaviour and Mental Health*, 6: pp.17—24, Sup-
plement, Whurr Publishers Ltd, 1996.

Emsley, John, 'The Trouble with Thallium', *New
Scientist*, 10 August 1978.

Faulk, Malcolm, 'After-Effects of the Graham Young
Case', *Criminal Behaviour and Mental Health*, 6:
43—49, Whurr Publishers Ltd, 1996.

Murder Casebook: Graham Young, Issue 59, Marshall
Cavendish, 1991.

Murder in Mind: Graham Young, Issue 30, Marshall
Cavendish, 1974.

Neal, Meg, 'Nature's Toxic Gifts: The Deadly Story
of Poison', *Popular Mechanics* website, 4 October
2020.

DOCUMENTARY AND FILMS

Born to Kill? Class of Evil: 'Graham Young', Series 1, Episode 5, Twofour Productions, 2017.

Crime Story: Terrible Coldness: 'Graham Young', Blue Heaven Productions, 1993.

Fred Dinenage Murder Casebook: 'The Teacup Poisoner', Series 1, Episode 2, Crime & Investigation Network, 2011.

The Young Poisoner's Handbook, Bavaria Film and Television Fund, British Screen Productions, 1995.